W9-AVC-609

The Latitudinarians and the Church of England, 1660–1700

John Tillotson, Archbishop of Canterbury (Boston Athenaeum)

The Latitudinarians and the Church of

England, 1660–1700 ❂ W. M. SPELLMAN

The University of Georgia Press   *Athens and London*

© 1993 by the University of Georgia Press
Athens, Georgia 30602
All rights reserved
Designed by Mary Mendell
Set in Baskerville by Tseng Information Systems, Inc.
Printed and bound by Thomson-Shore, Inc.
The paper in this book meets the guidelines for permanence and
durability of the Committee on Production Guidelines for
Book Longevity of the Council on Library Resources.
Printed in the United States of America
97 96 95 94 93   C   5 4 3 2 1
Library of Congress Cataloging in Publication Data
Spellman, W. M.
The Latitudinarians and the Church of England, 1660–1700 /
W. M. Spellman.
p.   cm.
Includes bibliographical references and index.
ISBN 0-8203-1429-3 (alk. paper)
1. Latitudinarianism (Church of England).   2. Church of England—History—17th
century.   3. Anglican Communion—History—17th century.   4. Great Britain—
Church history—17th century.   I. Title.
BX5085.S64   1993
283' .42' 09032—dc20   91-32384
CIP
British Library Cataloging in Publication Data available

for Nancy and Margaret

CONTENTS

ACKNOWLEDGMENTS

It is a pleasure to acknowledge many debts in writing this book. A number of individuals and foundations have generously supported my work over the past three years. Most of the research was carried out at the British Library and at the Bodleian Library. The staff at both institutions were, as usual, both kind and exceptionally helpful. Thanks are also due to the reference librarians at the Institute of Historical Research, London; the University of Tennessee, Knoxville; and the University of North Carolina, Asheville. I have attempted to acknowledge my debts to other Stuart scholars in the notes and select bibliography, but a special word of thanks goes to the authors of unpublished dissertations who are cited in the book. Final revisions were undertaken while I was a guest at Saint Benet's Hall, Oxford, during the summer of 1991, and I would like to express my appreciation to the master of Saint Benet's, Rev. Henry Wansbrough, for his gracious hospitality.

A one-year fellowship for college teachers and independent scholars from the National Endowment for the Humanities during 1989–90 enabled me to complete the bulk of the research for this project. Three grants supported by the University of North Carolina at Asheville, two from the Mills Faculty Research and Development Fund and another from the Intramural Faculty Fellowship Fund, allowed me to travel to Britain for extended visits on two occasions. UNC–Asheville Vice Chancellor Lauren Wilson, together with my colleagues in the Department of History, generously supported my application for a research leave during 1989–90 and worked unselfishly to secure a faculty replacement. Bruce Greenawalt, chairman of the department, has consistently and patiently approved all my requests for reassignment, research funding, and conference travel. His quiet support over the past three years has been essential to the completion of this book.

Earlier versions of chapters 4 and 5 were presented at the 1990 meeting of the Southern Conference on British Studies in New Orleans, where Barbara Shapiro offered a number of helpful suggestions, and at the 1988 Carolinas Conference on British Studies, hosted by James Madison University. Sections of chapter 7 were read at the eleventh Le Moyne Forum on Religion and Literature, Syracuse, New York, in September 1991. Parts of chapter 3 first appeared in my article "Archbishop John Tillotson and the Meaning of Moralism," *Anglican and Episcopal History* 56 (1987): 404–22. I wish to thank the editors for allowing me to use this material. Thanks are also due to the anonymous readers for the University of Georgia Press, both of whom identified areas where the text needed revision and clarification, and to Jane Powers Weldon, who copy edited the manuscript for the Press. Christine Waters offered helpful comments on drafts of the first four chapters, while Nancy Costello again assisted with finalizing the typescript, reading the proofs, making the index, and cheerfully supporting the entire undertaking from start to finish.

As seventeenth-century labels go, "Latitudinarianism" is as broad and as problematic a term to define as "Puritanism," although, fortunately perhaps, it has never generated anything like the heat which still characterizes the scholarly debate over the latter movement. From a synonym for religious moderation in Burnet's *History* to a derisive sobriquet in the hands of embittered Nonconformists, High Churchmen, and non-jurors, to a convenient but indeterminate historical description of the entire eighteenth-century Anglican establishment, Latitudinarianism has yet to receive the full critical attention that other areas of English religious thought have enjoyed in recent years.[1] Unhappily, the few earlier historical studies which discuss the "men of Latitude" focus almost exclusively on those aspects of the story which seem to presage later developments, stressing the purportedly close connections between Latitudinarianism and the subsequent religion of reason sponsored by the Deists. Products of a more confident time, most of these works are careful to emphasize the progressive nature of the movement, seeing in the Latitudinarian message a crucial bulwark of enlightenment and rational theology, a welcome antidote to the enthusiasm and intolerance of an age grown weary of religious dispute.[2]

Many contemporary scholars, on the other hand, while extending the impact of the movement well into the eighteenth century, have been much more critical of Latitudinarianism than their late nineteenth- and early twentieth-century counterparts. We are now told, for example, that the Latitudinarians, in their eager search for both a more reasonable faith and a more irenical church, deliberately downplayed or ignored some of the fundamental tenets of Reformed Christianity, including the important Protestant vision of fallen humanity. "It is surprising how many elements in Christianity the Latitudinarians ignored," writes the church historian G. R. Cragg: "Because they consistently minimised the power of evil, they felt little need to stress salvation. They had no conception of the Church as a divine society, and consequently laid little emphasis upon its worship and traditions. The sacraments played a modest and utilitarian role in their scheme, and mysteries were an embarrassment which was best avoided. They had little to say about the Incarnation and the Atonement, and almost nothing about Christ as Mediator."[3] One must wonder, on the basis of such a serious indictment, what there was about the movement that had anything to recommend it to serious Christians in the late seventeenth century. How, for example, could a defense of the faith purportedly based on calculating self-interest, where the sense of sin and the problems it raised were ignored, earn the respect of sensitive men and women when "all over England the grandeurs of Christianity were reduced to the modest proportions of prudential ethics."[4] For Horton Davies, Latitudinarianism was a movement "masquerading as authentic Christianity," its exponents left "to conceive of a contradiction, Christian discipleship without the taking up of a cross," and most scholars today, while normally avoiding such strong language, are inclined to agree with the general temper of this harsh estimate.[5]

Perhaps this is why so little attention has been devoted to the Latitudinarians in the recent scholarly literature on religious life and the official church during the Restoration. When contrasted with their intellectual forebears amongst the Cambridge Platonists, for example, the Latitudinarians seem to be without spiritual commitment or otherworldly direction, often emerging as little more than the complacent heralds of religious rationalism and tepid moralism.[6] And although there has never been a full-scale study of what even Cragg acknowledges was "one of the most significant movements of religious thought since the Reformation," the modern consensus seems to suggest that Latitudinarianism, with its primary concentration on Christianity as a way of life, its interest in morality and everyday conduct, its apparent desiccation of essential doctrine, and its alleged avoidance of sin and human depravity, was mainly

a corrosive force in the life of the church, thereby fully warrant-
ing its unfortunate association with the self-contented world of the
eighteenth-century Establishment.[7]

These modern criticisms of the Latitudinarian movement within
the Church of England, however, justified as they may appear in certain respects, present their own special interpretive difficulties for
the historian. The most important of these concerns the method-
ological problem inherent in any attempt to define what was, after
all, a late seventeenth-century phenomenon in terms of what became
the predominant emphasis of the official church during the course
of the eighteenth century.[8] This essentially teleological approach to
the inquiry fails to do full justice to the unique context in which the
movement originated, thereby distorting the import and the texture
of Latitudinarian thought both for those who formulated its central
principles and for those who assimilated its teaching. The impact of
the Civil War experience, particularly its violent sectarian component; the threat posed by a resurgent Catholicism; the rebirth of
academic skepticism; the development and attraction of the new science, with its vision of an orderly universe governed by omnipresent
law; and the danger of Cartesian mechanism and of Hobbesian ma-
terialism and ethical relativism are but a few of the more important
influences which helped to shape the nature of the Latitudinarian
message in the years after 1660.[9] To associate the most harmful developments in the life of the eighteenth-century church with the ascendancy of Latitudinarian thought at the close of the seventeenth,
I would suggest, is to ignore what the Latitudinarians were trying to
communicate in light of the very special challenges facing the Restoration Church after a half century of bitter religious quarrels and
flagging spiritual confidence in the face of alternative, and to many,
more philosophical and thus real, avenues to truth.

Gordon Rupp's recent study of religion in England during the
eighteenth century begins with an overview of church politics and
theology after the Restoration and presents a refreshing and meaningful, although brief, challenge to this modern critical consensus.
Recognizing the importance of placing the Latitude-men into a
proper historical context, Rupp vigorously defends their concentration on the faith of the moralist and their avoidance of vexatious
doctrinal issues. "In an age of dissolving moral standards," he writes

in reference to the London of Charles II, "there was an abundant need for plain and solid teaching." Rather than serving as a deleterious force in the Anglican communion, the moderate preachers of the late seventeenth century represented a solid "renewal in the Church, however temporary," where their numerous and instructive sermons and activities "spoke directly and very plainly to the evils of the day." Their interest in education as a force for moral and spiritual reformation, for example, signaled a special awareness of the problems peculiar to a rapidly changing economic and political environment.[10] And their refusal to separate saving faith from moral reform bespoke a firm commitment to a long-standing tradition in Reformed theology where faith and works became inseparable components of the gift of salvation.[11]

Others have continued to explore these suggestions. Alan Clifford has reexamined the theology of John Tillotson and concluded that the "arid dissertations" of this Latitudinarian archbishop of Canterbury never discounted "the pessimistic potential of human nature nor the necessity of divine grace to redeem it." John Spurr has reminded us how men who were labeled as Latitudinarians by their critics often embraced positions indistinguishable from those held by their supposedly more orthodox colleagues within the church, while Gerard Reedy's recent study of the Bible in Anglican thought during the late seventeenth century controverts a long-standing scholarly tradition which had argued for an alliance between the "rationalism" of the Enlightenment and the rational theology of the Restoration divines. The commonsense reason employed by Anglicans, Reedy maintains, "had little to do with the growing rationalism of later seventeenth-century England and Europe." According to Clifford, the Latitudinarian conception of reason amounted to nothing more "than the use of rational processes in perceiving facts and evaluating arguments."[12]

Observations such as these seem to suggest that the whole question of the nature of Latitudinarianism deserves another look. As a brief preliminary to such an undertaking, the present work seeks to extend some of these useful insights by reexamining two relatively neglected aspects of the movement: the Latitudinarian estimate of human nature—of man's place in God's creation, his nature and powers in the wake of the Fall—and the implications of Latitudinarian soteriology for the Deist challenge which confronted the church during the final decade of the seventeenth century. I refer to these issues as fundamental because one's picture of man's essential nature, his final end, and Christ's role in advancing that end invariably has implications not only for social and political theory, but for ideas about man's spiritual progress and about the desirability of change in his temporal "probationary" state. Current suggestions that the Latitudinarians were derelict in their adherence to the fundamental mysteries of the faith, that they did not emphasize salvation, the power of evil, Christ's work of atonement, and the value of worship and tradition, assume that these churchmen readily embraced a new, more optimistic picture of human nature and human potential which would soon displace the centuries-old orthodox Christian viewpoint. That a new—and empirically invalid—picture of man was emerging towards the close of the seventeenth century, that it would become one of the trademarks of Deism and place enormous strain on the intellectual life of the church in the eighteenth century, no one would deny. But before we accept the argument which places Latitudinarianism at the forefront of this transformation, we ought first to explore the movement exclusively in its original seventeenth-century setting, separating it from later, and in many respects, independent developments. To describe the final decades of the seventeenth century as simply "the Golden Age of natural theology and Deistical freethinking"[13] is to discount the significance of the theological affirmations of the moderate divines, while avoiding the special problems which were facing all religious moderates during the Restoration, particularly in their efforts to realize a comprehensive church.

From modest beginnings during the Interregnum, a self-conscious group of Latitudinarian churchmen spread their message from the pulpits of the expanding London parishes and at last reached the peak of their influence with the promotion of John Tillotson to the archbishopric of Canterbury in 1691. And by winning appointment to a number of episcopal sees in the wake of the deprivation of the non-juring bishops, the moderate churchmen for the first time enjoyed the opportunity to influence church policy in a compelling manner. Linked more by personal friendship and a common point of view than by a specific set of political or ecclesiological tenets, the membership of the school shifted as circumstances changed over the years.[14] Their brief ascendency in the 1690s was due to many factors, political sympathies being not the least significant of these, but equally important issues involving their understanding of man's contingent nature in a universe created and sustained by a personal God, the limits of reason in religious experience, the influence of grace in forwarding the goal of salvation, and the relationship between practical theology and human sinfulness all contributed to the intellectual and spiritual development of those who were called Latitudinarians.

Once these matters are addressed, once the conventional theological orientation of the Latitudinarians is restored to its proper context, it will become possible to suggest that the moderate churchmen were much less the precursors of Deism and the Age of Reason than traditionally has been supposed. Men such as John Tillotson, Edward Fowler, Edward Stillingfleet, John Moore, Simon Patrick, Joseph Glanvill, Mathew Hale, Robert Grove, and Thomas Tenison set an exceptionally severe standard by which men were expected to govern their lives as Christians and were much closer to a traditional Protestant view of man's essential nature and his subsequent need for divine assistance than critics of the movement are generally prepared to recognize. And while it may be true that they jettisoned much of the Puritan theology which had informed their earliest experiences, their reaction was not as sweeping as we have assumed, for they unquestionably retained that broader vision of human nature and human potential which so powerfully guided the Puritan mind.[15] Thus even the Latitudinarian call to reason and the emphasis on behavior in this life in no sense obscured their understanding of the function of evil, nor did this position diminish the gravity of their commitment to a Christian humanism where the stain of original sin effectively precluded the possibility of salvation without the unmerited saving grace of Christ. They knew something of the limits of nurture and environment in the effort to excise error and wickedness from the individual heart, and they refused to dismiss the centuries-old explanation for human wickedness provided by their faith. They referred to Christ's special sacrifice repeatedly in their sermons and taught that there was little efficacy in the doctrine of good works without faith. Their numerous innovations—the "plain" preaching style before the new commercial classes of London, the advocacy of a comprehension for moderate Dissenters, the commitment to education and parish schools, the adoption of a new criterion of truth and a "commonsense" rule of faith, and the promotion of science as an ally of true religion—all were designed to strengthen the basis for religious belief and to promote their interest in a revitalized Anglican communion where sectarian enthusiasm and the resulting obfuscation of the main truths of the faith would find little comfort.

The Latitudinarians devoted a great deal of energy to the issue of moral reform in an age when the example of the court was anything but salutary.[16] For the moderate churchmen, as for all of their Anglican counterparts throughout the seventeenth century, the Christian way of life could in no respect be reduced to an autonomous moral code. Concerned with every aspect of public and private conduct, and establishing a difficult standard by which their contemporaries must measure their actions, the Latitudinarians insisted that all behavior should issue from a genuine saving faith, a faith which rejected the emerging dichotomy between ethical and solely practical interests. They were rarely concerned with isolated moral problems, but sought instead to transform human character at large in the image of its original divine pattern, to reaffirm the validity of a Christian tradition which placed the requirements of the eternal before the exigencies of the merely mundane. In the face of powerful economic changes and the growth of an influential merchant and financial class, the Latitudinarians continued to champion a medieval inheritance where Christianity has a right and an obligation to govern and control the whole of the life of man under all circumstances and at all times. Ever ready to point out that property remains a trust and not an outright possession, viewing industry primarily as a religious service, and quick to remind their parishioners that economic activity is simply one department of human relations under the purview of a universal Christian standard, the Latitudinarians advanced a moral theology that was no simple judicial code whereby men might be enabled to keep on the right side of the moral law with the least effort.

The indispensable function of their practical theology was to teach men how to grow in Christian holiness and enjoy the grace of God through a strict, consistent, and living piety. There was to be no separation between the spheres of personal interest and Christian responsibility for the Latitudinarians, no convenient intersection where the values of the marketplace found sanction in the teachings of the church.[17] They were committed to educating laymen in the way to holiness, and, in step with a broader Anglican tradition, they tried "to give men a vision of the love and holiness of God, that they might grow more sensitive to the enormity of human sin."[18] Their tendency towards rigorism in light of man's sinful condition, together with an avoidance of the sort of mystical piety popular during the Interregnum, placed them firmly within the spiritual and intellectual boundaries of the historic Anglican communion.

The failures of the Latitudinarians were many, and to ignore these would be to repeat the errors of their earliest scholarly apologists. A comprehensive church was certainly one of their main goals, but they pursued this otherwise laudable vision on their own thoroughly Anglican terms, with little empathy for or understanding of the position of moderate Dissenters, men and women who struggled constantly to reconcile their own Nonconformity with the ideal of Protestant unity. As privileged and self-interested members of a re-established state church, the Latitudinarians repeatedly used their pulpits to inculcate unreserved obedience to authority and to counsel silent acceptance of a rigidly hierarchical social and economic order. Their disdain for the fruitless doctrinal quarrels of their youth often drove them in a direction where the purely spiritual and emotional aspects of religious experience were treated with extreme caution, thereby making their message appear somewhat less than impelling. Their focus on the life of reason and its verisimilitude with basic Christian tenets seemed to imply that all men could readily agree upon the specific dictates of universal reason, that the laws of nature were clear and immutable. Quite aside from the dangerous impact which such an outlook had upon the integrity of Scripture, the Latitudinarians assumed too readily the existence of absolute standards of good and evil which could be demonstrated by reflective reason, our special internal tribunal. Their casual assumptions sometimes obscured the real difficulty involved in reaching any doctrinal consensus in an age when religious belief and the essentials of godly worship were still very much a matter of intense concern to men not so far removed from the day when these differences had been settled by the sword.

But while it is important to discuss these and other flaws in a study of Latitudinarianism, one must do so with a clear recognition of the background against which these positions emerged and developed. The Latitudinarians' constant pursuit of the "middle way" between the Laudianism and Puritanism of their youth, their search for a comprehensive church whereby Dissenters could join in a unified front against the threat of Catholic insurgency, their dogged adherence to an essentially Augustinian picture of human nature, and their attempt to harness the discoveries of science and philosophy for the benefit of a theocentric view of the world made their overall task of renewal and reform somewhat less than enviable. The tendency of the Deists to appropriate elements of the Latitudinarian message for their own admittedly radical purposes unquestionably provided a constant irritant, particularly in the 1690s. The circumstances surrounding the rise of the moderate churchmen to the episcopal bench after 1689 made some long-standing charges of opportunism appear increasingly plausible, thus further frustrating efforts for reform at the very moment of ecclesiastical victory. And the friendship of Latitudinarians like John Wilkins, Benjamin Whichcote, Isaac Barrow, and Tillotson with the philosopher John Locke, whose novel epistemological ideas and alleged Unitarianism infuriated so many within the established church, placed added strain on the movement at the highest ranks.

In the end, however, despite the myriad criticisms centering on the rationalizing tendencies of the moderate churchmen and their willingness to forego large portions of the doctrinal canon, they retained much more of an older view of the limits of human reason and of man's essential nature than their opponents were ever willing to acknowledge. The Latitudinarian opposition to Puritanism, for example, was directed mainly against the spirit in which their Calvinist predecessors had made their case, not against the larger part of the message which they had to deliver and certainly not against their picture of the essential sinfulness and wilful depravity of man. The Latitudinarian call to action, the admonition to reform and works of charity, the "moral preaching" for which they have been so roundly criticized never signaled the adoption of a Christian anthropology where salvation was placed solely in the hands of men and where the position of the institutional church as a necessary guide in the search for salvation was abandoned. That position, that crucial elevation of man's status in the eyes of his maker without reference to human limits or divinely ordained institutions, constituted the core of the Deist challenge. The Latitude-men could never embrace such a position no matter how much they might champion the claims of reason and free will. The painful experience of the seventeenth century, the experience of their own youth, had made the vision of the Deists both unrealistic and untenable for the moderate churchmen, and regardless of what became of the movement during the course of the succeeding century, the Latitudinarian moment belongs to the seventeenth, to the revolutionary changes which made that moment possible, and to a view of human nature which had very little in common with the more confident assumptions rightly associated with the Age of Reason.

In a short pamphlet of 1662 which has been much quoted by
historians of the seventeenth-century Church of England, the
Cambridge divine Simon Patrick made the first use in print of
a term which seemed to be on everyone's lips because of its supposed association with religious heterodoxy and civil disobedience.
Responding to the query of an Oxford friend, Patrick sprang to the
defense of a movement with which he was already deeply involved.
"A Latitude-man," he wrote with a thinly veiled sense of indignity,
"is an image of clouts that men set up to encounter with for want of a
real enemy; it is a convenient name to reproach a man that you owe
a slight to, ('tis what you will, and you affix it upon whom you will)
'tis some thing will serve to talke of when all other discourse fails."[1]
Patrick was particularly disturbed by the hostile reaction against religious moderates taking place at Queens' College in the first year after
the Restoration, where his own recent election as master of Queens'
had been overridden by royal mandate in favor of the High Churchman Anthony Sparrow, and he recognized that this localized enmity
was symptomatic of a university-wide effort to remove from positions of power those considered suspect by returning Anglicans who,
for their part, had refused to "compromise" with the Interregnum
government. Men such as John Tillotson, for example, the future
Latitudinarian archbishop of Canterbury, were ejected from their
college fellowships for their Presbyterian sympathies, even after they
had received episcopal orders. For Patrick, it appeared as though
the extreme factiousness of religious debate, so marked during the
Interregnum period, was now in the process of recrudescence, carry-

ing on its troublesome and fruitless career despite the collapse of the Puritan experiment and the return of Crown authority in May of 1660. Sadly, the Cambridge Platonist Henry More was obliged to agree with Patrick's assessment, observing in 1663 how "there are some have a very aking tooth against such as they would brand with the nickname of latitudemen."[2]

In his brief pamphlet, Patrick identified the greatest part of the Latitudinarians as men "whose fortune it was to be born so late, as to have their education in the University, since the beginnings of the unhappy troubles of this kingdom." These young Cambridge divines, while receiving their ordination from bishops "in opposition to that hide-bound, strait-lac'd spirit that did then prevail," were dedicated to maintaining the liturgy, doctrine, government and worship of the Church of England despite the aspersions of their harshest critics.[3] On no account could they be found to dissent from the teachings of the church, "unless absolute reprobation be one, which they do not think themselves bound to believe."[4] And Patrick found nothing incongruous about the moderate churchmen's attempt to promote the claims of reason in religion while insisting upon the complete orthodoxy of such an enterprise, since in his mind the reason of the moderates was always guided by the wisdom of the ancient fathers and the councils of the church. There is no point in divinity, he insisted, "where that which is most ancient doth not prove the most rational, and the most rational the ancientest; for there is an eternal consanguinity between all verity. . . ."[5] The employment of reason in religion created a universal standard by which Anglicans must judge everything, a standard arrived at by deductions from our common, innate notions or through the evaluation of divine revelation and the interpretations of the ancient church.

Patrick's identification of the moderate church movement with mid-century Cambridge University is understandable from the point of view of his own peculiar situation in an increasingly hostile environment—nor was he alone in making such a connection—but it does not permit us a complete view of the wider intellectual backdrop which, extending far beyond the confines of the academy, supported the moderate churchmen in their struggle to position themselves as the legitimate heirs of an orthodox Anglican tradition.[6] It has recently been shown how the term "Latitudinarian" was primarily used during the early years of the Restoration as a reproach against clergymen and university dons who had conformed to the

Interregnum government while simultaneously embracing Arminian theological opinions.[7] Most often it was members of the dissenting community who equated Latitudinarianism with clerical time-serving and heterodoxy, and the attacks often called forth rejoinders similar to Patrick's *Brief Account*. These dangerous men of few convictions, it was thought, "indifferent what Religion others should be of," were no friends to either the reestablished church or the dissenting community.[8] But although Patrick's plea for an honest hearing may not have solicited a constructive response in those early years of delicate readjustment to monarchical government and a hierarchical church, it remains worth examining whether his protestation was simply a tendentious outpouring by a displaced academic or a fair picture of a much-maligned group of men whose unpopular response to the fury of religious contention obscured the fact of their steadfast commitment to a larger and more fundamental set of Protestant tenets, basic beliefs which were shared with the very men who sought to exclude them from leadership roles within the reestablished church.

The accused took no pleasure in the derogatory label attached to them by their critics, particularly since the "Latitudinarian" agenda, as we shall see, had much more to do with restoring an earlier seventeenth-century point of view than it did with amending the doctrinal axioms of the national church. The moderate "men of latitude" would distinguish themselves after 1660 both by their resistance to the persecutory spirit within the church and by their unremitting efforts to propagate a vision of God ultimately derived from the medieval Augustinian perspective. The earthly city of man was, for the Latitudinarians, to strive toward the likeness of the city of God, and mankind was to be infused with a longing for the peace of that eternal world, particularly in light of the recent fratricidal violence of their own.[9]

Even before the trials of the Reformation, northern humanists like Erasmus, Tyndale, and Colet had anticipated one of the objectives of moderate divines by attempting to integrate what they understood to be the foremost truths of Scripture with the dictate of reason, but that effort to avoid the labyrinth of scholasticism was soon overshadowed by the work of Protestant reformers who peremptorily set man's intellect to one side in the interest of magnifying God's power and inscrutable will.[10] For Luther and Calvin, for Beza and Knox, the propriety of God's actions had absolutely nothing to do with his purportedly rational nature. In abandoning the centuries-old Thomist idea that man might know God through the use of his reason and under the aegis of grace, and the belief that God had voluntarily conformed his charge for mankind to the rule of reason, the Reformers struck at the very heart of the reawakened humanist perspective.[11] By the close of the sixteenth century, the habit of free inquiry guided by reason, together with Erasmus's emphasis on the person and the life of Christ at the expense of scholastic erudition, both of which had marked the later stages of the Northern Renaissance, had succumbed before the collective weight of internecine quarreling over what precisely constituted a correct interpretation of God's inspired word. Erasmus's hope that Christian doctrine could be understood by the pious and resolute man guided by the Holy Spirit had proved to be unrealistic.

In the midst of the struggle, where variant transcriptions and translations of the Bible set the groundwork for later skepticism, the splintering Protestant churches, seeking to defend their respective understandings of Holy Writ, had, like their Catholic predecessors, hardened their positions into a clearly articulated and unmistakably authoritarian confessional dogma, one where no quarter was to be given to those who sought to maintain the inaugural goal of the Reformation: individual access to and interpretation of Scripture.[12] A foretaste of the coming struggle occurred when a conciliatory Erasmus informed Luther that disputes over issues beyond the pale of human knowledge must, in the interest of Christian unity, be held in abeyance. "I merely want to analyze and not to judge," Erasmus wrote, "to inquire and not to dogmatize. I am ready to learn from anyone who advances something more accurate or more reliable." Luther's confidence in the power of the Holy Spirit to inform those possessed of faith with solid truths, however, led him to reject all such pleas, insisting instead that "Not to delight in assertions is not the mark of a Christian heart. Indeed, one must delight in assertions to be a Christian at all!" It was a forbidding augury that would soon translate into the hateful religious wars of the sixteenth century and carry over, with equally tragic consequences, into mid-seventeenth-century England, where its malevolent impress would provide not a little of the background to the wider sentiment derisively referred to by its critics as Latitudinarianism.[13]

The reformed English Church, like its Continental counterparts, had initially turned to Scripture as the sole basis of the rule of faith. But when the problems inherent in the elevation of the Bible as a counter-authority to Roman pretense were made evident by the clash of conflicting interpretation within the larger Protestant community, and as apologists for a resurgent Catholic Church began to assert that the only certainty available in a congeries of subjective biblical exegesis was that embodied in an infallible papal tradition, some Anglicans turned their attention back towards human reason and early church tradition as possible alternatives to the inner light of the sects on the one hand and the authoritarianism of Rome on the other. They were aided in their search not only by the memory of Erasmian temperance but also, paradoxically, by the broader sixteenth-century revival of ancient Greek skepticism as it had first been articulated in the writings of Pyrrho of Elis (ca. 360–ca. 270 B.C.) and subsequently transmitted to the moderns by Sextus Empiricus (A.D. ca. 160–ca. 210) with the first publication of his works in 1569. Focusing primarily on the unreliability of the senses to provide accurate knowledge about the world around us and on the dubious power of the rational faculties to understand the real nature of things, skeptics like Michel de Montaigne (1533–92), his disciple Pierre Charron (1541–1603), and Pierre Gassendi (1592–1655) had argued that we can only really know the appearances of things, that we must freely acknowledge our immense ignorance of God's creation and eschew the vanity and presumption which governs our every action.[14] "Let us consider through what clouds," reflected Montaigne, "and how blindfold we are led to the knowledge of most things that pass through our hands. Verily we shall find it is rather custom than science that removeth the strangeness of them from us."[15]

Certainty on religious matters, it appeared, was bound to prove just as elusive as certainty in matters of sense due to our ultimate incapacity to discover an infallible standard by which to interpret God's transcendent will. The Catholic infallibilists had no reliable criterion by which to validate their position, no way to prove the inerrancy of the church. Similarly, all Protestant claimants to special illumination or election to salvation possessed insufficient means of testing their beliefs beyond the caprice of personal experience. Their subjective certainty of God's presence in their lives left the way open for all number of excesses in religious practice while precluding the possibility of limits to acceptable social behavior. As this skeptical tendency developed in the late sixteenth century, it tended to merge with a Christian antirationalist tradition which had first appeared as a powerful force in the medieval period. From Saint Paul's repeated thrusts at the pride of man's intellect, to Saint Augustine's deprecations of the reasoning faculty on behalf of grace and God's will, to the anti-Thomist fideism of William of Occam and Duns Scotus, to the recurrent mystical strain within the official church, the underlying suspicion of man's power to know, and to know unerringly, what it is that religion prescribes, provided a significant backdrop to the movement for religious charity emerging in the seventeenth century. It also afforded theologians an opportunity to find a suitable middle ground in the struggle between Pyrrhonism and dogmatism by employing a form of mitigated skepticism based upon the use of reason and the principle of moral certainty.[16]

The warnings of sixteenth-century skeptics, and in particular their reservations about the power of human reason to distinguish truth from falsehood in all matters, would be repeated by later English liberals, particularly during the years immediately preceding the Civil War. But in the early Stuart period, Richard Hooker's *Laws of Ecclesiastical Polity* was the most imposing example of the effort to find a renewed place for reason in the sphere of religion, and his influence within the official church expanded as the century progressed. Inspired by a tradition as old as Aristotle and as synthetic as the work of Aquinas, and faced with immediate threats from both Rome and Geneva, Hooker's Anglican universe was informed throughout by law, from the first law eternal which is the self-imposed rule of God's own nature to the law of man, which is the precept of reason. Troubled by the expanding influence of Calvinist theology within the Anglican communion during the late sixteenth century, Hooker insisted that "They err therefore who think that the will of God to do this or that, there is no reason besides his will," and he assured his readers that God's acting in accordance to a fixed rule was his own free and voluntary act. "The book of this law we are neither able nor worthy to open and look into. That little thereof which we darkly apprehend we admire, the rest with religious ignorance we humbly and meekly adore."[17] Our twofold nature makes it difficult for us to recognize and follow the law which identifies our greatest happiness and rest in God, and our corruption since the Fall has distorted our true character to the extent that we often see in those transitory pleasures of sense the supreme good of man. In fact, according to Hooker, it is our sinful nature which makes civil society necessary in the first place.[18] Nevertheless, even here in our probationary temporal state, the positive laws of the civil order must reflect the higher natural law, and that law is derived through the use of reason. As the state must not abridge natural law in carrying out its legitimate functions, so too must the teaching of the historic church conform to that same mandate.

Hooker believed that it was through the sacraments that man's real nature is moved toward a supernatural restoration of its original dignity. The role of the clergy was to administer these sacraments, to approach Scripture with the goal of separating fundamentals from accessories, and to serve in the difficult but all-important pastoral capacity as a living symbol of God's grace.[19] Thus the church and its ministry existed solely for man's spiritual well-being, and not the converse as seemed increasingly to be the case within Puritanism. As Peter Lake has remarked, Hooker's principal goal was to remove predestination from its central place in the theology of English churchmen and to replace it "by the sacrament-and-prayer-centered piety set out in the *Polity*."[20] And in matters of church polity where points of faith were not at issue, no single form or usage is mandatory. Hooker's Puritan opponents were wrong to conclude that specific ecclesiastical injunctions could be derived from Scripture, and wholesome devotional practice should never be abandoned simply because of its conformity with Roman tradition. In external forms of religion, Hooker insisted, "such things as are apparently, or can be sufficiently proved, effectual or generally fit to set forward godliness . . . may be reverently thought of; some few, rare, casual, and tolerable, or otherwise curable, inconveniences notwithstanding."[21] Offering the assistance of God's grace for all those who sought to reform their lives in accordance with the rule of reason, while eschewing questions regarding infallible guides, Hooker's *via media* would represent a fresh breeze to Restoration divines who were faced with similar challenges from a resurgent Catholic Church and a disgruntled and defeated Calvinist party.

Hooker's work, in some respects, was complemented by the efforts of Dutch thinkers who had also begun to reassess the validity of a Calvinist perspective which had become as imperious and dogmatic as Roman Catholicism. Jakob Hermanszoon—better known under the Latinized form of his name as Arminius—had studied in Geneva under Beza before taking up pastoral duties at the Reformed Church in Amsterdam, but by 1603, the year he was appointed professor at the University of Leiden, Arminius's doubts about unconditional election led to his censure as a Pelagian proponent of free will. For

Arminius, as for his successors among the growing community called Arminians or Remonstrants, mankind had doubtless experienced a fall and was in constant need of divine mercy and forgiveness, but Calvin's (and particularly Beza's) severe precepts appeared to view God as the author of sin while lessening man's moral responsibility in the face of infractions against the divine will. William Laud, whose own theology was inspired by the Dutch movement, addressed this issue directly when he confided to Lord Saye and Sele that the Calvinists' denial of universal atonement "makes God, the God of all mercies, to be the most fierce and unreasonable tyrant in the world." It seemed imperative to the Arminians, particularly after the outbreak of religious warfare in 1618, that Scripture be examined not with the Augustinian prepossessions of a Luther or a Calvin but by each individual and in pursuit of the most simple and direct meaning.[22] Hugo Grotius's *Truth of the Christian Religion* (1639) best exemplified that spirit in an age of crisis. Recognizing that proofs in matters of faith could never be as concrete as those in mathematics or in natural philosophy and shocked by the brutal excesses of the Thirty Years' War, Grotius argued that reasonable persons could still come to some understanding of the essential teachings in Scripture if only they would exercise mutual forbearance in pursuing their inquiries.[23] According to Grotius, Christians had less to fear from the legitimate differences of opinion with respect to matters of secondary consideration than they did from the hardness of heart incident to embroilments over doctrinal questions. Individual responsibility must be restored, he believed, if the Christian message was to have any substantive impact on the lives of his distressed contemporaries.

Edward, Lord Herbert of Cherbury (1583–1648), took the rationalizing theme further than any of his fellow Englishmen, utilizing the familiar and respected concept of innate ideas in order to establish what he accredited as the primary tenets behind all systems of belief and effectively reducing the church's Thirty-nine Articles to a scant five. That God exists, that he should be worshiped, that man should order his faculties as the principal part of divine worship, that everyone is duty bound to repent his sins, and that rewards and punishments will follow our brief passage here—such were the main principles which informed his 1625 *De Veritate*. The book, published in Latin while Herbert was completing a five-year tenure as English ambassador at the French Court, was the product of a mind sensitive to the threat posed by radical Pyrrhonism and committed to rescuing religion from the twin arenas of bloody conflict and hostile polemic. Herbert was adamant in the belief that fact could only be distinguished from error by referring all questions to the judicature of man's internal—and universal—truths of first impress.[24] By comparing the ideas common to all religions, universal consent would become the pacific test of truth in matters of faith, and since God has endowed each person with an inner faculty capable of knowing the divine mandate, there was no call for external arbiters of religious principle. "Retire into yourself and enter into your own faculties," was his advice to a Europe where violence had increasingly become the test of spiritual authenticity; "you will find there God, virtue and the other universal and eternal truths."[25] Herbert's faith in the existence of ideas innate and common to all men, irrespective of their circumstances in time or place, would remain a fixture of Protestant thought until challenged by John Locke during the last decade of the seventeenth century, but while his orthodoxy regarding the origin of ideas central to one's faith was obvious, no one within the early seventeenth-century Anglican communion could countenance Herbert's radical employment of innate ideas to dismantle the institutional framework of the church. His anticipation of Deism found few sympathizers in the 1620s, and his plea for a rational reconstruction of necessary belief was looked upon as an abandonment of the very fabric of the church's commission to guide and to discipline. Nevertheless, his call for a set of common principles of faith, a natural theology made possible by universal innate ideas, forwarded the interest of younger men who would later champion the use of reason in religion in order to achieve a greater comprehension for the national church.

The escalating intolerance and dissension within the various branches of the Protestant family were clearly in evidence at the city of Dort some seven years before the publication of Lord Herbert's book.[26] One English observer at this 1618 meeting of Reformed churches, John Hales, had expected to witness a full-scale debate between the Arminian supporters of free will and their Calvinist opposites, but instead of equanimity and intelligent discussion, he found those in the Calvinist majority engaging in such tendentious questioning and possessed of such prosecutory zeal as to leave him thoroughly disillusioned with the state of Reformed Christianity. The Five Articles of the Remonstrants, composed in 1610 after the death of Arminius and defending the ideas of universal atonement, the contingent nature of grace, and perseverance in following Christ's example, were firmly condemned by the majority of the assembled delegates.[27] For Hales, this wholesale abandonment of rational inquiry in religious matters for the sake of one group's arbitrary vision of correct understanding could only cultivate and inspire the worst aspects of the human personality.[28] The ostensible issue at Dort had involved the role of human agency in the process of salvation and the extent of Christ's atonement, but in the end the Calvinist party had triumphed, it seemed, only by exhibiting those very characteristics which appeared most in consort with the personality of their arbitrary God. For the emerging middle party in England, dogmatic precision and the struggle for the mastery of men's minds appeared to have little to do with the virtues which had been enjoined by Christ at the inception of the faith. "It hath been the common disease of Christians from the beginning," Hales wrote in 1636, "not to content themselves with that measure of faith, which God and the Scriptures have expressly afforded us," but upon the pretense of church authority or tradition to impose their arbitrary views on others.[29] Tragically, when it became apparent that one of the main hopes of the early Reformers—that subjective certainty would ultimately issue in an interpretive consensus—was an illusion, the old methods of enforced conformity, this time often with the full backing of the emerging nation-state, were reintroduced. The pleadings of men like Episcopius and Grotius received their most brutal response in a Europe seemingly bent on self-destruction between 1618 and 1648. Hales himself would feel the full impact of the forces of intolerance when, during the Civil War in England, he was stripped of both his fellowship at Eton and a canonry at Windsor before dying in poverty in 1656. The still small voice of reason had but few converts before mid-century.

In England during the 1620s and 1630s, with the chasm between the Puritans and the Church of William Laud deepening as it shifted from matters of ecclesiology to more fundamental questions involving theological orthodoxy, Hales was in contact with a little group of moderates whose thought has correctly been associated with the home of Lucius Cary, Viscount Falkland, at Great Tew in Oxfordshire.[30] The Tew circle, recognizing the potentially explosive nature of the sharp disagreements separating Protestants, set themselves two central tasks: the search for unity among the Reformed churches and the rebuttal of Catholic claims to infallibility in religious matters.[31]

Both goals were to be forwarded, it was hoped, by the development of a new epistemology whereby different standards of evidence would be employed depending upon the nature of the problem under investigation. Emerging from the skeptical crisis posed by Pyrrhonism, adopted by the natural philosophers of the Royal Society after the Restoration, and championed by virtually all the Latitudinarians, this epistemological perspective set the tone for a new and more modest estimation of human potential and the capacity to know, providing its exponents with a practical tool for the defense of Anglican rationalism and an explanation for man's continuing dependence upon the power of God's grace in his search for eternal happiness.[32]

William Chillingworth was one of those who visited at Tew, and his important contribution to the discussion, published in 1638 as *The Religion of Protestants a Safe Way to Salvation*, was facilitated by the fine library there and with the assistance of Falkland, who had already taken issue with the Catholic stand in his own unpublished writings.[33] After a brief flirtation with Catholicism during the early 1630s, Chillingworth, thanks in no small part to the efforts of Laud, had returned to the Anglican Communion and set out to defend his decision on the grounds that infallible certainty on religious matters was both unattainable and unnecessary. Certain knowledge, he pointed out, was accessible only in areas such as mathematics and metaphysics, whereupon understanding the meaning of the terms employed, one was compelled to assent to the truth of the propositions in question. But in all other matters outside mere opinion, and particularly in religious questions, moral certainty or belief had to suffice, for here our judgment was based upon the evidence of sense and the testimony of reliable witnesses. This moral certainty was the equivalent of the level of conviction which operated in our ordinary daily decisions and represented the position of sane, reasonable men who acted only after they had weighed and considered all the available evidence.

Chillingworth believed that since both Catholics and Protestants accept the divine inspiration of Scripture, it alone must serve as the standard by which to settle controversies, this despite the problems involved in accurately translating texts and the apparent contradictions to be found in certain passages. And human reason, not inspiration or some special illumination, must be our guide to those essential elements in Scripture which contain the teachings necessary for salvation. The fundamentals contained therein, he believed, will be apparent to every serious student and honest inquirer.[34] As Falkland wrote concerning our responsibility to exercise reason, even if one were to grant that the Catholic Church were infallible, "yet, me thinks, he that denies it, and imploys his reason to seeke if it be true, should be in as good case as he that believes it, and searcheth not at all the truth of the proposition he receives."[35] Chillingworth's book and the mitigated skepticism it advocated became immensely popular in the second half of the century, with the work reaching a seventh edition by 1704, but in 1638 such an appeal had little to recommend it either to his increasingly unpopular godfather or to those eager to undo the archbishop's work of Anglican reconstruction. By the summer of 1640 that dismantling process was underway in earnest, and by 1644 Chillingworth, like his friend Falkland, was dead, another unforgiving statistic in the grim cause of church and king. As his body was lowered into the earth, the Presbyterian rector of Petworth, Francis Cheynell, is alleged to have angrily tossed a copy of *The Religion of Protestants* on top, hoping to bury the pernicious idea with the man.[36] It was a vindictive gesture, surely, but one which nevertheless seemed to have more than a little prophetic substance during the succeeding two decades, when the thoughts of the moderates were disregarded by factions overscrupulous for their own unique vision of Christ's true communion. As men contended for the truth as they knew it after 1642, the proposition that churchmanship was intimately related to citizenship and public order—that religious doubt masked political expediency—strengthened its harmful grip on the consciousness of a nation at war.[37]

Implicit in both Falkland and Chillingworth's argument was the belief that moral certainty, although by no means inerrant, constituted the best grounds of demonstrating the sincerity of one's faith, just as there could be scant foundation for its employment if all elements were capable of being proved beyond the shadow of a doubt. The principle of moral certainty entailed just that measure of skepticism whereby a man's belief in the truthfulness of a benevolent creator could be tested. In addition, the epistemology of moral certainty, which would later be adopted by the Latitudinarian divines, embraced a solid recognition of man's limitations and the pressing need for compromise and tolerance in light of those limits. It was a standpoint that sharply circumscribed our intellectual claims while at the same time identifying both Catholic and sectarian attitudes as the very embodiment of arrogance and pride, the shameless attempt to know all things from the vantage point of the eternal. Catholic infallibility and Protestant subjective certainty represented the strongest examples of the real evil inherent in the human situation, a pretension to knowledge and virtue which mirrored the sin of Adam in Paradise. As the Latitudinarian divine John Wilkins informed his parishioners, it was surely just and equitable "that the Sons of Adam should for his ambition and curiosity be punished with a tantalizing desire; that the tree of knowledge should be within their view, but out of their reach." Men shall forever be "afflicted by the vexation of their imperfect knowledge," and the stubborn refusal to accept this simple fact was at the root of all England's religious troubles.[38]

Wilkins's own training in the "new philosophy" of natural science during his Oxford years in the 1630s, the "tentativeness of judgment and unwillingness to find solutions based on authority," were, as his biographer reminds us, "carried over from scientific investigation to religious thought." Ordained in 1637, Wilkins combined his pastoral duties with a keen interest in scientific activities. As warden of Wadham College during the 1650s, he was instrumental in organizing the activities of natural philosophers who would later form the core of the Royal Society. His moderation at Wadham, his abiding interest in promoting a plain, direct preaching style, and his commitment to reconciling natural and revealed religion made Wilkins one of the preceptors of the younger Latitudinarians, this despite the fact that he did not move to Cambridge (as master of Trinity) until 1659. Tillotson's marriage to Wilkins's stepdaughter Elizabeth in 1664 and his appointment that same year as Tuesday lecturer at Saint Lawrence Jewry, where Wilkins was rector, illustrate one aspect of Wilkins's larger relationship with the moderate churchmen. As one of the senior members of the group of Latitudinarian divines, Wilkins had refused during the 1640s and 1650s to accept that any single model of church government had been clearly designated by God. This position, together with his conviction that all such ecclesiastical problems ought to be settled on the basis of convenience, served to strengthen the resolve of younger men who embraced the irenical spirit.[39]

Other advocates of moderation were to be found within the Anglican camp during the Cromwellian period. Another visitor at Great Tew during the 1630s, Henry Hammond, worked throughout the difficult years of the church's eclipse to build a stronger and more rational base for the Anglican model. His influential *Practical Catechism*, later used by Patrick at Cambridge and recommended by Burnet in his own work on the subject of pastoral care, stressed the centrality of moral reform at the expense of narrow theological speculation where belief and knowledge were too often equated with sanctification.[40] Hammond was deeply concerned with reforming abuses within the discredited Laudian establishment, "for raising in the Clergy a due sense of the obligations they lay under," and despite his refusal to adjust church principles during the Interregnum, his death in 1660 doubtless narrowed the chances for a comprehension once the monarchy was restored.[41]

Like Hammond, Jeremy Taylor had been a faithful defender of the episcopal standard of church government during the years leading up to the outbreak of war between the king and Parliament. A favorite of Laud's who owed his fellowship at All Souls College, Oxford, to the intervention of the archbishop in 1635, Taylor's *Episcopacy Asserted* reaffirmed the divine institution of the bishops' office and identified the ecclesiastical hierarchy with the health and stability of the monarchy. By the mid-1640s, however, Taylor's loyalty to the Crown had resulted in the loss of his regular living and his eventual exile in Wales, where he established a school and published, in 1647, a work designed to heal the divisions between Christians in a society where theology could not easily be separated from politics.[42] In *A Discourse of the Liberty of Prophesying*, Taylor adopted the mitigated skepticism of his Oxford acquaintance Chillingworth to argue that while essential religious duties should be apparent to all reasonable men, there could be no infallible guide in religious matters. If our neighbors be Christians in their lives, Taylor asked, if they acknowledge the Son of God as their master and Lord and live as becomes persons making these professions, "why then should I hate such persons . . . because their understandings have not been brought up like mine, have not had the same masters, have not met with the same books, nor the same company."[43] Accepting as inevitable a relativity of belief due to the wide variety of educational experiences and individual tempers, Taylor concluded that only by permitting diversity over matters not essential to the core of belief could Englishmen extricate themselves from the chaos of civil war. "The variety of human understandings is so great," he observed, "what is plain and apparent to one, is difficult and obscure to another," making all attempts at coercion both unprofitable and otiose.[44] For men to be so in love with their particular opinions as to force them upon another is just one more sobering measure of the extent of our peccancy since the Fall.[45]

Taylor remained faithful to the persecuted Church of England during his exile, returning to serve Charles II after the Restoration, but with his powerful defense of the minimal creed, he won for himself no better reward than the distant bishopric of Down and Conner, a station where his irenical ideas would have a minimal impact on the shape of Archbishop Sheldon's reconstructed Establishment and even less influence upon the Presbyterian settlers who inhabited his troublesome diocese.[46]

Cambridge also played host to a few varied advocates of reconciliation during the years of civil war, and, as Patrick indicated in his *Brief Account of the New Sect of Latitude-Men*, the university town provided the immediate setting for the intellectual development of most of the moderate churchmen. Stillingfleet, Tillotson, Moore, Tenison, Fowler, and Patrick all received their education there at a time when the call for religious restraint and ecumenism was still affirmed thanks in large measure to the exertions of the group we call Cambridge Platonists. Many of the future Latitude-men had been reared in Puritan households, and their years at university became a time for serious and sometimes prolonged reevaluation. Joseph Glanvill, whose own university experience was at Oxford, recalled that as a youth in Puritan Plymouth, "I was continually instructed into a Religious and fast adherence to every thing that I was taught, and a dread of dissenting in the least Article. This discipline I underwent in my younger days and thought very strange of those that believed any different from the opinions of my instructors."[47]

The Cambridge Platonists—Benjamin Whichcote, Ralph Cudworth, John Smith, Henry More—actively encouraged just the sort of critical inquiry which had been forbidden Glanvill as a youth. Properly recognized by modern students for their lasting opposition to Hobbesian mechanism, their appeals to reason and a corollary disparagement of enthusiasm and the rigidities of formal worship, their rejection of man's total depravity, their ethical emphasis in the pulpit, and their preference for a religion made up of a few broad truths, the Platonists' contribution to the moderate church outlook has never been much in doubt.[48] A good example of that influence is provided by Patrick's own experience at Cambridge during the Civil War and Interregnum. He had originally sought to matriculate at King's College in 1644, but failing that was admitted to Queens' on the recommendation of Cudworth and the provost of King's, Benjamin Whichcote. While studying there, he became a close friend of John

Smith, maintaining regular contact until the latter's untimely death in
1652. It was Smith who reassured Patrick that predestination had no
place in God's benevolent plan for mankind, and it was Patrick who,
in turn, was entrusted with the oversight of Smith's undergraduate
students while Smith traveled to London for medical treatment.[49]
Selected by the fellows of Queens' to preach Smith's funeral sermon
in 1653, Patrick recalled that his friend "was always very urgent upon
us, that by the grace of God, and the help of the mighty Spirit of Jesus
Christ working in us, we would endeavour to purge out the corruption of our natures."[50] The special place reserved for the influence
of God's grace in the work of salvation may not be a commonplace
one normally associates with the ethical teaching of Cambridge Platonism, but that Patrick cared enough to identify it as a major theme
in the theology of his mentor is suggestive of one of the neglected
links between the moderate churchmen and their academic friends,
all of whom shared Smith's desire to highlight the role of unmerited
grace in the work of transforming man's nature preparatory to salvation.[51] The Platonists, despite their emphasis on the force of reason,
would not have their call for an ethical Christianity nullify the primacy of God's will in empowering sinful humanity to work towards a
partial obedience to the eternal law. Nor would they have their familiar "candle of the Lord" metaphor detract from the importance of
supernatural light and the relative insignificance of human reason in
the drama of salvation.[52] Theirs was a theology which undoubtedly
stressed the potential goodness of human nature, yet the work of
grace remained as the essential fulfillment of that nature, and bereft
of its influence, moral acts were of no consequence in man's search
for salvation.

In 1651 an important exchange took place between Whichcote
(who has long been considered the unofficial leader of the Cambridge
group) and his former Emmanuel College tutor Anthony Tuckney.[53]
The letters which passed between the two men have often been used
by historians to illustrate the scale of the break with Calvinism that
was characteristic for students of Whichcote's generation at Cambridge, but as a result, little attention has been directed towards
the points at which Whichcote outlined a more traditional picture
of the limits placed upon mankind in the search for salvation. Two
issues clearly divided Tuckney and his younger friend. The former's
concern over the rationalizing tendencies in Whichcote's sermons—

his references to pagan moralists, his apparent confidence in man's rational nature, the use of the "candle of the Lord" metaphor—are well known to students of the Platonists and certainly constitute an important point of departure for this school of thought.[54] But Tuckney was equally concerned that Whichcote's innovative theology was moving ineluctably towards an arrogant Arminianism where God's reconciliation with sinners was more the result of human volition than it was the exclusive product of divine will.

Whichcote, seeking to clarify his orthodox credentials on the question of the role of merit, apologized to Tuckney if in his recent sermons he had inadvertently "done prejudice to saving grace, by idolizing natural ingenuity" and protested that whatever steps he may have taken to restore man's capacity for rational behavior, he continued to "abhorre and detest from my soule all creature-magnifying self-sufficiencie." Despite his elevation of reason in his sermons, then, Whichcote insisted that "I attribute to the creature, upon itt's own accounte, nothing but unworthiness inabilitie and insufficiencie: and look at Christ, as the onlie ground of acceptance; and his spirit, as the onlie principle of enablement power and sufficiencie."[55] He acknowledged God in all his endeavors, saying that "there is nothing more written in my heart, than my sense of dependencie upon Him."[56] Tillotson, whose close association with Whichcote at the church of Saint Lawrence Jewry in London afforded him a special insight into the Platonist's preaching style, recalled that Whichcote "continually implored, and mightily relied upon" the assistance of God's grace in all his undertakings, inculcating the same sense of human dependency in his auditors at Saint Lawrence.[57] The rehabilitation of man's nature associated with Platonism did not include an abandonment of the principle, first associated with the writings of Saint Paul and integral to the fabric of Christian anthropology, that the grace of God, not man's moral freedom, provided the primary element in our work towards salvation, and this essential qualification was embraced by all of the Latitudinarian divines during the Restoration and into the eighteenth century.

It is true that the Platonists strongly underscored man's potential to act in accordance with the inborn principles of reason provided by a loving God, who, as Henry More declared, "communicates his own Nature [to man] so far forth as it is capable of receiving it."[58] But of equal importance to their picture of man's relationship with his maker was the belief that ethical conduct was not the natural product of man's present condition but rather the result of protracted and systematic training designed to restore his nature as it had first proceeded from the hands of the Creator in Paradise. Virtue may have been constitutive to human nature for the Platonists, but when they spoke of that nature they defined it in terms of what God had intended it to be prior to the Fall. "The soul of man," said Cudworth, who was master of Clare Hall while Tillotson was a student there, "was harmonical as God first made it, till sin, disordering the strings and faculties, put it out of tune, and marred the music of it."[59] It was abundantly clear to all the Platonists that man had repudiated his original nature with the Fall and that the true life of the soul was the recovery of the divine image in the individual. "A Man would think that rational nature would not be so depraved," wrote Whichcote sadly, "but that we have woeful experience of it."[60] Norman Sykes once observed that for the Platonists "the moral consciousness of man was a sure guide to salvation," but the fact remained that before such consciousness was awakened, there was little good to be expected from the offspring of Adam.[61] "That that which is Good indeed should be generally relished by the World," wrote More, "is as unlikely, as that Dead Men in their Graves should call out for Drink."[62]

In their reluctance to accept any simple resolution to the problem of man's present alienation from his God-given nature, the Platonists were not unlike Tillotson's college tutor, who (despite his Calvinist sympathies) was convinced that "the mind of man was the candle of the Lord." The soul, opined the Dissenter David Clarkson, "as it proceeded from God, was a clear lightsom beam, brighter than any ray of sun; but hereby [due to sin] it is become a noysom dunghill."[63] As educators, the Platonists recognized the importance of training into a Christian pattern of life. We are to become like God in the fulfillment of our duty, Whichcote advised, "as soon as we come to the use of reason and understanding," and the proper use of those faculties was not to be achieved without careful guidance.[64] They refused to oppose the spiritual to the rational in their theology, nor would they accept any abridgment of the potential of innate ideas or common notions to provide mankind with the fundamentals of a natural theology. Their faith clearly rested on rational grounds, but their natural theology took the full measure of the sinfulness of mankind and the importance of prevenient grace in making the ethical life possible. The moderate churchmen may have had little to learn from the mystical emphasis within Cambridge Platonism, but their plea for greater tolerance and a religion centered on conformity to the word of God, together with an orthodox picture of man with his constant need for divine assistance, had a lasting impact on the younger men who attended university during the years of civil war and political upheaval.[65]

The capstone of this long-term undertaking to restore the claims of reason and moderation in a world of sectarian feuding, while remaining steadfast in adherence to the Reformed view of man's status since the Fall (and the first such work by one of the moderate churchmen), appeared in the year the monarchy was restored under the title *Irenicum: A Weapon-Salve for the Church's Wounds* (1660). Its twenty-four-year-old author, Edward Stillingfleet, was the vicar of Sutton in Sussex and a recent graduate of Saint John's College, Cambridge. He had already decided in favor of episcopacy for himself by receiving ordination at the hands of the deprived bishop of Exeter, Dr. Ralph Brownrig, in 1657. But Stillingfleet's *Irenicum* reflects nothing of the partisanship soon to mark the restored Anglican Establishment, and it is evident that the Platonists' example at Cambridge was not without its influence on him.[66]

The protracted religious controversies of the previous decades, Stillingfleet lamented, "have brought at last even Religion its self into a Controversie," with weaker heads coming to the determination that faith itself has no sure foundation. His was an age, surely, "wherein Men talked of Religion most, and lived it least," and he was convinced that the sole solution to the crisis lay in following the example of the primitive church, where, it appeared, diversity had been permitted in things indifferent. Stillingfleet could discover no single form of church government prescribed by Scripture, nor did it appear that Christ had ever intended one pattern to prevail. He thought that the episcopal model best provided a dignified structure and rule whereby the worship of God could be performed with gravity and solemnity, but he insisted that "I am not for the asserting the necessity of any one form of that Government." His major criterion for evaluating any model was the extent to which its exponents pursued the search for the essentials of the faith in a tolerant manner, one that acknowledged men's inability to know with dogmatic certainty. The kingdom

of God consisted of righteousness and peace known by both an un-
alterable law of nature and positive precept; and the fractious men of
party, being for too long "very loath to put themselves to the trouble
of a Holy Life," must be persuaded to surrender their mistaken claim
to exemption from the sin of pride.[67]

Stillingfleet's timely work was certainly aimed at those who placed
their faith in the certainty of Scripture, but it was, in the end, essentially a skeptical argument which applied gentle pressure on anyone
who was bold enough to claim final authority for a particular form
of church polity. Burnet recalled that the work "took with many, but
was cried out upon by others as an attempt against the Church."[68]
Its practical counterpart was to be found in Charles Stuart's Breda
Declaration of 1660, but like that ill-fated olive branch, Stillingfleet's
youthful vision would remain just as unattainable in 1660 as it had
been in the days of Great Tew. Among many legacies, the Middle
Ages had left the early modern world a distinct conviction that loyalty to the state entailed membership in the church of that state.
Reformation Europe underlined this assumption with a vehement
suppression of all forms of dissent. Early Protestants had told men
and women to go to their Bibles, and with the help of translations
and the increasing availability of the printing press, the expansion
of lay knowledge was not inconsiderable. But the gates which had
been opened by the 1530s invariably led to the problematic realization that the truths contained in Scripture were matters of question
and debate. The acknowledgment of this stubborn reality and the
recognition that diversity over adiaphora did not pose a threat to the
integrity of either the polity or the church were slow to take hold in
the intellectual climate of the Restoration.[69] Simon Patrick's election
to the mastership of Queens' would be overridden in 1660, and the
new sect of Latitude-men would soon find themselves allied to a re-
established church whose actions during the 1660s seemed strangely
in concordance with those of the Presbyterian minister who in 1637
had buried Chillingworth's *Religion of Protestants* along with the man.
But while their calls for accommodation would not be respected,
while the advocacy of a simple creed with few essentials would be
looked upon as a cowardly capitulation to sectarian dissent, their
opponents within the established church would not be remiss in supporting a brand of practical theology difficult to distinguish from
that espoused by the Latitudinarians. The ethical and rational em-

phasis of Hooker's *Laws*, the pleas of the Dutch Arminians and the Cambridge Platonists for a return to a system of belief validated by behavior, and the new criterion of truth brought forward by the revival of ancient skepticism all played their part in shaping the ideals of the Restoration church.

More importantly for our estimation of Patrick's *Brief Account of the New Sect of Latitude-Men*, the various intellectual progenitors of the moderate churchmen accepted the doctrines of the church without reservation and communicated that loyalty to the men who would now be disowned by their ecclesiastical peers. The controversial liberty of conscience which the Latitude-men promoted, argued Patrick, was actually within the framework of the church's teachings and did not injure their commitment to the doctrinal canon. Narrow men who sought to impugn the orthodoxy of Anglicans like Patrick "would have all things bound up, and nothing free; they would fain be adding some ciphers to their [sic] significant Articles she now propounds, and instead of 39 would make 39000."[70] Acceptance of the Thirty-nine Articles, "and all other points of Doctrine contained either in the Liturgy or book of Homilies," placed the Latitude-men firmly within a tradition which viewed the depth of human sinfulness as a lasting bar to salvation through works and ethical behavior.[71] The unmerited grace of God, offered to mankind through the life and death of Christ, together with the faith of the believer who understood the sin of pride involved in works-righteousness, provided the intellectual framework for the Latitudinarian picture of Reformed Christianity.

For those who resented the willingness of the moderate churchmen to live in peace under a hostile regime, the attempt to reconcile a reasonable faith, a simple creed, a focus on ethics, and an interest in the new mechanical philosophy with the harsh realities of Article X, where the children of Adam "have no power to do good works . . . without the grace of God by Christ preventing us," seemed completely indefensible. But viewed within the context of the religious clashes of the mid–seventeenth century, any effort to retain the majesty and omnipotence of God without destroying his benevolence seemed to represent a step towards sanity. Hoping with Erasmus "to analyze and not to judge, to inquire and not to dogmatize," the churchmen who owned the derisive title "Latitude-men" entered the England of Charles II with thoughts of focusing the attention of

Protestants on the "ancient simplicity of the Church."[72] It was, then, to the past that the Latitude-men looked for their model of the ideal Christian life, to a church where the claims of reason neither compromised the work of the Redeemer nor released humanity from the crippling consequences of Adam's sinful disobedience.

When Charles Stuart issued his conciliatory Declaration of Breda on 4 April 1660, proponents of reconciliation within the Anglican communion, together with those moderate Presbyterians who had helped make the Restoration possible, had some reason to hope that strong support from the monarchy would be sufficient to blunt the forces of Cavalier reaction and resentment which had been stirring since the early years of the Long Parliament, forces intent upon managing both the spirit and structure of a re-established church order. Nobility and gentry who had once been eager to attack Laudian pretensions were by the late 1650s outraged over their loss of power under Cromwell and sought the restoration of episcopacy as a means of defending the traditional order in politics and society.[1] Before his return to England in May, Charles appeared to demonstrate his intention to settle the religious question without regard for the sensibilities of disgruntled Royalists by appointing some Nonconformists as royal chaplains and by making repeated promises of goodwill and peace to Presbyterians who had visited him in Holland. The prospect of a single communion was not entirely beyond the realm of possibility, especially if the situation on the eve of the Civil War is taken into account. For all its divisions, the church of Elizabeth and the first two Stuarts did "comprehend" all Englishmen with the exception of Roman Catholics. Before the outbreak of hostilities in 1642, Calvinists and Laudians still held out the hope that their respective positions would take permanent root within the official communion. Schism, at any rate, was unaccept-able to both sides in 1642. Unhappily for this admittedly strained union, the actions taken against the Laudian church during the war years—the 1642 exclusion of the bishops from the Lords, the abolition of the episcopal office in 1643, the sequestration of church lands—coupled with the internecine quarrels of the various Calvinist parties throughout the Interregnum created a situation in which talk of settling ecclesiastical differences was thought to be impractical.[2]

It soon became clear, in fact, that the king had set forth in the Breda Declaration an unselfish vision to which he had no deep personal commitment, fully aware as he was of his own delicate position in a fluid political climate, and seeking principally to placate a parliament intent upon restoring the rights and prerogatives of the Anglican hierarchy.[3] Whatever his personal religious convictions may have been, and despite his plea for conciliation after years of bitterness and bloodshed, Charles was not only powerless to override the wishes of the political nation, but he was also plainly indifferent to the philosophical argument being made by moderates like Stillingfleet in favor of a broadly comprehensive church whose polity and doctrine were based on utility rather than divine sanction.[4] And when Anglican exiles and sequestered High Church loyalists returned to London with the monarch in the spring of 1660, eager to resume their livings under the patronage of Cavalier gentry, older moderate churchmen like John Wilkins and members of the Platonist group at Cambridge, men who had to varying degrees consented to the Interregnum government and its religious program, found themselves outside the circles of power and suspected of having been little more than time-servers under a bankrupt regime. As Alan Clifford has written regarding Tillotson's critics, "a cool, conciliatory manner was viewed with suspicion by those for whom orthodoxy and pugnacity were all of a piece."[5] The council of the moderates, then, be they Anglican or Presbyterian, was both unwelcome and considered dangerous to men who had suffered with their monarch and whose own harsh experience buttressed the belief that compromise inevitably fueled dissent and bred ecclesiastical disorder, political upheaval, and civil strife.[6] Unlike the political sphere, where a willingness to bargain with those who had served the Commonwealth brought staunch Royalists into contact with a variety of opposing viewpoints, the Restoration Church lacked all semblance of balance during the crucial decade of the 1660s, making not only interdiction but active persecution of dissent the preferred policy of its frightened but resolute leadership.[7]

The appointment of the aged and infirm William Juxon—friend of Laud and devoted servant of Charles I—to the restored see of Canterbury was, perhaps, the symbolic gesture of thanks that the new king felt obliged to make on behalf of those who had endured humiliation and defeat alongside the Stuart family, but even as early as the royal coronation in the spring of 1661, the real power behind the revitalized Church of England was a former member of the Great Tew circle and now bishop of London, Gilbert Sheldon.[8] Burnet's tendentious claim that Sheldon "seemed not to have a deep sense of religion, if any at all, and spoke of it most commonly as of an engine of government" is certainly unwarranted, but the new bishop of London was definitely an abler statesman than a divine, and despite his earlier association with Falkland and Chillingworth, he possessed none of the conciliatory qualities which distinguished High Church Royalists like Hammond.[9] The latter's death in early 1660 robbed the church of that one universally respected High Church leader who might have proved critical during those negotiations with the Presbyterians that took place at the Savoy in April 1661.[10] Ostensibly a conference between equals called at the behest of a monarch still hoping to avoid a tragic breach in the national church communion, the newly restored bishops entered into the proceedings with all the confidence of those whose job it is to evaluate the protestations of a worried and beggarly suppliant.[11]

With the failed Fifth Monarchy insurrection of January 1661 as a sobering backdrop, religious dissent of any sort was invariably equated in the mind of the church with subversion,[12] and therefore it was not surprising that Richard Baxter's suggestions for a revised liturgy, together with several other points about episcopal reordination and required ceremony, were found to be without merit by the Anglican representatives, whose subsequent report to the king confidently declared that substantive concessions were unnecessary.[13] Seconded by a Convocation whose unedifying contribution to the whole affair was to propose a series of minor changes in the Book of Common Prayer, the overwhelmingly Cavalier Parliament which met in May 1662 accepted this inflexible package without debate, thereby setting the stage for the subsequent prolonged attack on the legitimacy of dissent known to history under the misnomer "Clarendon Code."[14] The preliminary steps in the direction of renewed intolerance had already been taken the year before, when the Commons passed a resolution excluding any member who refused to take communion according to the Anglican rite, but the legislation of 1662 confirmed Parliament's singularity of purpose in the face of royal efforts to stem the tide of angry bigotry.[15] The 1662 Act of Uniformity established a number of requirements on men who sought to maintain a benefice. Foremost among these was the acceptance of everything contained in the prayer book, episcopal ordination or reordination for non-Anglicans, and a renunciation of the Solemn League and Covenant. The prospect of reordination called into question the legitimacy of one's prior ministry, while the final requirement seemed to preclude any future amendment to the structure and doctrines of the church. It was a test, as W. H. Hutton wrote at the beginning of this century, born of the nervous conviction that all the troubles of the previous twenty years had been caused by the intrusion into government by men who harbored contempt for the official communion.[16]

For not a few Anglicans after 1660, it was self-evident that "the fanaticks know no other step to the magistry, but through the ruin of the ministry."[17] In order to forestall such a tragedy, on Saint Bartholomew's Day 1662 almost one thousand clergy were barred from the church for their refusal to consent to the Act of Uniformity, the full text of which many had not even been afforded sufficient time to read and digest.[18] It was undoubtedly a victory for the Sheldonians—men such as George Morley, Peter Gunning, and John Cosin—but it had been won at considerable cost in terms of both the church's larger autonomy and its spiritual prestige. No longer could a hierarchy which rejected dissent advance any plausible claim to speak for all Protestant believers in England, nor could that hierarchy continue to set the terms of its own internal discipline without the consent of members of Parliament who had transformed the sacrament of the Lord's Supper into a political test while treating the church as little more than an insurance policy against the great masses who would threaten their comfortable world.[19]

The leaders of the church in 1660 rejected religious pluralism and linked themselves to the wishes of the ruling class not only due to pluralism's association with sectarian violence and civil unrest during the Interregnum but also to a positive sense of evangelical conviction about the nature of divine worship and its place in the life of the nation. It is true that many of the worst elements of the old church order returned in 1660—lay impropriation of tithes and benefices, vast disparities in the wealth of the clergy, pluralism and nonresidence often made necessary by widespread penury—but as John Miller has recently pointed out, it is difficult for us to recognize that the church after 1660 "was in many respects militant and efforts to reimpose uniformity rested on a clearly perceived vision of the role of a Christian Church in a Christian society."[20] For Anglicans like Sheldon and the men who served under him in the restored episcopate, the mission of the church was to function as the central unifying force in the reconstructed national community, one where all Christians would be accorded equal status before God. But in order to realize such a goal, everyone must be made accountable to the moral and judicial authority of an all-inclusive church. The church, it was thought, would receive strong support from the civil power in its work as the guardian and teacher of the nation's religious sensibilities and in return would inculcate loyalty to the monarchy and the principle of indefeasible hereditary right.[21] To permit separation was to legitimize the arrogant and exclusivist notion, long embraced by Calvinists, that the godly community was to be sharply distinguished from the unregenerate majority.[22] Isaac Barrow confirmed this perspective when he observed that without episcopal control over church order, individual clergy "will say and do anything; they will in teaching please their own humour, or soothe the people, or serve their own interests."[23] Since only between 5 and 10 percent of Englishmen could be counted within the ranks of Nonconformity, the Anglican ideal of a truly national church in the service of God, king, morals, and social stability, particularly after the upheaval of the previous twenty years, seemed to many to be a realistic and positive goal in the 1660s, especially since the popularity of traditional religious forms had remained exceptional during the Interregnum.[24]

Another factor contributing to the hostility of the episcopate to proposals for comprehension involved the very practical and pressing problem of rebuilding both the fabric and the spirit of the Anglican communion after almost twenty years of desuetude. Only eleven English and Welsh bishops were still alive in 1659, and seven of these men were over seventy years of age.[25] There had been few ordinations of new clergy during the Interregnum as bishops hesitated to offend Cromwell's government by bringing attention to themselves, and over one thousand vacancies needed to be filled after the Act of Uniformity took effect. In Leicestershire alone, one-fourth of the parish incumbents were ejected by September 1660, while by 1662 half the county's parishes experienced clerical turnover.[26] Cathedrals and churches were in general disrepair, while many country parishes were without communion tables, surplices, fonts, or even Books of Common Prayer. Brian Duppa spent forty-six thousand pounds on the repair of churches in his diocese of Winchester, while Hacket of Litchfield spent much of his episcopal income over ten years on restoring a cathedral which had been besieged three times during the Civil War. Exeter Cathedral had been divided into two sections by a wall, with Presbyterians holding services in one end and Independents in the other. Thirteen out of eighteen city churches were unfit to hold congregations, while the bishop's palace was under lease to a private business.[27] In London the effects of Commonwealth neglect, together with the devastation of the fire of 1665, placed enormous financial strain on the church.

Throughout the country the spiritual desolation of the people was great. Two developments under Cromwell, the withdrawal of compulsory attendance at services between 1650 and 1657 and the introduction of civil marriage in 1653, had afforded Englishmen the opportunity to distance themselves altogether from the oversight responsibilities of the church.[28] Thomas Sprat, writing in the 1670s, observed that "it cannot be denied, but in this last Age, in most of our memories, our Nation has manifestly degenerated from the practice of former times, in many Moral Virtues, and Spiritual Graces."[29] The revived episcopal bench, strengthened by the appointment of younger "Laudian" sympathizers, was confronted by the need to ordain new men rapidly after the ejections; episcopal visitations had to be undertaken; and a host of judicial matters demanded immediate attention.[30] The duties of the bishops were enormous, and unfortunately, too much of their time and energy was expended fulfilling political obligations in the House of Lords.[31] The spirit of the Worcester House Declaration of August 1660, where suffragan bishops were proposed to assist their superiors, was unfortunately forgotten.[32] To spend valuable time wrangling over schemes for accommodation seemed folly when such simple but necessary tasks as curbing the practice of baptism in private homes, improving public catechizing, and increasing communion services for the laity remained to be addressed. In the end the simplest solution to the petitions of Dissenters appeared to lie in the proscription of their activities.

For those moderate churchmen like John Wilkins and his son-in-law John Tillotson, men who had not received episcopal ordination prior to 1660, acceptance of the settlement and the Act of Uniformity did not pose any special problems due to their conviction that one should not quarrel over things indifferent when the interests of peace and unity were at stake. Since the differences between Presbyterians and Anglicans did not concern important principles of theology but rather minor questions of order and practice, moderate Dissenters should welcome the opportunity to join with their friends in the church in order to present a united front against dangerous sectaries and papists. Future opportunities would surely present themselves for a successful resolution of all outstanding difficulties.[33] Barbara Shapiro has shown how John Wilkins was deeply disappointed when moderates like Richard Baxter, Edward Calamy, and Thomas Manton refused to follow his lead given their concurrence in the opinion that the issues separating Presbyterians from Anglicans were not clearly defined by Scripture. What Wilkins failed to appreciate was an opposing point of view which insisted that in such indifferent matters it was the obligation of the church to yield its coercive authority, that it was incumbent upon the ruling establishment to exercise charity wherever doubts are manifest. The failing was shared by the rest of the moderate churchmen throughout the Restoration period, as all of them repeatedly mistook Presbyterian adherence to principle for obstinacy and malign prejudice.[34]

The High-Church reaction at Cambridge after 1660 resulted in the relocation of many of the younger men who were derisively called Latitudinarians to London, where sympathetic lay patrons provided both moral assistance and important benefices.[35] Lord Keeper Heneage Finch was the most active supporter of the young divines, none of whom willingly appropriated the word "Latitudinarian" as a distinguishing label. John Moore and John Sharp were chaplains to the Finch family, Tillotson was made a prebend at Saint Paul's, and Patrick was nominated for the living at Saint Martin-in-the-Fields thanks to the recommendations of Sharp, who was entrusted with awarding the positions in the gift of the Lord Keeper. Members of the legal profession, long at odds with the church's disciplinary machinery, also provided opportunities for clerics who were willing to downplay the role of the church courts. During the early 1660s, what little influence these Latitudinarians exerted on the temper of religious life found its expression in the city, and particularly at the Church of Saint Lawrence Jewry, where both John Wilkins and then Benjamin Whichcote served as vicars between 1662 and 1683 and where John Locke's college friend John Mapletoft served from 1686 until 1721.

Wilkins's appointment in 1662 to this important parish close by the Guildhall was made possible by the influence of the incumbent, Seth Ward, who was vacating the cure to accept the bishopric of Exeter.[36] Tillotson, as noted earlier, was appointed Tuesday lecturer at Saint Lawrence under Wilkins in 1664, while the lay philanthropist and Unitarian Thomas Firmin often selected guest preachers after Tillotson's advancement to dean of Canterbury in 1672. An informal intellectual circle that formed around Wilkins included younger divines like Tillotson, Stillingfleet, Patrick, Mapletoft, William Lloyd, and sympathetic laymen like Locke and Firmin.

Other London churches also played host to Latitudinarian divines after the Restoration. Patrick became vicar of Saint Paul's, Covent Garden, in 1663, while Thomas Tenison was chosen to succeed William Lloyd at Saint Martin-in-the-Fields on the recommendation of Patrick to Heneage Finch. Their close personal ties, established in the capital largely due to their forced departure from Cambridge, served to unite the Latitudinarians in a casual alliance against the extremes of Anglican formalism and Catholic authoritarianism throughout the period 1660 to 1688. But with Sheldon's elevation to Canterbury at the death of Juxon in 1662, there was not much opportunity for this small group of moderates to receive a hearing, especially on such politically volatile issues as comprehension for Presbyterians. The London clergy, particularly those associated with Saint Lawrence, were clearly an exception to the rule of physical toil and personal hardship which characterized the lives of many rural clerics, where poverty too often meant "that their labors have no influence upon the Minds of Men, except it be those very few that are able to distinguish their Characters from their Circumstances."[37] The contributions of the Latitudinarians—their plain style in the pulpit, the erudite attacks against atheism, the spirited defense of Anglicanism in the face of Catholic criticism, the promulgation of a more rational religion—all had little bearing on the clergy outside the cities and university towns, men who had scant opportunity for intellectual pursuits and whose straitened circumstances precluded access to current literature on these issues.[38] Such men by and large were hostile towards dissent; shared no sympathy for schemes of comprehension, and, as the decade of the 1690s would prove, had prejudices that would effectively immobilize the reform schemes of their new, more moderate bishops.

On one occasion only did the moderate position receive a hearing in the 1660s, but the circumstances proved to be even less propitious than they had been at the time of the Restoration and the practical results even more humiliating. Direct persecution of Dissenters under the "Clarendon Code" had abated somewhat during the plague year of 1665 as Nonconformist ministers won the respect of many for their refusal to abandon London when many of their Anglican counterparts had fled. Despite Sheldon's attempt to set an example by remaining behind in the city, popular criticism of the episcopal bench intensified.[39] And in the aftermath of the Great Fire, with so many of London's churches destroyed, Nonconformist ministers began to preach openly.[40] The reprieve continued with the outbreak of war with the Dutch in 1666, as the government was anxious to cultivate the loyalty of English Calvinists in what for them might be an otherwise unpopular struggle against their religious kinsmen.[41] In addition, advocates of comprehension were not unaware that the king's personal desire to obtain concessions for Catholics through the mechanism of greater toleration for all Dissenters would be less apt to succeed if moderate Nonconformists were successfully integrated into the Anglican fold. Thus a strong anti-Catholic strain combined with more altruistic motives to further the goal of comprehension.[42]

With the fall of Clarendon on 30 August 1667, the members of the cabal government began to echo their monarch's growing frustration with the intransigence of the church over the problem of dissent. Charles, angered by Sheldon's rebukes concerning his lifestyle, banished the archbishop from court and undertook to exercise greater discretion in church appointments. But Sheldon's position in the House of Lords remained virtually impregnable, and his hardline attitude towards dissent was still being applauded by the country gentry who, although never passionate about the integrity of the Church of England, were receptive to the rhetoric of intellectually committed royalists who equated the cessation of persecution with political unrest and social instability.[43] A bill designed to alter the Act of Uniformity had in fact been prepared in the fall of 1667 by Sir Robert Atkins, the future chief baron of the exchequer under William III, but the M.P. who was supposed to introduce the proposal in the House lost heart at the last moment.[44]

Despite this adverse background, the duke of Buckingham, together with the earl of Manchester and Lord Keeper Orlando

Bridgeman, set out to pursue the issue, and they recruited the rector of Saint Lawrence to treat with the leaders of the Presbyterians in the hope that a workable plan might be presented before the archbishop could rally his parliamentary forces.[45] There was much confidence in the dissenting community at the time. According to Pepys, "the Nonconformists are mighty high and their meetings frequented and connived at; and they do expect to have their day now soon."[46] What eventually emerged from the January 1668 conference between Wilkins and Hezekiah Burton on the one side and Baxter, Thomas Manton, and William Bates on the other was a plan whereby ministers outside the Anglican communion would be afforded the option of avoiding formal reordination by a bishop. Wilkins suggested that the non-episcopally ordained ministers should be recognized with the words, "Take thou authority to preach the word of God and to administer the sacraments in any congregation of the Church of England where thou shalt be lawfully appointed thereto." Certain requirements—bowing at the name of Jesus, use of the cross in baptism, kneeling for communion—would also be relaxed, and revisions in the Book of Common Prayer would be entertained if the primary legislation was passed.[47] According to the proposals, it would only be necessary for Presbyterians to subscribe to "the doctrine, worship, and government established in the Church of England, as containing all things necessary to salvation." Wilkins also discussed the toleration of Independents with John Owen, who had evidently received support from Buckingham to draw up a separate bill on behalf of the Congregationalists.

When Sheldon received word of the discussions and the proposed legislation through Wilkins's friend Seth Ward, he alerted his Cavalier allies in Parliament, and the issue was immediately raised at the start of the parliamentary session.[48] A bill was drafted by Sir Matthew Hale, and the king recommended to Parliament "that you would sincerely think of some course to beget a better union and composure in the mind of my Protestant subjects in matters of Religion," but before Hale had the opportunity to bring the proposal forward, the Commons peremptorily forbade the introduction of any legislation designed to ameliorate the situation of Nonconformists, with some members angrily moving that anyone who sought to enact further statutes concerning religion might as well come "in as a proposer of new laws did in Athens, with ropes about their necks."[49] Riots took place in London in the wake of the defeat but were quickly suppressed, and by 1670 a new offensive had been launched by Sheldon against all dissent. A tougher Conventicle Act was passed imposing stiff fines on those who attended illegal religious meetings, and a single justice of the peace was now able to take punitive action against any Nonconformist on the word of an informant. The efforts of the Latitude-men to achieve modest reform through the legislative process were, for the moment, abandoned. Wilkins, whose willingness to consider the pleas of the Independents for a toleration had infuriated M.P.s who were otherwise willing to discuss comprehension, was subsequently (September 1668) elevated to the see of Chester against the protests of Sheldon, but the bishop had little further impact on church policy at the national level.[50]

While the question of the propriety of comprehension was being canvassed by Wilkins and his Presbyterian opposites in 1668, it was already becoming clear that there existed little genuine Latitudinarian empathy for nonconforming Protestants who refused to accept the moderate Anglican model for an inclusive church. Reservations born of the Civil War experience abounded within clerical ranks, and these memories were hard to efface so soon after the end of the Commonwealth experiment. Simon Patrick's view was illustrative of the general mood and suggests that many of the concerns of the Sheldonians were shared by the Latitude-men. In the very year of the comprehension and toleration scheme, Patrick published his *Friendly Debate Between a Conformist and a Non-conformist* in which Dissenters were described as men who would not "govern their passions, not reverence their elders, not fear to make a schism in the Church, being furiously bent to follow their own fancies, impatient of contradiction, conceited of their own gifts."[51] He referred disparagingly to the roots of dissent in the early part of the century, casting particular blame on the pretensions of Nonconformist ministers who criticized the official church. As soon as such men "had cast out of doors all that was old among us, if any fellow did but light upon some new and pretty fancy in religion, or some odd unusual expression, or perhaps some swelling words of vanity, presently he set up for a preacher, and cried up himself for a man that had made some new discovery."[52] The pretensions of the Dissenters to be "the only godly people, and we at the best but moral men," suggested the extent to which criticism normally made of the Latitudinarians (that they were mere preachers of moralism) could easily be extended to include the spirit of the entire Anglican establishment. Archbishop Sheldon, who had been angry with Patrick for contesting the king's selection of Anthony Sparrow for the presidency of Queens' College back in 1662, now warmly received the author of the *Friendly Debate* as a true defender of the Anglican ideal of peace through conformity.[53]

The strength of Patrick's performance was even conceded by Richard Baxter, who thought that the book had served to hearten not only "haters of Non-conformists" but also "all the prophane despisers and deriders of serious Godliness." The book, in its careless lumping of radical Independents with moderate Presbyterians, "was as fit an Engine to destroy Christian Love on both sides, and to engage men in those ways which still more destroy it, as any thing of long time hath been published."[54] More importantly, Baxter believed that the Latitudinarians had managed to betray their own principles by such thoughtless expositions. Whereas in their own case, "being not so strict in their Theology or way of piety as some others," the Latitudinarians thought that conformity was a reasonable price to pay in order to remain in the ministry, now they "grew into such a distaste" of men whose prayer, preaching, and discourse were different from their own that "they seemed to be out of Love with their very Doctrines, and their manner of worshipping God." Even Gilbert Burnet was critical of Patrick, believing that the book had needlessly heightened popular hostility against Dissenters.[55] For the Latitudinarians, the terms of a comprehension were strictly limited to what members of the Church of England, whose preeminent fear was the creation of a schism within the church, found permissible. The arguments of Dissenters, who sought to insure an independent identity for themselves within the church and whose scruples regarding the prayer book and certain ceremonies were both long-standing and determined, were never quite accepted as the ingenuous convictions of men equally dedicated to the realization of a broad-based communion.[56] The moderate churchmen would have a comprehensive church where adiaphora were settled exclusively by one side in the debate. Their plea for an inclusive Church of England may have stressed the futility and uncharitable nature of quarrels over nonessentials, but their readiness to concede the convenience, and thus the propriety, of Anglican forms after 1660 betrayed the limits of their ecumenical vision.

The alternative route to reform of the Restoration Settlement could not have pleased the Latitude-men, and on this point their views clearly intersected with those of the Sheldonian establishment, with many Presbyterians—and with the overwhelming majority in Parliament.[57] The nature and limits of the royal dispensing power had been left deliberately vague in 1660, and Charles was sensitive to the fact that any early exercise of such claims, given the memory of his father's behavior, would doubtless be challenged in Parliament. Having been rebuffed by Sheldon and his political allies in December 1662 after proposing a Declaration of Indulgence, and subsequently losing a vote in Parliament over a bill which would have granted him power to suspend penal laws in religious cases, Charles was loath to follow this route again during the course of the next decade.[58] But by March of 1672, having agreed to the secret Treaty of Dover with Louis XIV, eager to successfully prosecute another war against the Dutch while preempting possible Nonconformist unrest at home, and looking to establish a political counterweight to a Parliament still dominated by Anglican Cavaliers, Charles took the unilateral step of issuing a Declaration of Indulgence on the strength of his putative supreme power in ecclesiastical affairs.

According to the text of the declaration, religious coercion had been a "sad experience of twelve years" which had borne very little fruit; therefore it was only appropriate that the king exercise the dispensing power for "quieting the minds" of Englishmen in the interest of religious conciliation and for forwarding economic prosperity.[59] This preemptive suspension of all penal laws against Protestant Dissenters and Catholics was the boldest political gambit attempted by the monarch since the Restoration, and Charles received many addresses of thanks from dissenting congregations, the majority of whom immediately applied for the special licenses which would afford them security in their meetinghouses. But when Parliament reassembled in February of 1673 after a disappointing previous summer's military campaign against the Dutch, it was clear that the king's interpretation of his dispensing power would not go unchallenged. Soon after the appearance of the declaration, which had also granted Catholics the right to worship in private houses, the bishop of London ordered his clergy to preach against the threat from Roman Catholicism and to insist upon the supremacy of statute law.[60] With Sheldon commanding all bishops to be in attendance for the crucial deliberations, and with M.P.s insisting that statutes could only be repealed by the king in Parliament, Charles's pressing financial needs forced him to capitulate in March, and the declaration was withdrawn. The fury of the Cavaliers who saw in the king's tactics an ill-concealed design to advance the Catholic interest inspired the subsequent introduction and passage of a test act which effectively ended Roman Catholic influence at court by forcing all officeholders—including the duke of York—to repudiate transubstantiation and to receive communion according to the usage of the Church of England.[61]

The royal retreat from attempts to extend toleration continued under Danby's administration, and by 1675 even the king, sensitive to the unpopularity of his previous machinations on behalf of Dissenters—particularly Catholics—was at last reconciled to the church interest. The lord treasurer worked to effect better relations between the Crown and Lambeth Palace, using Secretary of State Williamson as liaison with the clergy. Licenses issued under the Declaration of Indulgence were formally withdrawn in 1675, and the government promised a stricter enforcement of laws against dissent.[62] William Sancroft succeeded Sheldon at Canterbury after the latter's death in 1677, and the new archbishop committed the church to a renewed sense of institutional loyalty to the Crown. But an inconsistently applied policy of repression and a dozen years of royal efforts to ameliorate the lot of Dissenters, together with a genuine popular revulsion at persecuting inoffensive neighbors who more often than not contributed to the local economy, had by the mid-1670s considerably weakened respect for the laws and made futile most efforts at coercing fellow Protestants.[63] Some fifteen hundred licenses had been issued to Dissenters under the provisions of the Declaration of Indulgence, and from March 1672 until February 1673, as new Presbyterian ordinations took place, Nonconformity was given such a boost that a good number of dissenting congregations subsequently dated their formation to that period.[64] Even during the struggle with the king over the Declaration of Indulgence, the Commons had approved a bill which would have afforded comprehension for Presbyterians and toleration for other Protestants if they would subscribe to the doctrinal parts of the Thirty-nine Articles and take a "non-resisting oath," but disputes with the House of Lords and a royal prorogation ended work on the measure.[65] Closer relations with Nonconformists seemed essential to many who worried about the royal penchant for leniency towards Catholics. Throughout the 1670s, enforcement of the laws against Protestant dissent were sporadic and depended upon the vigilance, or indifference, of local magistrates, churchwardens, constables, militiamen, and watchmen. Most efforts in London were focused against Quakers and Baptists, while moderate Presbyterians rarely appeared before the courts.[66]

Two factors—popery and arbitrary government—converged in the 1670s to meliorate temporarily the spirit of persecution, and each would contribute to the unprecedented rise of party conflict in England during the last quarter of the seventeenth century.[67] Danby's attempt to strengthen the power of the Crown through the management and bribery of Parliament, together with fears of a Catholic resurgence due to the king's close relations with absolutist France and the duke of York's marriage to Catholic Mary of Modena, served to alarm many members of Parliament who were concerned over the succession should the Catholic James follow his untrustworthy brother on the throne. In a climate of suspicion over the monarch's intentions, the idea of comprehension through legislative means was again in the air.[68] Toward the end of 1673 the earl of Orrery queried Baxter and encouraged him to draw up terms. Despite his deep reservations about the sincerity of the bishops and his wish that Tillotson and Stillingfleet had been invited to join the project, Baxter complied with the earl's request, and the proposals were submitted to Bishop Morley of Winchester. The sympathetic Wilkins had died in 1672, and Morley's willingness to flirt with schemes for comprehension at this particular juncture reflected more his concern over a possible Catholic resurgence than genuine irenical interest. In the event, the bishop could not bring himself to accept the terms of Baxter's statement.[69] And then in 1675 Baxter, who by then expected little from the episcopal bench, reluctantly agreed to meet with Tillotson and Stillingfleet. Tillotson was by that date dean of Canterbury, while Stillingfleet had been promoted to the prebendary of Newington in Saint Paul's Cathedral. After several meetings a draft proposal, possibly the work of Matthew Hale, was put together and submitted to Seth Ward for comment.[70] Once again Baxter and the moderates were to be disappointed, for the bishop thought the whole scheme impractical. Tillotson confided to Baxter that while he was still personally desirous of an accommodation, he preferred to maintain his anonymity in the affair, fearful lest the connection of his name with schemes for comprehension "be a prejudice to me and signify nothing to the effecting of the thing."[71] Despite the relaxation of persecution in the 1670s, then, the episcopal bench remained in near unanimity in its reluctance to make substantive concessions. When the bishop of Hereford, Herbert Croft, published his outspoken appeal for comprehension during the same year as Tillotson's and Stillingfleet's abortive efforts, it was immediately met by a storm of criticism.[72] Even Gilbert Burnet, while acknowledging that Croft "does sincerely desire the peace of our Church," believed that the work had only served to further divisions within the Establishment. He was sure that had Croft "shewed his papers, during all that time they lay by him, to any men of learning or judgement, they had so clearly convinced him of a great many mistakes, that this issue had turned abortive, and died before the birth."[73]

Under Sancroft's guidance, the church firmly supported the Crown's position during the Exclusion Crisis, but Whigs in the House of Commons, with strong approval from Dissenters, took steps to secure a resolution of differences between Protestants through comprehension. During the second "Exclusion Parliament" which began on 21 October 1680, five separate bills were to emerge designed to reconcile the established church and the Dissenters.[74] The long history of the perceived threat from Rome—including conspiracies against Elizabeth, the Gunpowder Plot, the Irish Rebellion of 1641, and, more recently, the London fire of 1666—gave plausibility to the story which originated in the unhealthy mind of Titus Oates and converted many Anglicans to the idea of compromise.[75] Even the previously hostile Patrick altered his position in the wake of the plot. The peaceful Dissenter, he wrote in October of 1680, should comply with legal requirements "so far as he is able with a safe conscience," but must be afforded broader freedoms so long as he refrains from attacking the public order.[76] Tillotson and Stillingfleet were again involved in meetings with Bates and John Howe, but their efforts were fruitless.[77] Throughout this crisis in government, as memories of "forty-one" returned to disquiet many members, it was Charles, with the support of bishops in the Lords, who refused to countenance changes in the Act of Uniformity, and the plans for comprehension died with the prorogation of Parliament in early January 1681.[78] Anglican intolerance was given further encouragement by the Crown after the dissolution of the Exclusion Parliament in 1681, as the king allied himself closely with the High Church clergy against Whigs and Dissenters who had become identified in the minds of the Tory leadership with dangerous republicanism.

During the reaction which followed the Exclusion Crisis, Crown control over ecclesiastical promotions assured that men sympathetic to the king and to James, duke of York, received the choicest preferments.[79] The laws against Nonconformity were enforced with more vigor, as Nonconformist meetings in London were broken up with regularity.[80] In addition, after 1682 Charles was able to bridge the divide between town and country by successfully issuing new charters to boroughs which in the past had returned M.P.s sympathetic to the cause of Nonconformity. Ignoring the terms of the 1664 Triennial Act, by 1685 the king had also gained considerable control over the internal affairs of many boroughs, enabling the Crown either to appoint sympathetic officials or to veto the election of hostile ones. This control over borough affairs, together with the further discrediting of the Whig cause in the aftermath of the 1683 Rye House Plot, contributed in no small measure to the return of a remarkably loyal Commons during the elections of March 1685. Out of a total of 513 M.P.s for England and Wales, only 57 Whigs were elected to office.[81]

Enjoying the solid backing of both church and Parliament, James succeeded to a position as powerful as any of his Tudor or Stuart predecessors, and in those early days of widespread Tory approval, he promised his privy council and Parliament that he would continue his brother's policy of punishing dissent while preserving the established order in church and state.[82] The goodwill and support which James enjoyed in 1685 was quickly forfeited, however, as the king embarked upon a policy of advancing the interests of English Catholics through the repeal of the penal laws and Test Acts of 1673 and 1678, regardless of popular and parliamentary opposition to these objectives.

On two separate occasions during the first year of his reign, James warned Sancroft to put an end to the anti-Catholic sermons which had become common at Anglican, particularly London, services. The Latitudinarian divines, most importantly Tillotson and Stillingfleet, were throughout the Restoration at the forefront of this polemical drive against Rome, using both pulpit and press to maximum advantage. The archbishop's failure to comply with the king's directives led in July of 1686 to the establishment of an ecclesiastical commission which was designed to curb the growing independence of the bishops.[83] But Anglican M.P.s who instinctively associated relief for Catholics with the opening of a design to extirpate Protestantism and to establish absolutism adamantly refused to grant concessions to James's coreligionists during the first two years of the reign.[84] Frustrated by the intransigence of his erstwhile Tory supporters, James reluctantly turned to the Dissenters as a political counterweight to the Anglican majority by issuing the first of two Declarations of Indulgence in 1687, freeing all non-Anglicans from the force of parliamentary laws against dissent.[85] For its part, the episcopal bench was now forced to reconsider not only its position towards Nonconformity but also its far more important policy of passive obedience to royal authority, of indefeasible hereditary right, and of the sinfulness of resistance. The political subservience of the Anglican clergy since the Restoration certainly had not been the monopoly of High Churchmen.[86] Even Tillotson, in his conference with Lord Russell before the latter's execution for treason in 1683, had warned that "the Christian religion doth plainly forbid the resistance of authority." None of the Latitudinarians, recalling the evils of civil war and the attendant social upheaval, scrupled over the requirement in the Act of Uniformity which obliged clergymen to "declare that it is not lawful upon any pretence whatsoever to take up arms against the King." [87]

When the second Declaration of Indulgence, promulgated on 3 May 1688, was ordered to be read from all pulpits on two consecutive Sundays, Sancroft found himself in the unenviable position of defending the prerogatives of a monarch who had committed himself to undermining the special position of the established church. Fearful lest Dissenters accept James's offer of toleration, the bishops began to emphasize the commonality of interest linking all Protestants in England and, like Halifax, stressed the insincerity of James's offer.[88] During 1688 the archbishop himself was personally engaged in efforts to achieve a comprehension, and for the first time since 1660 the search for a broader-based communion now became a "High Church" policy. Once again political expediency, rather than a genuine change of heart, would dictate the position of the established church towards dissent.[89] For their part, moderate Nonconformists expressed serious reservations about this latest Anglican olive branch. "I do not find that any of the tories, especially of the clergy," wrote the Presbyterian Roger Morris, "are come one inch further towards the Reformed Protestant interest, but still have as great an enmity and disgust against all the reformed churches as ever they had."[90] Clearly there was much work to do before the noisome practice of twenty-seven years could be reversed.

Nonetheless, the halcyon days of the "Church and King" Cavalier Parliament seemed quite distant in 1687. Whatever they may have felt about the ingenuousness of Anglican overtures toward reconciliation, those Dissenters who had originally welcomed James's declaration began to express reservations about the king's long-term commitment to liberty of conscience once his efforts to pack Parliament and repeal the Test Act became apparent. Few genuinely trusted James's sincerity about religious pluralism in light of his tarnished record, particularly given the backdrop of recent events in France, where the repeal of the Edict of Nantes only six months after James had succeeded to the throne exposed the arbitrary and inhumane face of Catholic rule.[91] As in 1673, when James's brother had capriciously reversed himself after claiming a prerogative right to dispense with acts of Parliament, Dissenters recognized that their new-found freedom was entirely dependent upon the caprice of a man who had only recently come to the throne with a pledge to realize their extirpation.

On 18 May 1688 a meeting took place at Lambeth to decide a course of action. Seven bishops, including the archbishop of Canterbury, were joined by leading representatives of the moderate London clergy—Robert Grove, John Tillotson, Edward Stillingfleet, Thomas Tenison, and Simon Patrick.[92] Later the same evening the bishops crossed the river and petitioned the king to excuse them from reading the second declaration, politely pointing out to James that the dispensing power on which the declaration was based had been declared illegal by Parliament as recently as 1673. Their "great averseness" to distributing and publishing the declaration proceeded "neither from any want of duty and obedience to your Majesty . . . nor yet from any want of due tenderness to Dissenters," but from constitutional scruples alone.[93] The king's rage at this show of clerical impudence was obvious to all in attendance as he declared that the petition "is a standard of rebellion," and the next day the bishops were charged with seditious libel.[94] Some clergy in London had already begun canvassing their colleagues about the declaration before the bishops' petition was delivered to Whitehall. "There were near twenty of us," recalled Patrick, "who were desired to feel the pulse of all the ministers in London." Tillotson, Stillingfleet, and Fowler were in attendance, and the last declared that he would not read the declaration regardless of what the majority decided.[95] The conclusion drawn from their survey was borne out on the following Sunday: few ministers read the declaration during services on 20 May, and the provincial clergy, who were ordered to announce it one week after the second reading in London, generally followed the lead of their city counterparts in refusing to obey.[96]

The arrest and trial of the seven bishops before the Court of King's Bench committed James to a final and, in the end, humiliating clash with the church leadership. When the seven defendants were acquitted and then greeted by the London crowd as popular heroes, the reputation of the king reached its nadir as his right to suspend and dispense with laws by prerogative right seemed to be repudiated.[97] The trial also provided a fillip to the cause of rapprochement between church leaders and moderate Nonconformists as several joint conferences were held during July in order to discuss future cooperation. In September, James attempted in vain to reverse the policies of the past two years. The ecclesiastical commission was disbanded, forfeited borough charters were to be restored, and, soon after William's landing, James promised a free Parliament from which Catholics would be excluded.[98] A now-desperate king had sacrificed all credibility in an effort to retain power, but his gestures were rebuffed by an incredulous and angry nation. His irresponsible flight from London on 10 December 1688 and final departure from England on 22 December created a power vacuum which made William "the indispensable agent in restoring order and government,"[99] although his ostensible reason for having invaded, cautiously outlined in his declaration issued from The Hague, had been only to secure the election of a free Parliament.[100]

With the collapse of James's rule in the fall of 1688, those members of the Church of England who as younger divines had been branded with the name of Latitudinarian would be afforded a unique opportunity—the first since 1660—to help refashion the Anglican communion in a manner which would win the support and allegiance of the majority of English Protestants. They had made their rather modest mark in the church of Sheldon and Sancroft as London clergymen committed to a simple homiletic style and the essentials of the faith.

It had been a long and at times inhospitable period of tuition, as repeated attempts to amend the terms of the Act of Uniformity had been frustrated by leaders of the church and their Parliamentary allies. Now they had won over the archbishop to the idea of comprehension, and expectations were high. It looked as though one of the central goals of the Latitudinarian clerics—a truly comprehensive church—might finally be achieved in the wake of a popular revolution in government, the very thought of which, paradoxically, all members of the Anglican communion had been condemning for almost thirty years.

The most pointed modern criticism of the Latitudinarian divines centers on their apparent efforts to elevate the position of mankind in terms of his relationship with God, to strengthen the claims of human reason, and to exaggerate the heights of human potential in direct contravention of the Calvinist theology which had first achieved its ascendency within the church as early as the reign of Elizabeth.[1] For Calvinists intent upon arresting the optimism of a Christian humanist tradition where the dignity of man remained exceptional, any suggestion that one could recognize the difference between good and evil and act according to the former implied that man had somehow remained undefiled by the Fall and introduced the dangerous and affected notion that self-directed moral reform—righteousness—was both possible and sufficient for salvation.[2] Calvin himself had insisted that "Man cannot arrogate any thing to himself, be it ever so little, without God being robbed of his honor, and himself being endangered by presumptuous temerity." The proposal that men might in fact participate in their own salvation indicated that we were guided "by the same counsellor, who excited in our first parents the desire of resembling gods, knowing good and evil."[3] Convinced that defenses of Latitudinarianism like Edward Fowler's *Design of Christianity* (1670) too readily assumed "the purity of our Nature, abstract and distinct from the sinful pollution that dwelleth in us," Calvinists argued that the infinite guilt contracted by our common parents meant that man must now be reborn from above, recreated by divine agency, saved by supernatural competence alone.[4] This point of view had been codified in

Article X of the Thirty-nine Articles, where man "cannot turn and prepare himself, by his own natural strength and good works, to faith and calling upon God." The Latitude-men of the Restoration era, because of their Arminian rejection of Calvinist soteriology and adoption of a synergism where human effort was completely rehabilitated, are thought to be among the principal late seventeenth-century laborers in a larger design to restore man's prelapsarian condition through independent effort. The start of the Enlightenment would have been impossible without the repudiation of Geneva, and the moderate churchmen, it is believed, were at the forefront of the anti-Calvinist assault.

Yet if we look closely at the specifics of the Latitudinarian estimate of man, we cannot fail to observe that in spite of their particular objections to church policy after 1660, and notwithstanding the many serious protests and challenges to religious authority in general throughout the seventeenth century, together with the important social, political, and scientific changes which were underway, it is evident that certain earlier patterns of thought, especially long-established ideas relating to man's place in God's creation, remained the common stock of virtually all educated laymen and religious figures in England, be they sympathetic to Latitudinarian ideals or not. Indeed, on this one issue more than most, inherited assumptions regarding man's state outside Paradise were rarely critically examined, so obvious did they appear to all sensible observers of the human condition. There was no wholesale abandonment of the Fall story after 1660 by the Latitudinarians, no amplification of claims on behalf of human merit or righteousness, no reevaluation of the role of sin in the wake of the advance of reason in religion. If anything, the Restoration period, with its characteristic suspicion of enthusiasm masked by ideals of religious purity, witnessed a resurgence of a view of man which placed sin at the forefront of all theological discussions, where the centuries-old tradition of Christian pessimism and contempt for this world remained a vital part of contemporary thought.[5] Here, as in other critical areas, the Latitudinarians were traditionalists seeking to restore the primitive simplicity of the Christian Fall story within the framework of the reformed Anglican communion.[6] Wary lest their benevolent God be implicated in the sinful deportment of his special creation, they accepted the Augustinian import of the Thirty-nine Articles on the nature of man and worked to harmonize this teaching with their program of active moral reform, a program based firmly on the humanistic values of the Northern Renaissance. Robert Grove's conviction that Latitudinarianism "is but an empty sound, and signifies nothing," has much to recommend it if Restoration, and in particular Latitudinarian, views of human nature are carefully examined.[7]

Despite an Arminian resurgence under Laud in the late 1620s and 1630s, Anglicans accepted without demur the Augustinian notion that with mankind's fall from grace in Adam, our natural powers had been so impaired that justification before God was solely the product of faith in Christ and in the efficacy of his saving grace.[8] That God was prepared to shed his mercy on "such vile, such sinful, such unthankful wretches," who deserved nothing of this favor, was for the Latitudinarian mind quite remarkable. "I loathe and abhore myself as unworthy to live and breathe upon the face of the earth," was Simon Patrick's response to the "foul blot and stain upon our nature" which all men received from their common parents.[9] All churchmen regarded the first three chapters in Genesis as a historically accurate description of the origins of the first sin and its consequences, just as the framers of the Thirty-nine Articles had believed before them. The ninth article of that official statement declared that original sin "is the fault and corruption of the nature of every man, that is naturally engendered of the offspring of Adam" and that every person is subsequently "very far gone from original righteousness." For Saint Paul, who was the first to detail the Adamic theory of the Fall, it was perfectly natural to accept the notion that all were involved in the sin of Adam; the Jewish belief in the solidarity of mankind made what appears to the modern mind as an arbitrary connection both acceptable and just.[10]

The Genesis story and its subsequent formal affirmation in the doctrines of the sixteenth-century church merely focused what was for English Protestants a universally accepted fact of ethical and spiritual experience. The constant moral striving which engaged every thoughtful Christian, the sense of deficiency, and the failure of all earthly schemes for happiness provided obstinate confirmation of mankind's self-imposed debility. During the first half of the seventeenth century, the pulpit constantly reminded men of this inherited sinfulness, and the severity of the ninth article continued to inform the sermons of the Latitudinarians and their Sheldonian opponents after the defeat of the Puritan order in 1660.[11] "We are not like the Creatures we were made," wrote the Latitudinarian propagandist for the Royal Society, Joseph Glanvill, "but have lost both our Makers image, and our own. And possibly the Beasts are not more inferior to us, than we are to our antient selves: A proud affecting to be like Gods, having made us unlike Men." [12] Human experience jarred uncomfortably with every alternative picture of the human situation, and no amount of knowledge or self-discipline, no timely intervention on the part of God's appointed ministry, no work of a practical nature provided by groups like the Royal Society—however laudable their goals of physical and social amelioration might be—could effect a transfer of this hard truth.

Glanvill's reference to the problem of irrepressible pride—of man's refusal to acknowledge his ontological dependence—had been at the heart of the biblical Fall as interpreted by theologians as diverse as Augustine and Aquinas, and it remained central to all estimates of the human condition in the years after the Restoration. [13] In their reflections on the historic Fall and its implications for mankind, the Latitudinarians shared a number of Pauline and Augustinian precedents with their Sheldonian and High Church counterparts, and the most important of these precedents unmistakably linked the first sin with the individual's conscious decision to violate God's eternal law rather than with ignorance or the passions of the body. [14] "So then God made man upright," Augustine had affirmed, "and consequently well-willed . . . but the evil will, which was in man before his evil work, was rather a falling from the work of God to its own works." [15] Edward Reynolds, the Presbyterian divine who accepted the nomination to Norwich in 1661, succinctly reaffirmed the bishop of Hippo's point when he wrote that man "hath an itch in him to be a god within himself, the fountain of his own goodness, the contriver of his own sufficiency," who without the aid of divine mercy would "repair that image of God which is so much distorted." [16] Tillotson coupled the fashionable skepticism of his day with a form of pride which takes pleasure "in unravelling almost all the received principles of both religion and reason," while his Nonconformist friend, Thomas Gouge, insisted that "confidence in our own strength is the fore-runner of a fall." [17] For another of Tillotson's friends, Gilbert Burnet, the malign influence of human pride led him to suggest that use of the word "merit" be avoided altogether in discussions of the process of salvation because it sounded "so daring, so little suitable to the humility of a Creature." Its mercenary flavor gives men an idea "of a buying and selling with God," and since there is "somewhat in the nature of man apt to raise and swell it self out of measure . . . no Indulgence ought to be given, in words that may flatter it."[18] The fundamental evil in the human situation, where men constantly pro-claim their independence from God, where humility and finiteness are dismissed as medieval encumbrances on the human spirit, was unequivocally condemned by all segments of the Protestant commu-nity. The drive for autonomy was explicitly linked to the first sin and, in the end, held responsible for the myriad pains and sufferings associated with the mortal state.

Even when the Latitudinarian divines stressed the dangers asso-ciated with the attractions of the senses, they were acutely aware that behind these appetitive impulses lay a deliberate preference for inde-pendence and spiritual self-sufficiency. When Patrick preached that the strength and violence of our passions was always met by "that forwardness in our wills to follow them, and to be led by them," the ultimate culpability of a free agent was unmistakable.[19] Like Saint Augustine, whose famous description in the *Confessions* of his theft of pears from a neighbor's garden, where he stole not out of hunger, but that he "might mimic a maimed liberty by doing with impunity things unpermitted me, a darkened likeness of Thy omnipotency," the statements of the Latitudinarians were the product of actual ex-perience of the power of sin, the unnatural condition of men in light of the example of Christ.[20]

Indeed, for all Protestants, the entire fabric of European history belied the easy assumptions about the rational nature of man which were being mooted by some opponents of Calvinist theology after 1660. When Bishop Sanderson wrote "that in this state of corruption the whole soul is out of frame, all the faculties thereof depraved," he was perhaps anticipating Robert South's description of fallen man as "a new kind or species; the plague of sin has even altered his nature, and eaten into his very essentials," but by the conclusion of the seventeenth century, this basic sentiment was widely and uncriti-cally shared.[21] The voice of the Latitudinarian Edward Fowler was certainly not dissentient. According to Fowler, Adam's "Contumacy, Pride, and Rebellion" are easily identified in his descendants, most of whom are "lost as to all true goodness . . . deeply sunk into sensu-ality and brutishness."[22] By our apostacy we have robbed God of His right to our obedience, a right "that he can never be willing to let go."[23] And while all other creatures take careful measures to protect the integrity of their beings, man alone is content to ignore his long-term safety, constantly preferring eternal ruin "for the gratifying of a brutish Appetite for a little while."[24] To John Wilkins, perhaps the most consistent champion of the moral aspects of Christianity and as we have seen the chief nemesis of Sheldon's reconstructed episcopate, no man could pretend to stand in judgment of another, since there was no outrage, no act of evil or cruelty to be seen in man or devil "but there are in our natures the principles and inclinations to it; the best of us being by nature as bad as the worst of sinners."[25] Most men would happily ignore the dread significance of original sin in their lives, thought Wilkins, "though it hath already brought so much mischief upon all mankinde, wholly depraved us in our faculties, and principles, and spread a curse and deformity upon the whole creation."[26] Indeed we not only have lost a capacity for good through our first parents but have contracted "a loathing and disliking of it: Not a liableness to evil, but also an inherent propension, and very strong desire to it."[27] The Pelagianism which so often has been associated with the moderate church movement, where the frailty of human nature is looked upon as a dishonest excuse for inaction and as an animadversion on the love of God for mankind, is not to be found in the orthodox anthropology outlined by Wilkins and his peers.

In spite of the bleak appraisal of human nature outlined by the Latitudinarians in their sermons and devotional works, Isaac Barrow thought that the representation of all men as "heinous sinners, void of all worth and merit, lapsed into a wretched state, altogether impotent, forlorn, and destitute of ability to help or relieve themselves" was actually one of the special strengths of the Christian story.[28] Like other moderate churchmen, Barrow was convinced that the first step into the Christian state had to be accompanied by an acute sense of our ruined condition, an awareness of moral evil as a constant of our mortal nature. In language which mirrors the harshest Puritan sermon of the first half of the century, he insisted that "we must discern and feel, that our mind is very blind and our reason very feeble; that our will is very impotent, lame, depraved, prone to evil, and averse from good: that our life is void of merit, and polluted with guilt; that our condition is deplorably sad and wretched; that of our selves we are insufficient to think, or do any good, in order to our recovery, or deliverance. . . ."[29] Only when the magnitude of man's voluntary declension had made an indelible impress on the mind of the sinner could the process of spiritual rehabilitation begin. Only with the abandonment of the conceit of righteousness, a conceit as old as the monk Pelagius and as immediate as the threat from Rome, could the children of Adam find hope in the work of a savior.

Barrow's manuscipts were edited and published after his death by John Tillotson, and it is therefore not surprising that in his own sermons the archbishop of Canterbury offered one of the most unambiguous and compelling statements of man's condition in the wake of the Fall.[30] We have been told that Tillotson "had no place for a doctrine of original sin and avoided any emphasis upon an evil inheritance transmitted from Adam," that he "gave encouragement to the view that moral virtues made up the sum of religion," but his 254 printed sermons controvert such a judgment.[31] The eighteenth-century Deist Anthony Collins may have been sincere in claiming the archbishop as one "whom all English Free-Thinkers own as their head," but it is quite another question to ask whether Tillotson would have welcomed the association or, for that matter, even have conceded the possibility of a connection between his own reasonable Christianity and the subsequent religion of reason.[32] As one of London's most popular preachers since the early 1660s, Tillotson communicated the Latitudinarian message of comprehension, the minimal creed, and the essential reasonableness of Christianity to a generation of Englishmen overtaxed by religious discord and the political instability occasioned by these quarrels.[33] But alongside his irenical message to congregations at Saint Lawrence Jewry and at Lincoln's Inn, where he had been elected preacher in 1663, Tillotson issued a stern warning, too often overlooked, about the boundaries of man's potential in light of his evil inheritance.

Like his fellow moderate churchmen, and in a manner as forthright as Augustine, Tillotson admitted that "there is a great degeneracy and corruption of human nature, from what it was originally framed when it came out of God's hands." Scripture informs us that our first parents voluntarily transgressed "a plain and easy command" and contracted on their posterity "inclinations to evil, and impotence to that which is good." All persons now invariably "partake of the bitterness and impurity of the foundation from whence we spring," and their accumulated habits of sin, being added to natural impotency, "are like so many diseases superintended upon a constitution already weak."[34] And whereas Adam and Eve faced only external snares in Paradise, mankind labors under a double difficulty, "being assaulted by temptations from without, and incited by evil inclinations from within."[35] Contrary to our proud boastings and pretended powers, sinful men "are but a little dust, and the least breath of God can dissipate us." We have become estranged from God because of the first sin, wrote Tillotson, "obnoxious to his wrath and displeasure" and utterly incapable of helping ourselves out of this miserable state. Such an estimate of man, he thought, had always been the "sad complaint" of the wisest part of mankind, and there was nothing in the Latitudinarian message designed to subvert it.[36] Each of Tillotson's "practical" sermons was built upon the conviction that motions towards moral reform on the part of the sinner were merely expressions of thoughtful contrition rather than claims to spiritual autonomy. Nowhere in those many sermons does Tillotson derogate the church's teaching on the mechanics of salvation in order to provide support for the Pelagian hypothesis.

The extent of the Latitudinarian adherence to the biblical Fall story is perhaps best revealed in their discussions of education. If, after all, their ambitious program of moral reform and a reasonable Christianity was to meet with any measure of success, it had to be based upon a theory of human malleability which would stress the importance of environmental factors—habit and custom—in shaping human personality. There was really no point in preaching spiritual renewal if a large part of man's predicament was not due to factors amenable to the instrument of Christian education. In this fundamental respect Latitudinarianism was guided by a strong faith in education, confident in those things which "by prudence and patience may be done towards the rectifying of a very perverse and crooked disposition."[37] Theirs was certainly not the later *philosophes'* view of education for autonomy, where the illiterate would be transformed into self-reliant and critically minded citizens, but rather a deliberate training into Christian culture, one where obedience and humility were the paramount goals.[38]

Despite the indispensable function of education for the success of the moderate church ideal, however, the chief exponents of that ideal steadfastly refused to compromise their Augustinian picture of the consequences of the Fall in order to exaggerate the power of instruction and amendment, even if that stand made the task of the educator exceptionally difficult in the face of enormous obstacles. Joseph Glanvill, for example, strongly disagreed with the argument which placed habit and custom at the core of the problem of human corruption. Notwithstanding his hopes for progress through the new science and collaborative enterprise, he was unswerving in his conviction that "there is scarce an instance of habitual vice, or villainy, but some or other are addicted to it by their particular make or natures." Vices were for Glanvill "the first-born of our natures" and would never be completely eradicated regardless of remedial action.[39] "We carry all the beasts of prey within us," he wrote, and without the assistance of supernatural gifts our best hope remains "that we can die, and mingle with insensible rottenness and corruption."[40] Isaac Barrow believed that even in the best dispositions there is "much averseness from good, and great proneness to evil," while Stilling-fleet could not accept "that bare example were enough to corrupt the World if there were not some antecedent inclination in humane nature to the practice of evil," and compared man's "natural propensity to evil" with the desire "of the thirsty Travellor to drink of the Brook that he meets in his way."[41]

Clearly the mind was no blank slate wanting an inclination to either virtue or vice, and the challenge facing the educator was to arrest the natural tendency in children to violate the eternal laws of right reason before the tragic experiences of mid-century were repeated. Even Tillotson's friend John Locke, whose *Some Thoughts Concerning Education* (1693) had posited the optimistic notion that "all the men we meet with, nine parts of ten, or perhaps ninety-nine of one hundred, are what they are, good or evil, useful or not, by their education," later conceded in the same work that "few of Adam's Children are so happy, as not to be born with some Byass in their natural Temper, which it is the Business of Education either to take off, or counter-balance."[42] For Locke, it was clear that the learning process was a life-long struggle for each man "to gain a mastery of his Inclinations, and submit his Appetite to Reason." He was convinced that virtue was more difficult to acquire than knowledge of the world, "and if lost in a Young Man, is seldom recovered."[43]

Gilbert Burnet had produced an early work on education in which he too confirmed "a natural byas and propensity to corruption" in children,[44] but again it was the popular Tillotson who gave the clearest exposition of the Latitudinarian position on the relationship between education and original sin. Tillotson devoted considerable attention to the problem in his sermons, and of all the particular duties required of Christians, he thought none more difficult than the education of the young.[45] Indeed, it might not be unfair to say that his overriding concern in the pulpit was with the process of educating individuals into the exercise of reason, whereby they might be empowered to realize the Latitudinarian ideal of enlightened Christianity.[46] Three sermons, first published in 1694 but preached earlier at Saint Lawrence, were devoted exclusively to the question, although the larger issue of counterbalancing man's natural proneness to evil was raised on a number of occasions. Parents, he warned, have conveyed a sad inheritance to their children "in those corrupt and evil inclinations which they have derived from us," and if their education be ignored, if they remain by nature "children of wrath," then the evil which they commit will be charged directly to their natural guardians on the day of judgment.[47] Ever hostile to what he interpreted to be the Puritan predilection for instantaneous conversion into a state of grace, Tillotson cautioned that spiritual regeneration was a work of many years of uninterrupted sacrifice.[48] The corrupt nature of man, he said, "is a rank soil, to which vice takes easily and wherein it thrives apace." Likened to weeds that grow wild, human vices were "natural to the soil, and, therefore, they need not be planted and watered; it is sufficient if they be neglected and let alone."[49] Tillotson made it clear that there was no natural disposition towards goodness in children, no principles of religion or virtue; all was the product of deliberate effort. Because of this sad fact it was essential that children be informed of their "great degeneracy" at an early age, in order that they might dedicate themselves to a course of virtue while always acknowledging the inadequacy of human merit as a necessary check on irrepressible pride. Unfortunately, said Tillotson, even with the best will in the world, and the most careful and diligent tuition in Christian principles, there would in the end be only a few fortunate individuals who would be able to avoid the worst excesses of natural depravity through the influence of a thorough education and the working of God's grace. Education would never serve as a universal palliative to a problem whose roots were coterminous with the historic Fall of Adam.[50]

While much of the emphasis of Pauline and Augustinian ideas as interpreted by sixteenth- and seventeenth-century Calvinist theologians moved Restoration divines towards an exceptionally harsh picture of human nature, another equally powerful perspective pointed in the direction of a more confident understanding of man, one where fragments of the divine nature remained to enhance the self-respect of Adam's descendants. Saint Paul had observed that through sin men "come short of the glory of God," and his reference recalled the story of creation in Genesis, where God fashioned man in his own image and likeness. Clearly, men had fallen below their potential through the malevolent power of sin.[51] In addition to their study of Saint Paul and Saint Augustine, Anglicans were accustomed, due in large measure to the enduring influence of Hooker, to drawing upon the medieval Thomist tradition in constructing their picture of man's station outside Paradise. And for Saint Thomas, who freely adopted the teleological framework pioneered by Aristotle, man's perfection and end were now to be found in the contemplation of truth, a rational knowledge of God or participation in the divine beatitude which constituted the most sublime wisdom.[52] Disobedient man was yet capable of entering into society with God through the exercise of his rational faculties and with the help of divine grace, should we elect to take hold of God's assistance in our lives.

The Fall, according to Aquinas, had not so completely extinguished our natural reason that it was no longer of service in this holy enterprise. It was true that in the first transgression Adam had exercised his free will in the choice of a lesser good, preferring himself to God and bringing moral evil into the world. And it was impossible to deny that every subsequent sin was a renewal of this act of revolt against God, linking each generation with the primal sin of disobedience and furthering disorder in the universe.[53] But even with the debilitating power of sin lodged at the very center of our personality, the Second Adam demanded the constant employment of our still-considerable rational faculties—that partial likeness of God's eternal reason—if the gift of grace was to be efficacious. This essentially semi-Pelagian position both reclaimed the power of reason in the work of salvation and deliberately exaggerated the extent of human culpability in the act of sin, thereby sharply circumscribing alleged sins of ignorance or those committed out of weakness. With God's grace now available to comfort all who would exercise their talents, the interpretation of sin as direct rebellion, with the flesh simply the instrument of a corrupt will, helped to confirm the place of moral reform in the drama of salvation while preserving Christ's instrumental role in its attainment. "For whatsoever we have hitherto taught," said Hooker, "concerning the force of man's natural understanding, there is no kind of faculty or power in man or in any other creature, which can rightly perform the functions alloted to it, without perpetual aid and concurrence of that Supreme Cause of all things."[54] The renewal of the power of reason complemented by grace which was carried out by Aquinas in the thirteenth century, then, together with the forceful and articulate recapitulation of this standpoint by Hooker at the close of the sixteenth, made it likely that some sort of synthesis with the Augustinianism propounded by English Calvinists would be attempted by men committed to a comprehensive Anglican church.

It is not difficult to identify the powerful strain of optimism in the Thomist position and why it would appeal to Anglicans in particular. In addition to the intrinsic value of the human soul as the repository of the rational faculty, the faith of Christians in the salvation of the whole person—both body and soul—elevated the worth of the individual by defining man as a special unity capable of resurrection.[55] Like all Anglicans, the Latitudinarian churchmen were loath to abandon the anthropocentrism which had been at the heart of the medieval world view. In the divine hierarchy of forms, the human species occupied that crucial nexus between the spiritual and the material, the rational and the sentient, the immortal and the perishable. "God was pleased," wrote Tillotson, "to advance us to the top and perfection of the visible universe." Man was God's special creation, his chief concern, and the universe remained the great stage upon which a magnificent drama was being enacted.[56] The redemption of sinful mankind, the rectification of his nature after his initial apostacy, was the master theme. Indeed, in spite of the first sin and its consequences, the medieval church had given its sanction to the idea that a loving God remained firmly committed to the well-being of his most precious handiwork. Man's connection to God through his soul and the faculty of reason spoke well of his potential, as did the incomparable fact that the Son of God had sacrificed himself in order to restore our fractured relationship with the eternal Father.

The implications of this belief in man's special status were expounded by a wide spectrum of writers during the Restoration. The Nonjuror George Hickes, author of several vitriolic attacks on the Latitudinarian churchmen during the 1690s, indicated that man's spiritual side connects him most closely with the divine. That spiritual quality "is the resemblance of God. . . . God himself was the original after which she was drawn." Given our special nature, it would be "horrid Ingratitude and Blasphemy against God" for anyone to ridicule human nature as it left the hands of the Creator.[57] Christians, he thought, have a special obligation to live up to the dignity of their primordial character and to avoid those sins and passions which transform men into little better than beasts. "And as we are made like Angels, after the image of God, so like God we ought to be very jealous of our own Honor, and to think and act as it becomes such Angelical Creatures to do."[58] Even Tillotson, one of Hickes's most frequent targets, preached that while our rational faculties and powers had been "much weakened and disordered" by the Fall, they had not been completely extinguished by it. The impressions of the natural law were "still legible upon our hearts," he said, and although men were "assaulted by temptations from without, and incited by evil inclinations from within," the obligation of fallen humanity to continue in its efforts to work towards the ideal of full obedience remained unshaken.[59] Richard Baxter spoke for moderate Dissenters when he warned his readers against "unreasonable thoughts of the workmanship of God" which would make the Creator responsible for such flaws as the inveterate selfishness of men. To believe that God had made man in such a state "doth make the image of Satan to be the image of God."[60] And Gilbert Burnet suggested, in words redolent of the spirit of Aquinas and Hooker, that the most effective way for man to frame an adequate idea of his Creator "is to consider our own Souls, which are said to be made after the image of God."[61] If man were in fact as depraved as the Calvinists alleged, thought Burnet, he would never have been aware of his corruption or even considered the importance of moral struggle in the process of election to salvation.

The optimism of the Thomist view can also be seen in the numerous Anglican references to a loving, merciful God who finds as much satisfaction in the act of forgiveness as in the process of design. John Cosin expressed a simple commonplace when he said that God's dealings with sinners would be no more rigorous than the frailties of human nature could bear.[62] The Fall itself, while inexcusable in the context of man's contumacy against his sovereign, was from the vantage point of God's character an opportunity to magnify his own glory through the exercise of infinite compassion. This "paradox of the fortunate fall," as it has been aptly described by Arthur Lovejoy, was explored by Clarendon when he observed that "If we could live without Sin, and offending God at all, it may be we should be more perfect than God intended to make us, his Majesty delighting and magnifying himself no less in the Exercise of his Mercy, than in the Power of his Creation."[63] Such an analysis of man's situation relative to his maker enjoyed a long history in Christian thought and doubtless provided needed reserves of comfort for the weak of heart throughout the ages, but it could easily be abused should our privileged position at the center of creation lead us into the sort of complacency and confidence preliminary to the sin of pride. It certainly complicated the Latitudinarian estimate of man after 1660, as the moderate churchmen—no less than their Sheldonian counterparts—struggled to find a suitable balance between the pessimism of an Augustinian stand which seemed to leave the way open for reckless Antinomianism and an equally unacceptable Pelagianism where men claim their own salvation without an outpouring of preventing or assisting grace.

Much of the current confusion over the Latitudinarian image of man, then, can be attributed to our own failure to recognize the importance of this tension between the Augustinian and medieval Thomist inheritance for the men of the later seventeenth century. When the moderate churchmen employed their matter-of-course references to the rational nature of man, they were (like their Platonist counterparts) describing an ideal condition which had obtained prior to the Fall, a necessary aspiration of depraved humanity rather than a concrete reality. Adam diminished his own humanity through his act of disobedience, departed from the rationality of his first nature, and "brought disorder into divine order."[64] The order of justice, Aquinas believed, "lay in man's will being subjected to God" under all circumstances. "This subjection first of all and chiefly was through the will, to which belongs the moving of all other powers towards the final end. From the will's turning away from God, then, the disorder in all other powers of the soul followed."[65]

Whichcote had been one of the first of the moderate divines to observe this fact, and the point was surely made to his auditors at Saint Lawrence Jewry after the Restoration. For while no one doubts that he always underscored the rational side of the medieval synthesis throughout his lifetime, he was also careful to make a timely distinction between the prelapsarian norm and the present unhappy situation. When he spoke of man's similitude with the divine when directed by reason, insisting that "Man, as man, is Averse to what is Evil and Wicked," it was with the firm recognition that none of his contemporaries had attained this state in their lives.[66] Sadly, we must declare the nature of man "not from what it is, by Defection and Apostacy; but from what God made it: what it was, and what it should be."[67] To appeal to the best in human nature was a laudable tactic for the seventeenth-century reformer who had witnessed the futility of more violent measures, but to recognize the practical corruption of that nature and to try to redress it through specific warnings and directives was of much more immediate concern.

Like Whichcote, the younger Latitudinarian divines were careful to emphasize that their ministry was in large part the product of the absolute failure of their contemporaries to approach, through discipline and holiness, the elevated nature that God had originally granted them. Early in his career Stillingfleet wrote that "a man may be as well bound not to be a man, as not to act according to principles of reason," but sixteen years later he confessed that only those who looked exclusively at man's rational side "would expect to find the world much better than it is."[68] Hezekiah Burton spoke of a "true natural state" where reason predominated over the passions and claimed that many mistake "the Depravation and Corruption of it, for our true Nature." He cautioned against calling that a natural inclination "which is an unnatural Appetite or Inclination, as every one is, that is immoderate, inordinate, that is destructive, or but hurtful to the whole man, or to the Society, the Community, of which he is a member," and he warned that as repentant sinners we must look upon ourselves "as in an unnatural state, so long as I do what does not become me, or neglect to do what does."[69] Similarly Tillotson preached that as Christ assumed human form for our benefit, so men must "re-assume humanity, which we have in great measure depraved and put off."[70] Men were "so far from that pitch of goodness and virtue which the Christian religion is apt to raise men to," he lamented, "that a great part are degenerated into beasts and devils . . . as if the grace of God had never appeared to us to teach us the contrary."[71] In his much-quoted sermon, "The Wisdom of Religion," Tillotson stressed the enormity of the task facing his fellow Christians, and its laconic tone as well as its stern contents suggest the dimensions of the problem facing the children of Adam: "What a conflict and struggling do the best men find between their inclination and their duty! How hard to reconcile our practice and our knowledge, and to make our lives to agree with the reason of our minds, and the clear conviction of our consciences! How difficult for a man, in this dangerous and imperfect state, to be, in any measure, either so wise or so good as he ought!"[72]

That "the reason of our minds" would more often than not fail to dictate effectively the substance of our actions was no less a truism for the Latitude-men than it was for those allies of archbishop Sheldon who sought to exclude them from positions of power within the revived church establishment. A common Christian anthropology superseded differences over matters of lesser concern to the life of the faith, and that shared understanding necessarily informed, as we shall see, all discussions of man's spiritual recourse in the light of his contracted impotency and cosmic disgrace.

There were, of course, less laudable reasons for propagating the idea of the general sinfulness of man after the experience of civil war and the anarchy of the sects. Preaching depravity, asceticism, and the probationary nature of earthly existence may have been of a piece with the otherworldly orientation of medieval thought, but it had also been one of the more time-honored and serviceable methods of buttressing the existing social and political order, and it remained the habit of Anglican bishops and their Calvinist opponents alike during the course of the seventeenth century.[73] The ancient Greek and medieval conviction which associated all change with decay had been under serious attack since the days of Francis Bacon and George Hakewill, but enough of that old identification lingered to add intellectual credibility to Restoration fears of further violent upheaval, as it undoubtedly had for Cromwellians during the war years.[74] The bitter tests of the 1640s, when radicals like Gerald Winstanley repudiated the idea of original sin and took advantage of the breakdown of censorship in order to challenge the predestinarianism of "respectable" Calvinists, shocked members of the elect. The dangerous social implications of such thinking quickly became apparent to men who saw in any attempt to establish spiritual equality a prelude to demands for political and economic parity as well. If order and civil peace were the great ends of society, then hierarchy and subordination were essential; if property was not to be held in common, then Adam's Fall must be associated with man's covetousness and pride.[75] Arminianism and Antinomianism spelled disaster for the natural leaders of society before 1660, and as the promptings of the inner light made headway among the poor, the idea of a hierarchical order, a great chain of being which conjoined the whole social sphere and assigned each his fixed place, appeared ready to surrender its hold to those who were poised to abolish sin.[76]

With the Restoration, the notion of the sinfulness of man returned with a vengeance as Royalists struggled to restore the intellectual and religious scaffolding of the monarchical order, and the Latitudinarians were every bit as impatient as their High Church opponents to employ the "depravity factor" in the interests of social cohesion and political stability. It certainly informed their Erastian politics. The existence of the state itself and the lawful exercise of its coercive authority were clearly made necessary by the sinfulness of man. Hooker had insisted that laws "are never framed as they should be . . . unless presuming men to be in regard of his depraved mind little better than a wild beast," while the Puritan John Pym was convinced that "if you take away the law, all things will fall into a confusion, every man will become a law unto himself, which in the depraved condition of human nature must needs produce many great enormities."[77] Tillotson echoed these earlier analyses when he said that without strong government "human society would presently disband, and all things would run into confusion."[78]

In man's present degenerated state neither rational appeals to the goodness and propriety of God's law nor, quite often, even the promise of eternal happiness was apt to influence the behavior of most self-professed Christians. Since men have lost "in a good measure, the love and relish of true happiness," only fear, the ominous threat of immediate and eternal torments, would engage them to practice a living faith with any consistency. Fear alone, not appeals to reason, "is the strongest bond of laws, and the great security of our duty."[79] Few of the Latitudinarians would have disagreed with the High Churchman Robert South's maxim which affirmed that if there were not godly ministers assigned to every parish in the country, then the state would quickly find cause to increase the number of constables.[80] Latitudinarian Christian discipleship operated on the unshakable premise that appeals to reasonable self-interest would fail to inspire most men to obey God's law. More traditional sanctions— with all the unflattering assumptions about human nature they implied—remained very much a part of the theological outlook of the moderate churchmen.

In assessing Adam's bequest to the seventeenth century and beyond, the Latitudinarians could not escape the disturbing lessons of their personal historical experience. Their own lives—the bitterness of religious struggle in an age when theology still shaped politics, the unwillingness of Anglicans and moderate Presbyterians to transcend their differences in the interests of Protestant unity, the sullen intransigence and bold contumacy of radical Dissenters—all seemed to give tragic confirmation to a view of man which left little room for optimism about the future. Important events like the organization of the Royal Society may have done much to further a Baconian hope in the prospects for "technical perfection," the mastery of this small stage upon which the real business of life was conducted, but in that real business, "teleological perfection"—man's reaching his true natural end in the knowledge of God—was quite simply out of the question in the England of the Latitude-men.[81] The medieval picture of the world as evil, doomed to destruction along with mankind, may have been displaced by a new natural philosophy which saw God's perfections exhibited in his handiwork, but the goal of escape from the present probationary existence which had for so long animated the thought of Christian Europe was still very much at the center of Latitudinarian thought.

Standing between the goods of this world and those of another, the moderate churchmen continued to insist that no human talent, no concentration of effort or denial of self could qualify the children of Adam for what had become, since the Fall, the "gift" of salvation. Genuine perfection for the Latitude-men remained unattainable as long as that goal was pursued without reference to the providential blessing of Christ's sacrifice. The facts of human nature, revealed by Scripture and affirmed by experience, had placed man's natural end well beyond the prospect of all except the humble sinner who was content to surrender himself to the work of one who would redeem us for no other reason but the power of divine love.[82] Preaching the depravity of man was, for the Latitudinarians, the beginning of enlightenment.

In 1675, as Charles was accommodating himself to Danby's policy of reconciliation and alliance with the Church of England, one of the royal chaplains delivered an intemperate sermon at Whitehall warning of the growing tendency within the official church to "supplant Christian Religion with Natural Theologie; and turn the Grace of God into a wanton Notion of Morality . . . making Reason, Reason, Reason, their only Trinity, and sole Standard, whereby to measure both the Principles and Conclusions of Faith."[1] And although John Standish failed to identify the guilty party after raising the alarm in so bold a fashion, Simon Patrick, who had also recently been appointed one of the king's chaplains, sensed that yet another attempt to discredit liberal churchmen was underway and responded to the calumny without delay. Patrick demanded that Standish reveal the names of those clerics who had been teaching such dangerous notions, for until this elemental information was made public, the entire clerical community suffered under the onus of unwarranted suspicion.[2] And he took to the offensive against what he saw as a thoughtless disparagement of reason by requesting that Standish "oblige us so far as to tell us by the way why you scorn reason so much; which distinguishes you from a beast, and hath made you choose, I hope, to be a Christian."[3]

The Latitudinarian churchmen could not have shared a common perspective on man's essential nature with their High Church colleagues had they ignored the role of divine assistance in the process of salvation, nor could their treatment of the nature and compass of grace be complete without a thorough examination of human reason and its proper limits in the wake of the Fall. The inherited sinfulness of each human being, the inablility of man to merit the least measure of forgiveness for his repeated offenses, made these issues critically important to Restoration divines. In their efforts to propagate what they took to be the essential task of the church in the aftermath of the mid-century upheavals and in response to sweeping attacks like the one launched by Standish, the moderate churchmen were obliged to address the nature of the relationship between reason and revelation, to clarify their understanding of God's providential work and support to man.

Confronted by challenges from Deists who denied that special revelation was in any sense necessary in order to arrive at credenda, to fideists—both Protestant and Catholic—who insisted that reason had absolutely no role to play in matters of religion, the response of the Latitudinarians would be of considerable importance to the integrity of the Anglican tradition.[4] Voicing an unmistakable adherence to a familiar orthodoxy regarding grace and reason, their collective reply placed the Latitudinarians sharply at odds with the more extreme forms of natural religion which marked the last decade of the seventeenth century. It was a reply which reaffirmed their unconditional acceptance of a special revelation dealing with historic time as well as a supernatural technique for the redemption of sinful man. The moderate churchmen agreed with Standish that as "the Jew cannot be saved by the Law of Moses, much less the Gentile by all the Works of the Law of Nature," but they sought nevertheless to find a modest place for human effort based on the dictates of God-given reason.[5] And while later Deists like Anthony Collins may have pointed to Tillotson and the moderate church bishops as their intellectual forebears, the Latitudinarian message of the archbishop and his friends, had the Deists paused in their confident pursuit of a religion without mystery to consider it in its entirety, contained small comfort for anyone committed to the resolute new world of eighteenth-century religious rationalism.[6]

As we mentioned in the previous chapter, few within the Restoration Anglican community rejected the important role entrusted to human reason in the work of uncovering and putting into practice the central tenets of the faith. Despite the clash with Deists over their exaggerated claims on behalf of reason in the 1690s, there was never any suggestion within the mainstream of English Protestantism that reason and revelation were somehow incompatible, that to embrace the mysteries of the faith one had to abandon the instrument of reason. The importance of natural religion proceeded from the logical grounds it provided for the acceptance of revelation, a special guarantee that the Word of God was in fact truthful.[7] This effort to balance the facts of reason against the rule of revelation had been at the heart of Renaissance humanism and constituted one of the prime targets of Calvinist Reformers.[8] In fact, reason during the second half of the century continued to be identified with the tradition of "right reason," where the thinking faculty was conceived as the arbiter not only of intellectual choices but of moral ones as well.[9] So when the Presbyterian bishop Edward Reynolds confidently declared that "there is nothing more profoundly and exactly rational than true religion," most leaders within the Restoration church were thinking in terms of this expanded definition of the rational faculty as an epistemological and moral instrument.[10]

The majority of English Protestants continued to accept what Hershel Baker has described as the medieval "axiom of knowledge," a widespread belief that a rational God had created the universe for entirely benevolent ends.[11] It included the great Thomistic assumption that God and his work of creation were capable of being comprehended, albeit imperfectly, by sinful men who remained in possession of the remains of reason after the Fall. Man's earthly tenure was to be dominated by his overriding teleological goal: happiness through the contemplation of truth or the knowledge of God.[12] "Right reason" enabled him to unite the knowledge of the good with the desire to pursue that good, thereby facilitating a larger process of recovery which was only completed through the agency of divine assistance. Even Saint Augustine, despite his theology of original sin, believed that mankind continued to enjoy a spark of reason and a capacity for moral knowledge. Hooker, whose universe was informed by law, had forcefully defended this scholastic position in his quarrel with Puritans who questioned the scriptural basis of Anglican Church organization, ceremony, and rights.[13] Thanks largely to the corrosive work of the Puritans, Hooker lamented, "the name of the light of nature is made hateful with men; the 'star of reason and learning,' and all other such like helps, beginneth no otherwise to be thought of than if it were an unlucky comet; or as if God had so accursed it, that it should never shine or give light in things concerning our duty any way towards him."[14] The English followers of Calvin had encouraged the novel and dangerous opinion that "the way to be ripe in faith were to be raw in wit and judgment; as if reason were an enemy unto religion, childish simplicity the mother of ghostly and divine wisdom."[15] They would equate law with the capricious will of a nonrational Creator, stripping those who had no access to the word of God of any touchstone by which they might guide their actions.

Hooker was convinced, like Aquinas before him, that the gap between God and man created by the Fall was not limitless, that some fundamental truths could still be discovered by unassisted reason.[16] For example, the existence and attributes of God, the immortality of the soul, mankind's chief moral duties, and the need for repentance all constituted the essential elements of natural theology and were available to us without the help of revelation. Reason, in proving the existence of God, established sufficient "motives of credibility" or grounds upon which to accept the supernatural truths which came to us through Scripture.[17] It also assisted us in better interpreting and understanding the divine text. "Unto the word of God," he said, "we do not add reason as a supplement of any maim or defect therein, but as a necessary instrument, without which we could not reap by the Scripture's perfection that fruit and benefit which it yieldeth."[18] Hooker even went so far as to suggest that most things necessary to salvation were available to natural reason working on the simple words of Scripture, a position not too far distant from the one promoted by rationalists at the close of the seventeenth century. "Some things are so familiar and plain," he stated, "that truth from falsehood, and good from evil, is most easily discerned in them, even by men of no deep capacity. And of that nature, for the most part, are things absolutely unto all men's salvation necessary, either to be held or denied, either to be done or avoided."[19] Such had been the conviction of Saint Augustine, Hooker stated, and such had always been the view of the Church of England. That the respect for reason which had survived repeated attacks within the family of Christians from Tertullian to Occam to Calvin found a congenial home within an otherwise factious Anglican community during the course of the seventeenth century was due in good measure to the authority of Hooker's appeal. Mankind may once have been capable of union with God through "the observing of, and obedience to, the laws inherent in his instrument, nature," but the fact that our final end could no longer be realized without supernatural assistance was no excuse for the abandonment of this special endowment.[20]

We can trace the scholastic components in Hooker's thought to the work of both Sheldonian churchmen and their Latitudinarian peers after 1660, for it provided these clergymen with a powerful weapon against opponents as diverse as Protestant sectarians, Catholic fideists, Deists, and suspected atheists. Hooker's rationalism also assisted in the clergy's efforts to give an account of the faith which they hoped would save theology from nature by arresting the tendency in some scientific and philosophic circles to disregard religious explanations of the world in favor of mechanistic and deterministic ones. As a conscientious member of the Restoration episcopate, Bishop Sanderson was not unique in acknowledging that reason cannot comprehend the full extent of the heavenly mysteries, but he was also not alone in insisting that "We have use of our Reason (and they are unreasonable, that would deny us the use of it) in Religion, as well as in other things. And that not only in Agenis, in matters of Duty and Morality, wherein it is of a more necessary and constant use . . . but even in Credentis too, in such points as are more properly of Faith, in matters Doctrinal and Dogmatical."[21]

The instrument of reason was to be employed by Anglicans even in the settlement of difficult questions concerning belief and practice, particularly where the word of Scripture is silent or ambiguous. Bishop Cosin, certainly no friend of the moderate churchmen after the return of the king, nonetheless repeated what most scholars have come to accept as a Latitudinarian commonplace when he stated that Anglicans cannot believe anything against their reason. Unlike Catholics, members of England's state church are not asked to believe "they know not what, nor any mysteries of the kingdom of heaven, they know not why." Rather, Englishmen must be "ready to give an account and to render a reason of what we believe." God had not given any man so much ease in this life "as to let him sit still there and make no use of his reason for the mysteries of the other life. We call it not faith, that is not grounded upon reason. . . ."[22] Even Thomas Sprat, whose staunch opposition to Latitudinarian schemes for comprehension resulted in his abrupt departure from the Royal Ecclesiastical Commission in 1689, recognized that Christian doctrines "are very agreeable to the reason of Mankind; its Precepts most becoming the purest, and the strictest Laws of Nature, and Virtue, and Morality." God deals with mankind, said Sprat, "by a steady, plain, declared, written Rule of Justice and Righteousness." Tillotson and the Latitudinarian bishops, all heirs to this common tradition of Christian humanism, could not have agreed more. As Gerard Reedy has recently observed, we easily misrepresent the late seventeenth-century Anglican divines if we do not recognize "that their insistence on the reasonableness of Christianity was not an iron grip on a deistic future but on the traditional past." And that past included a respect for the instrument of God-given reason which could be abandoned only at the risk of ignoring the one gift which distinguished man from the merely sentient and appetitive.[23]

Anglican rationalists used Hooker's arguments repeatedly in their undertakings against Protestants who rejected reason in the drive to magnify the claims of spirit and individual inspiration and against Catholic apologists who insisted that papal authority was the only sure guide in matters of faith. In the case of Protestant sectaries, their abandonment of the authority of the institutional church struck Anglicans as being every bit as self-righteous and sinful as the deci-sion of our common parents in their proud desire to know good and evil without God's leave. Dispensing with the sacraments, ignoring liturgical expression, and disparaging the intellect in favor of some subjective inward experience, the exclusivism of the sectaries stood as a worrisome affront to the whole fabric of Thomist theology.[24] According to representatives of the church, prophesy and gifts of the spirit had ceased with the apostolic age; thus the claims of the sectaries were little better than intolerable manifestations of man's depraved and rebellious state.[25] Fowler's reminder "that men cannot receive the things of God's Spirit, till by the assistance thereof, their Reason hath regained its authority, and be able to keep under their brutish affections" served as a warning to all Dissenters who would place conscience before the collective wisdom of the historic church.[26]

The High Churchman Robert South sought to put an end to this flagrant abuse of the Spirit by defining "conscience" and the "light within us" in terms which were exactly opposite those known by the religious Independents of the 1640s. For South, both designations were to be considered synonymous with the dictate of reason.[27] Man's capacity to reason may be weak and not "universally sufficient to direct us to what to do"; it was doubtless a "diminutive light com-pared to Revelation," but that was no excuse for ignoring it in our religion, for despite its limits it remains "a ray of divinity directed into the soul." In words reminiscent of Whichcote, South described reason as "the candle of the Lord . . . and God never lights us up a candle either to put out or to sleep by."[28] In decrying the use of rea-son in religion, the more radical Dissenters were unwittingly abetting the Catholic cause by strengthening the case for fideism. Those who put religion above the grasp of reason, said Glanvill, "beyond sobriety and sense," distort Christ's simple message for their own ends. In such schools "The way to be a Christian, is first to be a Brute, and to be a true Believer . . . is to be fit for Bedlam."[29]

In addition to these serious theological concerns, equally compelling political ones commanded the attention of Anglicans. After 1660 all forms of "enthusiasm" came to be equated with the social and political disorder of the Interregnum period, posing a threat to both person and property.[30] Many had been conscious of the problem during the Interregnum itself. In 1644, for example, William Prynne wondered whether Congregationalism, by making each individual sovereign in religion, would not ultimately destroy all public order. Congregationalists insisted that the true church consisted of gathered, self-governing associations of the godly answerable to no human authority. Such voluntarism, as Ellen More has indicated, invariably pointed in the direction of instability and confusion in society, fueling every disintegrative tendency and making the job of the magistrate a formidable one.[31] Glanvill spoke for many churchmen after 1660 when he said that the disparagement of reason in religion was "the Spring-Head of most of the Waters of Bitterness and Strife; and here the Fountain of the Great Deeps of Atheism and Fanaticism, that are broken up upon us."[32] Without some curb upon the claims of nonrational avenues to religious experience, the Restoration settlement itself would be extremely short-lived.

Glanvill's concern about the benefits provided to the Catholic cause by unsuspecting Dissenters was not completely unfounded, for the threat to the integrity of reason from sectarian enthusiasts was matched by the fideistic claims of a resurgent Catholicism. Dryden's *Religio Laici* was the best-known English expression of the fideist position, but it was by no means the only one.[33] The debate between defenders of the principle of moral certainty and Catholic infallibilists accelerated after the Restoration, and virtually every one of the moderate churchmen had occasion to enter the fray. Most did so willingly, believing that theirs was a struggle both to vindicate individual freedom in matters of interpretation and to reclaim for the Anglican communion its identification with a view of man where salvation, although beyond the purview of frail and fallen humanity, was nonetheless contingent upon the responsible employment of God-given reason.

Edward Stillingfleet devoted much of his career to fighting skepticism and infidelity under all its guises, and his well-received *Origines Sacrae: or A Rational Account of the Grounds of the Protestant Religion* (1665) continued the explorations of Chillingworth into the limits of knowledge and the proper basis of belief, exemplifying the approach taken by all the Anglicans who engaged in the controversy.[34] Genuine faith, said Stillingfleet, can be based only on rational assent to proper evidence, but to demand the wrong sort of evidence—say, mathematical certainty or concrete sense experience—for proving matters of fact was to distort God's requirements for mankind. There can be no demonstration of a matter of fact in the Bible, yet we can be certain of the truth contained therein on the basis of the evidence offered to the diligent student. We are assured that Christ was the Messiah because the miracles he performed were confirmed by credible witnesses who have passed their testimony down to us through Scripture. Men accept without difficulty the principle of moral certainty in virtually every aspect of their lives, making daily decisions on the same type of probable evidence which obtains in matters of religion. We do not doubt the existence of Ireland or America, for example, simply because we have never visited those lands. To demand an infallible guide in religion is to apply an inappropriate standard of evidence; it means that men "must destroy all historical faith out of the world," adopt a complete skepticism, and surrender their reasons to the fiat of an arbitrary authority such as the Roman Church.[35] Such a state of affairs would be tantamount to renouncing the one divine gift that separated men from the beasts.

Bishop Pearson's defining faith as "an Assent unto truths credible upon the testimony of God delivered unto us in the writings of the Apostles and Prophets" and a "habit of the intellectual part of man" reflected the unanimity which Anglicans—and some Presbyterians—maintained on this question of utilizing the best evidence available to human reason in advancing the cause of religious understanding.[36] As Richard Baxter argued in his first direction to the graceless sinner, in order to receive Christ's helping grace, one must "remain not in a state of ignorance; but do thy best to come into the light, and understand the Word of God, in the matters of salvation."[37] Anglicans and moderate Nonconformists were agreed "that objective Religion is to be received by Man's Reasonable Intellect, and is, when so received, the light and guide, the advancement and perfecting of our Reason." For Baxter, the most religious person is he who is "truly, and nobly rational."[38] Sounding not unlike his friends among the Latitudinarians, Baxter encouraged his readers to use their best reason in order to search the works of God in nature, to determine which are the truly canonical scriptures, and to gather just conclusions and rules of action for daily life.[39] However, once divine authorship is established, "we must believe and submit to all that is in it, without any more reason for our belief."[40] Things equally true may not be capable of the same degree of evidence, but because God seeks not to deceive men, we have the greatest reason in the world to believe all that he has revealed in Scripture, even though our own unstable intellects cannot comprehend how some articles of faith can be possible. As South insisted, the most intricate and mysterious passages in the Bible "are vouched by an infinite veracity; and truth is truth, though clotted in riddles, and surrounded with darkness and obscurity."[41] The fact that there are many mysteries in Christianity should not discourage anyone, for such a state of affairs has never deterred natural philosophers. Anglicans, said Cosin, "ask no more in divinity than otherwise they ask in nature; where the mysteries be oftentimes so abstruse and hidden in themselves, that no man's reason is able to reach them, nor the light of nature clear enough to find out the secrets of nature itself."[42] Our doubts concerning Scripture serve as a testament to our own ignorance rather than to the irrational nature of God, to the fact that scriptural truths—like so many truths in nature—are above but not contrary to reason, and this inability to comprehend the divine mysteries encourages us to depend upon our spiritual guides within the official church for instruction and advancement.[43] Moral certainty in matters of religion may appear less satisfying to men than the absolute certainty or certainty of demonstration available in mathematics or philosophy, but this situation simply reflects the competence of human reason and not the veracity of revelation.

Such a position regarding the role of reason in religion, where the Protestant follows the dictate of reason until persuaded of the truth of Scripture but defers to authority once that truth is established, obviously served the Church of England in its ongoing struggle against a wide variety of opponents. The emphasis given to the wonderfully ambiguous word "reason" could be conveniently varied to serve the institutional needs of the church, alternatively elevating its competence against enthusiasts and fideists and restricting it when faced with the challenge from Deism.[44] In the end the authority of the church, the intellectual ascendancy of the clergy, and the respectability of religion within the context of the new science could all be significantly enhanced by the skillful employment of reason in carefully defined contexts. The Church of England would serve as the indispensible link between the province of natural theology and the much more expansive domain of truths which transcended the frail grasp of debilitated human reason.

Underpinning every Anglican reference to the reasonable nature of man was the long-established and rarely questioned assumption that each individual possesses certain innate ideas or first principles whereby the soul is predisposed to a rational life and where man is able to discern the moral good, the content of the natural law, and oftentimes the existence of God as well. The doctrine of innate knowledge was widespread in the seventeenth century and considered to be essential for the stability of religion and morality.[45] To question whether ideas of God, or ideas of good and evil, were part of our natural endowment seemed to leave the way open for the sort of moral relativism which members of the Platonist group at Cambridge espied and condemned in the work of Hobbes.

Innate ideas were thought to be the essential buttress of the moral order, providing men with a ubiquitous and lasting touchstone by which they might guide their actions. When Tillotson, for example, in his preface to Wilkins's *Principles and Duties of Natural Theology*, announced that "the great Duties of Piety and Justice are written upon our hearts, and every man feels a secret obligation to them in his own Conscience," his foremost concern was with solidifying adherence to established norms of conduct by referring men to the dictates of universal conscience as reflected in their own souls.[46] The foundation of morality, then, was to be discovered not in custom, legislation, or edict, but in the unvarying internal nature of man himself.

Some of the moderates, like Matthew Hale and Edward Stillingfleet, subscribed to a form of simple innatism, where God impresses complete ideas on the mind of children at birth. Hale believed that "There are some truths so plain and evident, and open, that need not any process of ratiocination to evidence or evince them."[47] These "connate Principles," although "weakened by the Fall, and the Contracted Corruption of Humane Nature," were nevertheless "engraven in the Soul, born with it, and growing up with it till they receive a check by ill customs or education, or an improvement and advancement by the due exercise of the Faculties."[48] Such a view of innate ideas was the exception, however, as the majority of churchmen preferred a modified or dispositional version of the theory, one where the mind is predisposed to accept the truth of certain ideas and principles of morality once they are presented to our experience. While natural law was ultimately fixed in the rational soul, the modified version of the theory required that men reflect upon their ideas in order to discover their innate principles.

Isaac Barrow succinctly described this dispositional form of innatism when he wrote that the ways of truth, right, and virtue "are very legible characters graven by the finger of God on our hearts and consciences, so that by any considerable reflection inwards we may easily read them."[49] The need for a modicum of ratiocination in the process of uncovering connatural ideas was reiterated by Archbishop Sancroft when he wrote that all men were learners "and so indued with Faculties of Reason; Powers of a Soul capable of Learning; stampt, and possest with first Principles, and common Notions which deeply searc'd and duly improv'd, and cultivated, might teach us Much of Righteousness."[50] Even the Dissenter Baxter agreed that there is in the nature of man's soul "a certain aptitude to understand certain truths as soon as they are revealed . . . and it is true that this disposition is brought to actual knowledge as soon as the mind comes to actual consideration of the things."[51] The advocate of dispositional innatism was acutely aware of the important role played by education in the development of the individual's innate capacity to know; without constant activity and self-discipline there was little prospect that connatural ideas would materially affect our behavior.

Belief in the doctrine of innate ideas certainly strengthened the Anglican faith in man's capacity to exercise reason despite the lachrymose implications of the Fall. With the inborn capacity to distinguish moral good and evil, men were unequivocally obliged to cultivate that capacity for their own temporal and spiritual well-being and for the greater glory of their maker. To ignore such a special endowment would be the highest impudence, the final abjuration of their very nature as rational beings. Tillotson spoke for most of his peers when he preached that even the worst of men have a natural sense of the evil and unreasonableness of sin which can hardly ever be extinguished from human nature.[52] This innate knowledge made the sinner's plea of ignorance of the law completely indefensible; there was no excuse for those who violated the promptings of their own conscience even after taking into account the intellectual and spiritual infirmity occasioned by the actions of our first parents. Innatism demanded a rigoristic ethics.

But regardless of the presence of mankind's purportedly innate disposition to that which is in accordance with God's eternal law, the Latitudinarian churchmen had no illusions about the strength of innate ideas as a guide to behavior and belief. Given their view of human nature, they were obliged to acknowledge that precious few of their contemporaries would be apt to reflect on their ideas before acting in what they took to be their best interest; the Latitudinarians could never accept the Deist claim that reason provided all of the necessary grounds of religion. Churchmen like John Moore may have accepted that "the great Duties of our Religion [are] all writ upon our own Nature," but experience forced him to admit that natural religion can give us but "obscure" and "uncertain" ideas of the next life.[53] By the use of reason alone the ancient philosophers had come to some right notions regarding God, but their polytheism and idolotry indicated the problems which all men faced in attempting to establish a natural theology without divine assistance.[54] It took an "extraordinary Revelation published by the miraculous Power of God" to cleanse the souls of men from these false opinions.[55] Tillotson and Stillingfleet agreed. Careful guidance and instruction were "never more necessary than in this degenerate Age" when the natural obligation of moral duties seemed to have but little practical impact on the lives of most. These purportedly natural promptings were so weak, in fact, that God felt obliged to supplement them with his holy word, an "unspeakable advantage" in clarifying the knowledge and enjoining the performance of civilized action.[56] Tillotson's successor at Canterbury, Thomas Tenison, preached that reason ruled in exceptionally few men, while daily experience "shews how narrow-minded, how unjust, how biassed men are, how they judge by their affections, and instead of doing nothing by Partiality, they scarce do anything otherwise."[57]

Not surprisingly, the Sheldonian High Churchmen stood shoulder to shoulder with the Latitudinarians on this question. According to Sanderson, for example, God may have implanted innate characters of the law of nature in every person, "yet so desperately wicked is the heart of man, that if it should be left to the wildness of its own corruption, without any other bridle than the light of natural principles only, it would estsoons shake off that also: and quite raze out all impressions of the Law of Nature; at least so blur and confound the Characters, that the Conscience should be able to spell very little (or nothing at all) of Duty out of them."[58] Deliberate and careful instruction in the duties of Christianity was clearly a necessary labor in a world where innate ideas had a negligible impact on actual behavior. And the central text in that work of education had graciously been provided by a loving Savior, for "when we had blurr'd the Original, defac'd the first Traces of Righteousness upon our Souls, he was pleas'd to provide Expedients to teach it us again the second time, that we might be renewed unto Knowledge after the Image of him, that created us in Righteousness."[59] Scripture would instruct and enjoin those very precepts which we had failed to discover in our own nature.

Given such serious reservations about the potential of reason, it was little wonder that Tillotson's friend Locke was beginning to question the whole notion of putative innate ideas after which so few men patterned their lives. Seeking a new basis for the establishment of the moral law through a radical empiricism which denied any place for inborn knowledge, Locke's critique, published in 1690 as *An Essay Concerning Human Understanding*, won few adherents and much derision during the 1690s.[60] By attempting to rebuild knowledge—including practical and speculative principles—on the foundation of observation and experience, Locke found himself charged with reintroducing the sort of moral relativism found in Hobbes. That none of his friends among the Latitudinarians were willing to accept Locke's alternative to innate ideas and that one of them, Bishop Stillingfleet, thought that the *Essay* actually undermined the force of Christianity are important indications of just how central innatism was to their picture of man's rational nature. Innate ideas, despite their obvious impuissance in the arena of everyday affairs, remained the crucial nexus between man and his creator, the guarantor of the integrity of Scholastic anthropology.

Still, the implications of innatism for the Latitudinarian picture of human nature, particularly given the obvious failure of men to act in accordance with the promptings of their conscience, were not particularly sanguine. Unhappily, continued adherence to the doctrine of innate ideas could only enhance the validity of an interpretation of sin as wilful and malign rebellion against God's known laws. Faced with the paradox where belief in innate ideas as man's foremost link with God had the effect of magnifying the contumacy involved in even the smallest sin, the Latitudinarians, like so many of their fellow churchmen, instinctively embraced that epistemology which authenticated the centuries-old Christian indictment of human nature.

Regardless of the conquests of reason in the seventeenth century—the apparent advances in natural theology no less than the successes in experimental science—developments which suggested an expanded role for philosophy at the expense of theology did not signal the abandonment of a tradition of thought where the distrust of reason remained paramount. When Puritans during the first half of the century stressed that the employment of reason without the help of spiritual assistance would invariably lead men astray, they were reaffirming a broader point of view which found its roots in the warnings of Saint Paul and the early church fathers against the vanity of worldly learning and the need to humble the intellect before the soul can receive true knowledge from God. The anti-rationalist strain found in such critics of Thomism as William of Occam and Duns Scotus stressed that the knowledge obtainable through the use of philosophy had nothing to do with the certitude of faith.[61] Together with the revival of ancient skepticism during the Renaissance, when the arguments of Pyrrho and Sextus Empiricus were once again employed to deflate the claims of ever-changeable man and his deceptive senses, antirationalism remained a powerful force throughout the Restoration and into the eighteenth century. Rochester's *Satyr Against Mankind* was, perhaps, the most striking of the literary attacks, and one could mention Swift and Pope in a later context, but the suspicion of human reason was an important theme in theology as well.[62] Hooker had been careful to remind his contemporaries that even with the exceptional potential of natural theology, the weakness of reason in most men made it necessary that further assistance be provided through special revelation.[63] Man's reason had been so compromised by the Fall that few individuals now possessed the self-discipline and intellectual strength to search out and follow the precepts of natural theology, even though the simple fundamentals of the faith were amenable to rational inquiry. In Hooker's judgment, as in the minds of his sevententh-century Anglican successors, revelation remained the foremost channel whereby the essential truths of religion were made available to all men and which served to legitimize those special truths which transcended the grasp of mere reason.[64]

The many problems attendant upon referring to natural theology as a guide to faith and conduct, particularly when not combined with the gift of revelation, had been further explored by Jeremy Taylor during the Interregnum. He touched the core of the issue which would face Restoration divines and even anticipated some of the concerns of Hume in the eighteenth century when he described reason as "such a box of quicksilver that it abides nowhere; it dwells in no settled mansion; it is like a dove's neck, or a changeable taffata; it looks to me otherwise than to you who do not stand in the same light that I do; and if we enquire after the law of nature by the rules of our reason, we shall be as uncertain as the discourse of the people, or the dreams of disturbed fancies."[65]

William Sherlock later pointed to this same dangerous subjectivism and cautioned that "Natural Reason" can be a troublesome guide because "different men reason very differently, and very absurdly too." One had to be careful when employing such a delicate tool in the most important business in life. "Most men think themselves Masters of as much Reason as their Neighbors; and, if they have no Instructors but Men, will judge for themselves, and take what they like, and leave the rest." It was little wonder that most churchmen turned to divine revelation to "give new Power and Authority" to the laws of nature available to man through the use of reason.[66] Reason, it seemed, was on many occasions just as untrustworthy and fluid a guide as the "inner light" of the much-derided sectaries. "The rules and directions of a holy life," said Tillotson, "were very obscure before," because the general corruption of mankind, "and the vicious practice of the world, had in great measure blurred and defaced the natural law." In consequence, our motives to virtue were but weak and ineffectual "in comparison of what they are now rendered by the Revelation of the gospel."[67] Tillotson and the other Latitudinarians would have agreed with Bishop Sanderson's observation that men were prevented from knowing God's eternal purposes through the use of reason because of both their limited understandings and the errors of their vain imaginations. But the Holy Scripture, "fitted to our capacity, speaketh of the things of God in such language, and under such notions, as best agree with our weak conceptions, but far below the dignity and majesty of the things themselves."[68]

Unlike the earlier Puritans, however, it was more the inadequacy of human reason rather than its inherent wickedness which compelled Anglicans to focus on the importance of special revelation.[69] "I cannot allow," wrote the layman Boyle, "that the intellect of man is the genuine standard of truth, so that whatever surpasses his comprehension must not be admitted to be."[70] The deficiencies of human reason which were obvious to virtuosi like Boyle were repeatedly contrasted with the sufficiency of supernatural knowledge. John Cosin's assurance that the will of God as revealed in Scripture, because of its inherent majesty, justice, and harmony, would commend itself to the assent of all reasonable men, was no different from the faith of the Latitudinarian layman John Locke's position in his controversial, and much misunderstood, *Reasonableness of Christianity*. For Locke, the devout Christian will humbly concede the sharply prescribed compass of human knowledge and turn to the supernatural word of God whenever reason fails him, confident in the promise that everything necessary for salvation can be found there. Natural religion "in its full extent, was nowhere, that I know, taken care of by the force of natural reason." It was much the better course that a rule coming directly from God and avoiding "the sometimes intricate deductions of reason" serve as man's principal guide.[71] Men must build upon their reasonable nature as a first step in searching for the key to salvation, argued Cosin. "It is the light of faith that shews the right way to be saved," he wrote, "but in that way faith is not on this side of knowledge, but beyond it, and we must necessarily come to the light of knowledge and reason first; though when we are come thither we must not stay in it, but make use of it to lead us to a better and higher light than it."[72]

The light of reason, then, enjoyed but a subsidiary role as a guide to God's everlasting truths when compared to the faith which is anchored to man's fully developed rational nature. For the Latitudinarians, the employment of reason itself was not to be viewed as the arrogant tool of individuals seeking to separate themselves from God's eternal governance and affecting an independent virtue and knowledge. Man's subordination extended even to the powers of his mind, for as Patrick remarked, "when I speak of reason, I do not mean bare natural reason without the guidance of God's grace."[73] While reason doubtless elevated man above the other creatures, it was always accepted as the gift of God, a special trust one day to be returned to its divine original and acting as a brake on one's pride in merely human accomplishments.[74] The honest man has no conceits about his reason, and "he knows nothing more undoubtedly than that he is a weak and shallow creature."[75] In fact, insisted Glanvill, men trust their reasons only "because we have them from God, who cannot mistake, and will not deceive." In following the promptings of human reason, men are relying entirely on God's "veracity and goodness, and that is an exercise of faith."[76]

Whatever confidence the Latitude-men had in the power of reason, then, was ultimately based on their unshakable faith in the goodness of God's will and superintendence, in the belief that human reason differed in extent, but not in kind, from its divine original. Given this relationship, it would be little better than blasphemous to pretend to rival God's omniscience, since all human knowledge is but a poor reflection of that deiform standard. Rational "self-control" as first understood by the Greeks, and much later by their Deist heirs, was impossible for Latitudinarians who viewed every instance of reasonable behavior as the complementary outgrowth of divine and human agency. Tillotson emphasized the disjunction between the classical view of reason as the supreme authority and the measure of man's integrity and the Christian awareness of human contingency when he observed that "whatever natural power we have to do any thing is from God, an effect of his goodness."[77] A habit of holiness through the exercise of reason, wrote the High Churchman Robert South, "Must needs be produced by supernatural infusion, and consequently proceed, not from acquisition, but gift. It must be brought into the soul, it cannot grow or spring out of it."[78] There was, for Anglicans, no independent role for reason without the constant assistance of the very being who had endowed us with that now much-diminished faculty. Reason was but an empty term without the constant infusion of God's saving grace, assistance made available through the unmerited sacrifice of his only son. Just at that point where reasonable religion seemed to intersect with the Deistic religion of reason, late seventeenth-century Anglicans, including those derisively referred to as Latitudinarians, declared for a prospect of human reason which sharply distinguished the truths of theology from those of emulous philosophy. The vision of God would remain for the moderate churchmen what it had been for Aquinas—at once man's natural end and a supernatural gift. Deists would not be welcome in the world of Thomism inhabited by such thinkers.

W e are miserable, despicable creatures," stated the Latitudinarian John Wilkins, "and we can hope for nothing from
God, but upon account of Bounty; without his mercy we
are all of us lost and undone."[1] The man who caused Archbishop
Sheldon such distress during the 1660s as a result of his indefati-
gable work towards a comprehensive church entertained few illusions
about the competence of human effort in the work of salvation. "Our
Righteousness be as filty rags," was the essence of his somber message, and "If there be any particular sin which we have not fallen
into in our lives, 'tis not for want of corrupt principles and dispositions in our natures, which do incline us to all, but by reason of God's
restraining grace, which hath yet with-held us from them; without
which we should break out into as great abominations, as were ever
committed by the vilest sons of men."[2] The Latitudinarian picture of
human nature and the problems attendant upon the use of reason in
religion invariably moved the question of supernatural agency to the
forefront of late seventeenth-century discussions concerning man's
teleological home. The storm over the sufficiency of merit first raised
by the fifth-century monk Pelagius, just as the harsh contours of
Augustinian anthropology were overspreading the crumbling city of
man, had by no means dissipated in the more self-assured intellectual
climate of Restoration England. While firmly denying that all natural
goodness had been forfeited at the Fall, Anglicans found themselves
obliged to detail once again the nature of the relationship between
free will and divine grace, between the efficacy of works guided by
reason and the sufficiency of unmerited sacrifice on the part of God's

only son. Since the strength of the charge of preaching "moralism" and ignoring Christ's sacrifice, so frequently made against the Latitudinarian divines, rests largely upon the position occupied by grace in their overall theology, an examination of the extent of their divergence from the generally accepted orthodoxy on the subject deserves further consideration.[3]

It is well known that the Latitudinarians often referred to Greek moralists in their sermons, and it is not difficult to understand why they did so. Both Greeks and Christians recognized the importance of man's binary nature, and both believed that the life of the soul was superior to the temporal exigencies of the flesh. But as Basil Willey has observed, there are three characteristics of Christianity which sharply distinguish it from the spirit of classical Greek humanism: a special revelation dealing with historic time, a doctrine of original sin, and a technique for redemption.[4] All three are interrelated, of course, but it is the last which is perhaps the most fundamental to the Christian's picture of man and his place in creation. Aristotle had not called for a redeemer because he felt no need of redemption and was not obsessed by a sense of sin. Such was not the situation with Saint Paul, however, who remained deeply affected by his own unrighteousness, by the frailty of human intellect and will, and by God's omnipotence.[5] "There is none righteous, no, not one," had been his warning to a world where obedience to the law had been nullified by the tryanny of sin which dwells in every individual.[6] Paul's own dramatic escape from the exacting requirements of that law through faith in the grace which was made available by Christ had a compelling impact on the institutional church throughout the medieval period.[7] For while many of the early church fathers thought that Adam's Fall had not deprived man of his freedom of will to the point where he could no longer begin the process towards righteousness on his own, Augustine powerfully reconfirmed the Pauline view in his famous clash with the monk Pelagius.[8] In the mind of Pelagius, grace was merely a juridical forgiveness of sin, a divine pardon, rather than an interior transformation of the heart of the offender. Christ's passion and death served merely as moral examples to men who remain capable of achieving their own salvation through proper conduct and self-discipline, with grace becoming simply the nature in which we were created. Christ was necessary for Pelagius "that by His gospel we may learn how we ought to live; but not that we may be also assisted by His grace."[9]

This tendency towards naturalism, where Christ was reduced to preaching a code of behavior for man, and where, because grace is inherent in the constitution of our nature, full adherence to the law remains within our grasp, reminded Augustine of the false righteousness of the Pharisees, men who so often boasted of their own meritorious works. For the bishop of Hippo, grace was an unmerited election, a desire for and delight in the good reserved for a few, "a new form of liberty that required an internal modification of the human will."[10] No longer did justification merely signify God's accounting the Elect righteous, as was the case with Paul, but it now involved making them so, a process of progressive sanctification instead of preliminary absolution. For Augustine the elect of God received a power or gift which was infused into their souls in order to make possible their moral advancement; the justified man "is given a will capable of desiring good, and subsequently cooperates with that good will to perform good works, to bring that justification to perfection."[11] The way was now clear for a more dynamic view of the saving power of God while stressing the importance of moral reform for those granted the gift of grace. The medieval church, by and large, accepted the broad outlines of Augustine's position, particularly his insistence upon the necessity of works after justification, while simultaneously taking swift action against the misguided promoters of human self-sufficiency.[12] All varieties of Pelagianism were officially condemned at the Council of Orange in 529, where the assembled bishops strongly reasserted the necessity of prevenient grace in the final canons. The sentiments of Christ as repeated by Saint John, "Without me ye can do nothing," became the basic position of the church throughout the course of the Middle Ages.[13]

Thus, even with the Scholastic rehabilitation of reason during the thirteenth century, there remained within the church a clear acknowledgment of the futility of works in the drama of salvation. Grace continued to be identified with the condescending love of the Creator towards an undeserving mankind, and it was believed that he not only provided the opportunity for reform but also operated to create man's very willingness to accept this assistance. The human mind, "however perfect it may be," indicated Aquinas, "cannot know the truth by reasoning without divine illumination. And this belongs to the assistance of grace."[14] Both for the knowledge of any truth and the beginning of any good work, sinners must first seek divine help. Such was mankind's spiritual declension that no one could even prepare himself to receive the light of grace "except by the gratuitous assistance of God moving him within." [15] There was, then, no preparation available to man independent of God's charity; conversion began with faith, and faith itself was a prevenient grace, the free gift of God. And even after obtaining grace, man subsequently "needs habitual grace to heal nature, so as wholly to refrain from sin." [16] Every individual "needs to be conserved by God in the goodness which it has received from him." [17] For the sixteenth- and seventeenth-century Protestant heirs to this enduring theological perspective, *sola fide* meant that the gulf between God and sinner is too great for men to cross of their own strength. "The will is so bound by the slavery of sin," warned Calvin, "that it cannot excite itself, much less devote itself to anything good . . . which in the Scriptures is attributed solely to Divine grace." [18] Man's sanctification— the alliance of his behavior with the will of God—must be preceded by justification or the imputation of Christ's righteousness to him. [19] Meritorious acts were the delusion of the unregenerate who would experience the harshest divine justice for the temerity which infected their lives.

Under such a reading of the human drama, faith became the first and greatest Christian duty, faith in what Christ has done for us and faith in God's promise to us under the generous terms of the Second Covenant. In an outpouring of mercy towards his disobedient subjects, God freely takes the initiative and sends his son as a sacrifice for our sins and as our redeemer. Our trust in that redeemer is what justifies because it signals a voluntary submergence of the self in God, the submission of a finite will to an infinite one and the apperception of the crippling magnitude of our common parents' act of disobedience. [20] But as with Saint Thomas, faith for the seventeenth-century Protestant was exclusively a divine work *in* man; it changes him and redirects his life before he can begin the process of reestablishing the supremacy of reason over appetite. Moral perfection, as Perry Miller indicated in his pioneering treatment of the Puritan mind, "required a previous infusion of supernatural grace." Unless the depraved will of man is regenerated by grace, there will be no easy transition from the rule of reason to the practice of virtue. To know the good was scant guarantee that we would live according to its mandate, much less that such knowledge would restore us to a prelapsarian arcadia. [21] "Man lost by sin the integrity of his nature," stated that nemesis of the Puritans, William Laud, "and can not have

light enough to see the way to heaven but by grace."[22] Ordained
clergy acting in their capacity as counselors might do much to help
quicken our response to the influence of the Spirit, but in the end
no human agency could effect what had been a gratuitous divine act
since the Fall of Man.[23] Arminius had illustrated the point when he
wrote that "a rich man bestows, on a poor and famishing beggar,
alms by which he may be able to maintain himself. Does it cease to be
a pure gift, because the beggar extends his hand to receive it?"[24] Few
English Protestants would quarrel with such a judgment, even when
it was uttered by an alleged champion of heretical Arminianism like
Laud. Latitudinarians such as Wilkins were not the only members
of the seventeenth-century Church of England whose theology was
misrepresented by hostile critics.

One of the principal ways that sixteenth-century Protestant reformers distinguished themselves from their Catholic opponents on
the nature of grace was by emphasizing the predestinarian components of Augustine's thought and by insisting that God's special gift
did nothing to heal human nature from within or restore it to an
original purity. As part of a larger protest against the localization
of divine power within the institutional Catholic Church—and in
order to establish the absolute transcendence of God—justification
for the first Protestants was defined as a purely extrinsic imputation
of the merits of Christ where the sinner, for no reason known to frail
humanity, was gratuitously protected by God's mercy. No internal
transformation of the individual took place, and no healing power or
divine life was communicated to him; for the Protestant there could
not be a real change *in* the man who, at that special moment of justification, receives assurance of his eternal salvation without reference
to his previous condition.[25] "The elect are the children of God," wrote
Ulrich Zwingli, "even before they believe." Irresistible grace and the
unfathomable wisdom of God became the watchwords of the earliest
Protestant understanding of the conversion process, confirming the
absolute depravity of man in the aftermath of Adam's sin.[26] The elect
of God engage in good works as a result of their privileged status,
and these works have no relation whatsoever to the process of election. The saved man can thus perform works without worrying over
the self-sanctifying aspects of his actions.

With this reading of the process of divine assistance, the church's
role as a custodian and conduit of grace was undermined as the spiritual autonomy of the individual, alone before his maker, redefined

the nature of the religious experience. The first English reformers were deeply influenced by these Continental ideas when they were initially introduced by men like Martin Bucer and Peter Martyr, and Englishmen absorbed this novel theology of grace into the official doctrinal statements of the church.[27] In the final formulation of the Thirty-nine Articles (1563), for example, the Elizabethan bishops incorporated the purport of reformed theology on grace into the church's canon by insisting that "The condition of man after the Fall of Adam is such, that he can not turn and prepare himself, by his own natural strength and good works, to faith, and calling upon God," while works done in anticipation of grace "are not pleasing to God" and "have the nature of sin."[28] For the earliest Protestants, "preparation" in any form was tantamount to "works righteousness" and the egregious errors of Rome.

The Catholic response to this radical departure from a powerful medieval perspective which had placed inward spiritual renewal at the center of man's justification was formulated at the Council of Trent. Recognizing in the reformed theology a divine determinism which seemed to invalidate human responsibility, the representatives of the Roman Church rejected the idea of forensic grace or pardon where the sacrifice of Christ covers the sins of select individuals and affirmed that the moral life of the Christian was in fact the clear expression of the interior power of grace. Good works were not simply signs of previous conversion but products of the activity of justifying grace within the soul where, without violence or sudden action, the temperament and personality of the sinner are transformed.[29] As Augustine had written centuries earlier, grace is a gift of the Spirit to the inner man, "by whom there is formed in his mind a delight in, and love of, that supreme and unchangeable good which is God . . . [by which] he may conceive an ardent desire to cleave to his Maker, and may burn to enter upon the participation in that true light, that it may go well with Him to whom he owes his existence."[30] Human nature, insufficient for its proper end, needs to be augmented by a transcendent power before it can enjoy the goodness which is the vision of God. And while man cannot take the first step toward righteousness without divine assistance in the form of prevenient grace, he must respond to this gratuitous initiative by consenting to it and cooperating with it.[31] Thus God gives to man a freedom of self-determination even in the realm of grace; the burden of decision to accept its healing power is his alone.

Medieval theologians—and particularly Aquinas—had drawn convincing analogies between Aristotle's picture of unformed matter receiving its form through a process of generation and the soul of man moving towards its maker through the instrument of divine grace. According to this view, God was the Supreme Mover who restores the free will of disobedient man, grace being a disposition in God that becomes active in its object, and this process is often extended over a considerable period of time. "Since a man cannot prepare himself for grace unless God . . . move him to good," wrote Aquinas, "it is of no account whether anyone arrive at perfect preparation instantaneously, or step by step."[32] God chose not to be the sole agent in some arbitrary process of salvation where human freedom and individual moral responsibility are nullified; for the Catholic, grace must transform men into new creatures capable of responding to the pardon which is available to them through Christ's sacrifice. Using the metaphor of the light of the sun and the power of sight, Aquinas compared grace to the light from the sun without which man could not see but upheld the need for human response by observing that "He who has his eyes turned away from the light of the sun prepares himself to receive the light of the sun by turning his eyes thither."[33] Works became coeval with conversion rather than consequent to it, and men were empowered to follow Saint Paul's exhortation to reform, living in "repentance toward God, and faith toward our Lord Jesus Christ."[34]

Although the early Protestant reformers had condemned the idea of preparation for grace as another otiose pretense of Roman Catholicism, by the late sixteenth and early seventeenth centuries, even English Puritans began to express the possibility of such preparation taking place in the soul of depraved man. Proof texts to fit either doctrinal stance could be found in Scripture, but as a reforming and proselytizing community eager to transform their society, Puritans found themselves increasingly engaged in the work of exhorting men to prepare the heart for saving grace. The Pauline model of instantaneous conversion, much admired during the early stages of the Reformation, did not easily lend itself to such an animated, yet orderly vision of spiritual remediation. Paul himself had not insisted on his own conversion experience as normative, often preaching that man's faith could often be weak before preparation. By preparation the Puritan normally meant a period of intense introspection and meditation before one turned to God for assistance, but by the seventeenth century there was general agreement on the need for prolonged discipline and instruction before the saving power of grace could be effectual.[35] Even at the Calvinist Synod of Dort, where hostility to any form of synergism ran deep, one English delegate sympathetic to the anti-Arminian findings of the conference could not accept the majority decision on grace. Joseph Hall, soon to be appointed bishop of Exeter, recognized man's inability to work his own salvation but nevertheless maintained that "there are yet certain foregoing acts that are pre-required to the conversion of a man . . . as the knowledge of God's will, the feeling of our sin, the fear of hell, the thought of deliverance, some hope of pardon." According to Hall, the grace of God "doth not use to work upon a man immediately by sudden raptures, but by meet preparations."[36]

The paradox involved in a position which counseled reform while flatly rejecting sinful man's ability to influence God had been resolved to the satisfaction of most seventeenth-century English Protestants by ascribing all impulses toward reform to the power of preventing grace.[37] Paul's advice to the Philippians—"work out your own salvation with fear and trembling. For it is God that worketh in you both to will and to do of his good pleasure"—seemed to provide Protestants with a theologically plausible basis on which to fuse the sufficiency of grace with a summons to conversion. Such "preparation" avoided association with the Pelagian doctrine of works by ascribing man's first impulse toward reform to the work of the Spirit within his soul. In the same article where the Elizabethan bishops had denied that man could turn to God by his own strength, they had also stated that with the grace of God preventing us, "we may have a good will, and working with us, when we have that good will."[38] Saving grace not only preceded man's liberty but actually created it, leaving no quarter for the pretensions associated with human merit. Faith and holiness remained free gifts, an interior transformation of the soul unencumbered by the strivings of lapsed humanity and distinguished from any sign of moral virtue.

The possibility of preparation for grace, together with an acceptance of its renewing and sanative power, continued to inform Anglican thought throughout the period of Puritan ascendancy. Indeed, opponents of predestination within the church tended to look upon the innovations of the first Protestant reformers as indefensible intrusions into an orthodox theology of grace which had guided the Christian community since the patristic age, an orthodoxy which had obliged men to dispose themselves for the healing power of divine assistance and to avoid the pitfalls of irreversible justification. "We have no warrant in Scripture," Ralph Cudworth reminded the House of Commons in 1647, "to peep into those hidden roles and volumes of eternity . . . before we see the image of God, in righteousness and true holiness shaped in our hearts."[39] The rule of the saints betrayed the intensity of worldly ambition hiding behind the mantle of religious devotion, and the arrogance of the victors seemed to be the logical result of their exclusivist notions regarding the nature of grace. Herbert Thorndike was one who repeatedly warned against the Antinomian consequences of Calvinism and blamed the breakdown in moral standards to predestinarian theology, while the most important apologist for High Anglicanism, Henry Hammond, chastised both sides in the debate over the nature of election for their unchristian temper.[40] In an address to Robert Sanderson published at the close of the Commonwealth era, Hammond rejected the idea of irresistible grace and argued that salvation is conditional upon reform and the obedience which is made possible through divine assistance.[41] Sanderson himself, while similarly convinced of the importance of reform, felt that our boasting of any ability in ourselves to merit forgiveness and win God's favor through our own natural strength was a dangerous delusion. "Nature it self in the last resolution is of grace," he insisted, "for God gave thee that." Our power and determination at the start of reform "cometh merely from the good will and pleasure of that free spirit, which bloweth where, and when, and how he listeth."[42] Sanderson's colleague on the episcopal bench after 1660, Edward Reynolds, also reminded his parishioners that the grace of God must not only assist us in our works, but "giveth us both the strength and first act, whereby we are qualified to work."[43] Both men firmly rejected the Pelagian notion that preparation begins with the sinner and elected instead to return to a pre-Reformation theology of grace where the descendants of Adam are obliged to cooperate with prevenient divine favor in the work of salvation. They would have agreed with Robert South in his observation that man's confidence in the merit of his works evidenced the "sottishness" of his corrupt nature.[44] It was a perspective at once deeply medieval in orientation and virtually indistinguishable from that put forward by their moderate church counterparts after 1660.

Due in part to the controversial nature of their ideas regarding comprehension and the minimal creed, the prominent place devoted to the work of moral reform in the sermons of the Latitudinarians re-opened the whole question of Arminianism during the Restoration; the memory of the Laudians and their efforts to restore the "dig-nity of religion" through a wide range of purportedly "Romanizing" innovations had not been erased by the temporary rule of the saints. Moderate divines, while certainly at the forefront of the hostilities against Catholic apologists during the second half of the century, still had to remain wary lest their own moral theology be equated with the "corrupt" Catholic doctrine of works and sacramental tests. Moral preaching was also conveniently associated with the facile solution to man's dilemma offered by Deists and Socinians. The sixteenth-century anti-trinitarian Faustus Socinus had combined a strict bibli-cism with an acknowledgment of the rights of reason in religion to fashion a theology where obedience to God's will—possible for all who followed Christ's example—constituted the sum and substance of Christianity. The tolerance and practical spirit of the Socinians had much to recommend them to moderate churchmen during the Civil War years and after the Restoration, but their peculiar doctrinal beliefs repulsed High Anglicans and Low Churchmen alike.[45]

Anxious to distance their own theological outlook from the legal-ism inherent in Deism and Socinianism, and resolute in acknowledg-ing the supremacy of divine forces beyond the purview and control of man, Latitudinarians like Hezekiah Burton insisted that "noth-ing but the Infinite Goodness, and the omnipotent grace of God can save me from utter destruction." The truly penitent sinner "confesses himself so obnoxious, and so corrupted, that nothing less than the goodness of God can save him from Misery; and nothing less power-ful than the Blessed Spirit, can renew and restore the decays of his nature."[46] The Reformed concept of forensic grace was replaced by the restorative, transforming power of the Spirit familiar to a longer Catholic tradition, but Burton made it clear that even after God had sent his only son to serve as a sacrifice for the sins of Adam, men remained unable to perform the easy conditions outlined in the Gospel until they were relieved by the gift of that Holy Spirit; the "justice" inhering in the individual signifies that God has taken hold of our lives for the forwarding of his benevolent ends.[47] According to Edward Fowler, neither Anglicans nor moderate Dissenters de-sired to attribute any more to man in the process of salvation than absolutely necessary, and charges of Socinianism made against them were nothing but the petulant caluminations of those who sought to promote predestinarian theology.[48] Men who hold "that the Christian Religion designeth to set forth and glorifie the infinite grace of God in Jesus Christ to wretched sinners . . . assert the very same thing that I have done," said Fowler. Works were necessary for salvation, "But that we can, of ourselves, turn our own wills from the ways of sin to the ways of God, is peremptorily denied by us."[49]

In his book of devotions written in order to provide devout laymen with a selection of prayers for every occasion, Patrick made the theme of God's free grace central to the message of virtually all of the individual petitions.[50] He was so convinced of the supererogatory nature of grace that he informed his congregation at Saint Paul's, Covent Garden, that even their prayers could not move God, who saves men exclusively for his own sake.[51] The theme of man's crying need for the grace of God runs throughout the work of Latitudinarian laymen as well, as is evidenced in the religious meditations of Wilkins's friend, the jurist Matthew Hale. Without the help of God, wrote Hale, our sinful soul "will never rise out of that state of impotency, yea of rebellion, into which it is fallen, but would multiply sin upon sin to all eternity."[52] Saving grace and the incapacity of man to do the least work to merit salvation were at the very center of the Latitudinarian estimate of man, underpinning every call to the life of holiness and transforming their alleged moralism into an obedience to the divine will made possible by an initial gift of God. It was a point of view which they shared even with their non-juring critics within Anglicanism, for as the much-admired Thomas Ken observed,

> But Lord, my Sins turn thee away,
> And I, by thee abandon'd, stray;
> Thou first, my God, must turn to me,
> E're thou canst turn my Heart to thee.[53]

The spiritual warfare of the Latitude-men, their unwavering concern with the actual practice of Christianity, their conviction that one universal moral code was applicable to all of the varied aspects of human experience, was in the end made possible by the promptings of their Creator whose love for disobedient man overrode his anger at their declension. Regardless of the significant intellectual advances made by their contemporaries in the late seventeenth century, despite the talk of historians about being on the threshold of the Enlightenment, the Latitude-men knew that eternal salvation was not the product of their own labor. Their righteousness, as Wilkins had properly noted, "be as filty rags," and the words of Saint Paul to the Corinthians—"What do you have that you did not receive? And if you received it, why do you boast as if it were not a gift?"—provided the starting point for their "moral" theology.[54] In was within this severe Pauline framework that John Moore could speak for all of the Latitudinarians when he observed that "A Man never loseth himself sooner, than by a Presumption of his own Ability; and he never stands so firmly and securely, as, when out of an humble Sense of his Weakness, he places his Trust in God."[55] In affirming that God wills the salvation of all, and in denying that the grace proffered to mankind is irresistible, the Latitude-men undeniably broke ranks with a strong current within English Calvinism, but that these convictions attenuated their reliance upon a theology of grace is a charge both unsubstantiated and undeserved.

Recent scholarship has sharply disparaged the soteriology of the Latitudinarians, claiming that their consuming interest in practical theology had the ineluctable effect of marginalizing the importance of Christ's atonement. Such a view is unfortunate, for it unaccountably fails to accept the veracity of the declarations made by moderate churchmen on the question, preferring instead to repeat the accusations of their hostile contemporaries. Seeking to avoid the pitfalls of Socinianism on the one hand and the self-assurance of solifidianism on the other, Anglicans were obliged to approach the problematic question of Christ's role as mediator with extreme caution. For example, should one place too much emphasis upon the value of autonomous moral reform through the application of reason to human action, and he risked being identified with the temper of Socinianism. But equally unacceptable was the Antinomian claim that the truly justified individual is freed from the requirements of the law altogether, that the moral standards of the unregenerate have no application to those which guide the elect.[56] The obvious dangers for the stability of church and state inherent in such a position, not to mention the implicit acceptance of a radical subjectivism which amounted to religious anarchism, had been sufficiently demonstrated during the 1640s. In an environment where every form of religious experience could be identified with genuine directives from God, where "authentic" manifestations of grace were left to the individual's determination, the pseudoreligious finds ample opportunity to magnify its claims, and "illuminism quickly descends into illusionism."[57] It was not easy to recognize the legitimate influence of God in one's life, and if the personal element in Protestant theology were not subject to more critical and pragmatic criteria, then the Church of England's institutional mandate, not to mention autonomus rational judgment, would become untenable.

Socinus had taught that by retaining the idea of Christ's satisfaction for sin, one virtually obviated the need for forgiveness or repentance. If Christ had in fact atoned for the sins of men with his own ignominious death, what need remained for them to adapt their behavior to the pattern enjoined by Scripture? By stressing the prophetic function of Christ's life and avoiding his work of reconciliation, Socinus hoped to improve the tone of Christian living along more rational and humane lines.[58] In order to clear themselves from allegations of lending support to this view of the mission of Christ, the Latitudinarians regularly preached sermons on the theme of atonement, following in the steps of the Platonists and members of the Tew circle.[59] In doing so, however, they were confronted with a variety of perspectives on atonement, each of which had at some point in the past won considerable support within the wider Christian community. Early church fathers like Irenaeus and Athanasius had focused on God's decision to enter human life through the incarnation, where a loving God and sinful humanity meet in the person of Jesus. Human nature was restored when the divine being took on characteristics of the human in an act of unsurpassed charity. Others like Justin Martyr and Origen saw the locus of atonement in the defeat of evil and demonic forces by the Son of God. Even Augustine believed that "The cross of the Lord became a trap for the devil; the death of the Lord was the food by which he was ensnared." This had become the common image of Christ's work in the early Middle Ages.[60] And finally the idea of unparalleled sacrifice, of Christ's death as an expiation for our sins, appears prominently in the New Testament and was given its most forceful presentation by Saint Anselm.[61] According to Anselm's legalistic approach to the problem, man alone can never make an adequate payment for the sins he has committed. Since all of our good deeds are already owed to God out of simple obedience to his will, the offering of a sinless human being was required to overcome death. This latter theme of a debt repaid by a sinless man became a recurrent one in the homiletics of the Latitudinarians.

Tillotson delivered one such sermon at Saint Lawrence Jewry in December 1679, and in order to rebut critics who questioned his orthodoxy after he had been elevated to Canterbury, he had it published in 1693.[62] The archbishop was unequivocal in his estimate of the benefits which Christ's life and death had for mankind. "He hath rescued us from the bondage of sin, and from the slavery of Satan," was the lesson which had been delivered to the congregation at Saint Lawrence, since all the services we can possibly perform "are infinitely beneath those infinite obligations which the Son of God hath laid upon the sons of men."[63] By reflecting on the supreme sacrifice, Burnet wrote, "we can only imagine a vast sense of the heinousness of Sin . . . a melting Apprehension of the Corruption and Miseries of Mankind by reason of Sin."[64] Simon Patrick followed Tillotson's lead in impressing upon his own clergy in the diocese of Ely the rule that their chief objective in the pulpit was to stress the nature of Christ's full satisfaction and suffering on our behalf. None should countenance any suggestion that Christ's life was merely an example of moral excellence within the reach of mankind and sufficient for their salvation. Why would a benevolent God permit a teacher to suffer the pains of persecution and death? God's justice was only served by the oblation of his son, and the power of original sin over the will of man was broken through this one act of infinite love.[65]

The attention which the Latitudinarian bishops devoted to the doctrine of Christ's atonement was, as Tillotson's sermon suggests, a clear indication of the depth of their disagreement with the Deists and Socinians. Like Tillotson, Patrick had spoken out on the issue years before reaching the episcopal bench. His *Book for Beginners*, published in 1679, was designed to help young children prepare for the sacrament of communion, that central commemoration of Christ's death for mankind. Having lost his first child only a year earlier, Patrick reintroduced the important theme of Christ's propitiatory sacrifice, first discussed in his earlier *Mensa Mystica* (1659), for the benefit of a new generation of Anglicans who were to lead the church into a brighter age, one he hoped was innocent of the bitter memories engendered by earlier seventeenth-century religious conflicts. In the *Mensa Mystica*, Patrick had employed a quaint metaphor to describe the position of disobedient mankind. Comparing the sinner to the poor man who petitions his king to grant him a favor on the strength of the worthy deeds of some distant ancestor, when we now come before God to request mercy of him, "we can hope to prevail for nothing, but through the name of our Lord, whom we can never mention with so much advantage as when we solemnly commemorate his sufferings and deservings."[66] The *Book for Beginners* pursued this point, arguing that one of the prime goals of communion was to give thanks to God for sending his only son "to be a propitiation for our sins." Children must be made to recognize that Christ "offered his own body, to put away our sins by the sacrifice of himself."[67] Youngsters should not become disheartened over their unworthiness to receive God's forgiveness, said Patrick, for men will always be unworthy "in the strictest sense of the word," but each child should be made constantly aware that as he pursues his life's goals, whatever blessings he receives are the gratuitous outpourings of divine love.[68]

By emphasizing the sacrificial nature of Christ's decision to assume the human form, Latitudinarians sought to clarify further their picture of human nature in the wake of the primal Fall. In a representative passage, Isaac Barrow said that the thought of God offering his only son to be a sacrifice for man should render us sensible of "our weakness, our vileness, or wretchedness" in the face of our sins: "For how low was that our fall, from which we could not be raised without such a depression of God's only son? how great is that impotency, which did need such a succor to relieve it? how abominable must be that iniquity, which must not be expiated without so costly a sacrifice?"[69] If man's guilt had been as nugatory as the modern followers of Pelagius suggested, God surely would have found some less drastic means of bringing sinners back into his favor. "Is it not madness of us," Barrow asked, "to be conceited for any worth in our selves, to confide in any merit of our works, to glory in anything belonging to us?[70] None of the Latitudinarians would have responded to this query in the negative.[71] To do so would have been to rend the intellectual fabric of their collective heritage on the doctrine of grace and proclaim for a vision of human potential that was alien to their own religious experience.

In addition to their concern with the sacrificial aspects of Christ's death, the Latitudinarians also shared an awareness of a "moral influence" component in the doctrine of the atonement, an idea which was first given forceful expression by Peter Abelard in the twelfth century. Abelard was repulsed by the cruel implications of Anselm's theory of a God who demanded the death of an innocent person for the sake of guilty humanity, preferring instead to view atonement in terms of loving reconciliation. God's gift of himself in the life and death of Jesus, his refusal to abandon us to our own sinful nature, empowers us to change our hearts and enjoy a new freedom to strive after a union with the eternal.[72] Christ binds us to himself by love, "with the result that our hearts should be enkindled by such a gift of divine grace, and true charity should not now shrink from enduring anything for him."[73] While the Latitudinarians were often, and unjustly, viewed as lending support to Socinianism and an Arminian "covenant of works," it was the deeply rooted Antinomian strain in English Protestantism which posed the most serious challenge to their cherished vision of a comprehensive church and elicited their use of the model of Christ's work formulated by Abelard.

Certainly no Anglican could accept the notion that the assistance of grace was forced upon men who had no intention of using it for the improvement of their corrupt lives. Such a view of justification would make a mockery of Christ's sufferings. Like many of the earlier Puritan preachers and in keeping with Abelard's "moral influence" argument, Restoration Anglican divines insisted that men must turn their hearts to God once the experience of regeneration through Christ had begun. Even moderate Dissenters like Baxter believed that in the process of conversion, the Spirit of God or Holy Ghost worked first upon the intellect of man and next upon his heart. The Spirit opens men's eyes to the mysteries of the gospel and subsequently brings about a change of being.[74] The Latitudinarian divines, in their characteristic determination to maintain individual moral accountability, felt especially compelled to strike out against all traces of Antinomianism and the dangerous implications of solifidianism. Some men "would make religion to be a very short and easy business, and to consist only in believing what Christ hath done for us," but such a radical reading of Scripture was for the Latitudemen "the very definition of presumption."[75] Tillotson believed that if this theological outlook were to be entertained within the Church of England, it would make about as much sense for the clergyman to preach in the graveyard as to hold regular services in the church.[76]

Tillotson thought that the best exposition of the relationship between works and the grace brought forward by Christ's sacrifice could be found in the epistles of Paul to the Corinthians. That the grace of God is never bestowed in vain had been the apostle's argument, for the sinner who receives this gift must labor to cooperate with it, cognizant that all the good he does is owing to the quickening power of the Spirit within him. "By the grace of God I am what I am," had been Paul's reminder, "and His grace, which was bestowed upon me, was not in vain; but I labored more abundantly than they all; yet not I, but the grace of God which was with me."[77] Claims of instantaneous conversion and justification only demonstrated the indolence of those who would not subject themselves to the rigors of genuine moral reform. Their indifference toward the pains suffered by Christ on their behalf was fully expressed by their refusal to welcome the assisting power of grace into their lives, for the normal course of grace was to act upon the conscience of man gradually, thereby habituating him to a new life. "Grace imitatith nature," wrote Baxter, "in beginning, usually, in small degrees, and growing up to maturity by leisurely proceeding." [78] We best glorify God when we are rendered most like him by his aid.

Simon Patrick, perhaps, best expressed the Latitudinarian effort to link Christ's satisfaction and mankind's obligation to action in his *Parable of the Pilgrim*. Why had Christ shed his blood for us at all, he wondered. "Was it only that our sins might be pardoned? Did he bear the cross that we might bear none? Did he deny his own will that we might have liberty to do ours? Is his death to excuse us from holy living?" [79] If Protestantism was to avoid the very sin of spiritual arrogance which had been associated with Roman Catholicism during the course of the early sixteenth century, and if the significance of the atonement was not to be debased by the presumption of particular, irreversible justification, then a return to an understanding of grace which incorporated moral striving had to be undertaken by a church struggling to recapture the hearts of a people distracted and disillusioned after two decades of internecine civil and religious struggle. The Latitudinarians did not abandon grace for moralism as their many critics have suggested. Given their belief in the unity of humanity with a corrupted Adam and the deleterious consequences of that corruption on the power of reason, the moderate churchmen found the sole solution to man's spiritual dilemma in the free gift of divine assistance. And that assistance, while evidenced mainly in the internal working of the Spirit within the individual, was also displayed within the larger arena of supernatural providence, those explicit warnings and encouragements to mankind living in what was increasingly thought to be a "clockwork" universe.

The idea of a level of supernatural truth and action which permanently transcended human comprehension—historically referred to as providence—was one of the habitual assumptions of all seventeenth-century divines. Like so much within the corpus of Christian tradition, the idea of providence found its earliest roots in classical antiquity, particularly in the thought of Plato, who insisted that it was impossible to admit that the gods exist and yet express no interest in human affairs. Everything in the universe was ordered according to the good of the whole, he believed, and man's experience of evil must ultimately be viewed from the perspective of the harmony of creation.[80] The God of the Old Testament certainly ruled as a jealous and concerned master who involved himself in the mundane affairs of his creatures, and this more personal and dramatic view of divine interaction clearly informed Augustine's apprehension of history as God's management of human affairs for his own glory; the being who made the world according to specific standards understands that creation down to the smallest details and directs whatever proceeds from his will to its proper end. Adopted by Aquinas and given new force in the theological voluntarism of Calvin, providence assured men of God's unwavering interest in the welfare of his creation.[81] "God governs the world," explained Calvin, "not merely because he preserves the order of nature fixed by himself, but because he exercises a peculiar care over every one of his works." Nothing escaped divine scrutiny or obviated the possibility that the full force of God's justice might be visited upon individuals at any moment in their lives. In a world which is upheld and sustained by the power of God, where, "there can be no such thing as fortuitous contingence," events were the manifestations of divine judgment and controlling will, the most cogent reminder of human dependency.[82]

This picture of personal prerogative within history, so difficult for the modern mind to recapture, remained a vital concept to the Restoration church, and especially to the Latitudinarians, despite their sympathetic interest in the power of reason and the "philosophic" explanations of reality which were so popular after 1660. By the close of the seventeenth century, the mystery which had for centuries shrouded the natural world had largely been accounted for to the satisfaction of contemporaries; nature's laws were increasingly being construed along mechanistic lines by the practitioners of the new science, men who were nevertheless convinced that their bold inquiries were simply alternative avenues to divine truth, a complement rather than a challenge to Scripture. Professor Willey has argued that a truly novel "climate of opinion" emerged before 1700, one where "supernatural and occult explanations of natural phenomena ceased to satisfy" and where the transcendent, "in both its divine and diabolical forms, was banished from Nature."[83] Newton's universe, where a single principle seemed to govern all movement, suggested a supreme mechanic who resembled less a personal deity than a remote first cause. A world of order and mathematical regularity where the antecedents to every event could be empirically verified seemed to bespeak a God who had no call to interfere with the workings of his creation on a regular basis, and attempts to preserve God's special intervention seemed increasingly artificial.

Contemporaries certainly seemed to notice the shift away from arbitrary causation in the realm of nature, and the Latitudinarians lamented the dangerous implications of the trend toward naturalism as much as any within the church. As early as 1678, for example, Stillingfleet complained that "We live in an Age not over prone to admire and take notice of any remarkable instances of Divine providence," most men preferring to ignore acts of God in history which were contrary to the course of nature.[84] The waning of anthropocentrism was surely regrettable, he thought, asserting much later that "The Tranquillity of our Minds in this World depends very much upon the Esteem we have of Providence."[85] Even Robert Boyle, perhaps the most important figure in the development of a mechanical conception of nature which seemed to make God's regular attention supernumerary, was chary of abandoning a place for divine intervention in the actions of men.[86] Without a sense of God's imminence in the world, his power to interfere with the regular course of nature in order to correct and to reprimand in the name of eternal justice, man's sense of constant reliance upon God for his spiritual and physical well being would be diminished and his proclivity for sinful behavior afforded wider opportunity for release.

Naturalistic accounts of reality and the study of secondary causes may have appealed to the inquisitive and skeptical temper of the age, and most individuals found no difficulty in reconciling the idea of general providence—God's supervision of his creation—with the mechanical hypothesis, but for those churchmen who thought about the implications of science for a theocentric worldview, God's presence in creation, his constant activity and occasional interference with the cosmic machine, was thought to be imperative lest the omnipotence of the Creator be called into question. On the Continent, Leibnitz may have sought to vindicate the Almighty's power with the doctrine of preestablished harmony, but few within the Anglican community would have agreed with a description of sovereignty which precluded the right to alter one's creation. As Jacob Viner has reminded us, it was for many men in the seventeenth and eighteenth centuries "psychologically impossible to believe that God did not constantly have men in his providential care, and that the physical order of the cosmos was not one of the tools he had designed to serve that purpose."[87] Jeremy Taylor expressed his doubts about the Baconian interest with secondary causes when he cautioned that despite the claims of scientific analysis, "whatsoever is disposed to happen by the order of natural causes, or civil counsels, may be rescinded by a peculiar decree of providence."[88] The use of particular providence as an explanatory device, despite its unscientific and figurative quality, was still a satisfying alternative to many late seventeenth-century Englishmen whenever events seemed to defy "philosophic" analysis.[89] There was no felt need to question or to analyze God's providence on these occasions, since to do so would simply evidence the old sin of pride along with a rejection of the limits placed upon human nature. "God's will" might no longer suffice as an explanation of planetary motion for members and patrons of the Royal Society, but it could still satisfy, as an interpretation of events like the malicious Gunpowder Treason, the disasters associated with the Civil War, the restoration of the king, the recurrence of plague, and, at a more personal level, the lingering death of a loved one.[90] The eternal "why" question had not been entirely superseded by the growing concern with deterministic causation, nor was there any universal longing to be rid of what could not be understood, to abolish fear of a God whose reason so often transcended the purview of its human counterpart. The providence of God was still accepted as the manifestation of truth at a level beyond the capacity of human reason to master, a different quality of justice which ultimately accorded with eternal reason. The physical world might be reduced to mathematics by the virtuosi, but the mechanical explanation of nature invariably failed mankind at the stage of life's central questions. Intimate knowledge of God was still possible in this life, but it was not to be gleaned exclusively from the postulates of the new science, which at best would afford men a glimpse at the artisanal skills of the Creator, the particular and the contingent rather than the meaningful and the eternal.

John Wilkins, in his *Principles and Duties of Natural Religion*, indicated how belief in particular providence served to reinforce some of the central reformed ideas about human nature and potential while strengthening our bond of trust in God's care. His constant advocacy of natural philosophy did not prevent him from stressing the importance of maintaining a place for a particular providence in the lives of men because of its importance in confirming our sinful nature. "It would not be consistent with our dependent conditions," Wilkins wrote, "that worldly prosperity should be so infallibly under the power of our own endeavors, as that God himself might not sometimes interpose for our disappointment."[91] The belief in particular providence was necessary "unto that adoration which we owe to the divine nature," and we must resign ourselves to any evil we suffer in this life, for "the greatest judgement that can befal us in this life, is farre less than our deserts."[92] Isaac Barrow and John Moore agreed with Wilkins's assessment. According to Barrow, it was often necessary for God to cross our inclinations and frustrate our best-laid plans through the power of his particular providence, "for if human transactions passed on as do the motions of nature, without any rub or disturbance . . . men commonly would no more think of God than they do when they behold the sun rising."[93] Moore thought that God's particular providence required of man a measure of resignation which left no room for complaint when we were afflicted with sorrow and pain, for "How terrible soever any Calamity may appear to us, yet it is fitted to our Circumstances." Troubles, he warned, do not spring out of the earth, "But God in his Wisdom does order the time when we shall be afflicted; he determines the kind of Evil which shall fall to our Lot, and metes the very Quantity that we must suffer." And the man who would deny that God concerns himself with the affairs of the world, wrote Moore, "can never truly reverence him, nor worship him sincerely."[94] God's personal interposition in the lives and fortunes of men confounded suggestions that one's best-laid plans for independent spiritual renewal might be of any value in attaining either worldly success or, more to the point, eternal happiness.

According to the Latitudinarians, then, God's judgments against mankind, no matter how severe, were always designed with the intention of reclaiming them from the power of sin. The Father preferred to exercise mercy towards us in our repeated failings, but his long-suffering with men too often goes unheeded. Were it not that most men "are such perverse creatures as not to be wrought upon by kindness," said Tillotson, "so wild as not to be treated by gentle usage, God would not handle us in any other way." It is our sheer obstinacy and intransigence to reasonable entreaties which "almost forceth him against his inclination to take the rod into his hand, and to chastise us with it."[95] Particular providence remained an essential tool of divine management in a world where the power of sin often overwhelmed the call of reason and conscience. Belief in this special prerogative should be a great comfort and happiness to men, since it assured them of their importance in God's creation despite the Fall of Adam and their own repeated affronts against the law of nature. From a more intimate perspective, we can see the crucial role that particular providence played in the thought of the Latitudinarians by looking at Patrick's well-known autobiography. The bishop of Ely unhesitatingly attributed such disparate and mundane events as his unlikely advance to study at Cambridge while a young man, his friendship with the Platonist John Smith, and his fortunate survival while living in the midst of London during the Great Plague, to God's direct intervention in his life.[96] Throughout his many sermons and longer treatises, the miraculous effects of providence serve as a constant warning both to individuals and to the unrepentant English nation. Everything from the Great Fire of 1666 to the Great Storm of November 1703 was for Patrick "clearly the voice of God."[97] But perhaps the most momentous example of immediate divine power was the "rescue" of the English nation from the grip of the "Romish butchers" in 1688, an event "in which if we do not see a finger of God, it is because we are blind, or, which is worse, shut our eyes against the most evident tokens of a divine hand." The popish party, he was convinced, was on the verge of extinguishing the last vestiges of English liberty "When behold! the outstreched hand of Heaven appeared against them, to confound the Babel which they had been so many years a building."[98]

Connecting great natural disasters and political turns with the work of the Almighty was the most common, and the safest, mode of employing God's personal superintendence and intervention. We can see in those things which Patrick's list excluded from the power of providence a typical Anglican reluctance to indulge in the more audacious claims associated with sectarian views of God's work in the lives of men. In particular, accounts of dramatic interior transformation brought about through the intervention of the Spirit were seen as an abuse of providence, the tool of men who would avoid the work of serious moral reform advocated by the Latitudinarians. One could not wait upon providential renewal while ignoring personal correction without risking the rebuke of providence and the weakening of the social and political fabric in the process. The preaching of the Latitudinarians placed the right of God to interfere with his orderly universe strictly within the context of encouraging the very model of moral reform that was so much disparaged by their critics. Baxter recognized the value of their position, however, writing that the Latitudinarians' "profitable Preaching" was itself a prime example of God's particular providence at work in the world, designed "to keep up the Publick Interest of Religion, and refresh the discerning sort of Auditors."[99] Such a compliment, coming as it did from one who well understood the dangers posed by an exaggerated picture of God's work in the lives of men, reflects the desire of the moderate churchmen to maintain a place for supernatural interposition in a world where the Judeo-Christian picture of history as a manifestation of the love of God was becoming something less than axiomatic.

By including the idea of saving grace as a central component of their homiletics, in declining the overtures of Deists and Socinians who would place salvation within the grasp of Adam's children, and with the retention of particular providence despite its incongruity with an emerging mechanistic model of the universe, the Latitudinarians shared with the rest of their peers within the Church of England a powerful acknowledgment of human contingency and spiritual impotence. A genuine theology of grace is an essential correlate of any picture of human nature which assumes a stain inherited from the Fall. When the consequences of that Fall include an impairment of man's reason and will, as it certainly did for the moderate churchmen, then a supernatural—and entirely gratuitous—formula for salvation becomes unavoidable. The succor of grace, of God's condescending love evidenced by the death of his only son and the transforming power of the Spirit, was the indisputable prerequisite to their program of moral reform. That the strength of their commitment to a theology of grace has long been disputed is certainly one measure of how much the Deist interpretation of events has come to influence our own.

In response to queries from the new bishop of Lincoln regarding the state of spiritual affairs in his diocese, the vicar of Caddington, Edward Bowerman, reported a situation which affords us some insight into the scale of the task facing the Church of England after the Revolution of 1688. Bishop Thomas Tenison must have been discouraged to hear from Bowerman that in the wake of English Protestantism's great triumph over the Romanizing schemes of James II, "I found ye people over run with ignorance and irreligion and wholly unconcern'd for their souls, that one would think they had conversed their lives with ye wild men of America. . . . when I discoursed with some of the more knowing sort, they were so far from relishing ye severer Precepts of Christianity that I could scarce convince them anything was their duty that gave any disturbance to their carelessness and ease, or thwarted their inclinations."[1] The bitter century-long controversies over the nature of Christ's message to mankind, what one should believe and how best to honor God, seemed of little import to the lives of many by the time a Dutch Calvinist assumed the position of supreme governor of the English church.

For the Latitudinarians who were to enjoy advancement under the patronage of this distrustful monarch, the accounts of clerics like Bowerman dramatically pointed up the futility of all attempts to strengthen the brotherhood of Christians by uninterrupted and acrimonious attention to theological detail. True religion "consisteth not in fair professions and glorious pretenses," for the experience of these had been disasterous, "but in real practice . . . in an inward good complexion of the mind, exerting itself in works of devotion and charity."[2] Latitudinarian "moralism" involved first and foremost a transformation of the inner person brought about by an infusion of grace which was wholly unmerited, a transformation proved genuine by the eradication of scandalous situations like the one which obtained in the parish of Caddington. Edward Fowler's belief that "the free grace of God is infinitely more magnified, in renewing our natures, then it could be in the bare justification of our persons," set the tone for the moderate church program after 1660.[3] If the Renaissance picture of man's preeminence in what was still looked upon as a theocentric universe were to be maintained, then a living demonstration of his identification with a God of love had to be undertaken.

The Latitudinarian focus on the tropological sense of Scripture, on practical divinity as an instrument to encourage men along the road to Christian perfection, was by no means an ingenious or radical departure from the tradition of the Church of England. Article XII of the Thirty-nine Articles had stated that while works could not endure the severity of God's judgment, they are pleasing to God "and do spring out necessarily of a true and lively Faith; insomuch that by them a lively faith may be as evidently known as a tree discerned by the fruit." The man who has accepted forgiveness through the sacrifice of Christ must be prepared to serve him and by serving him to become like him.[4] This commonsense theological orientation enlisted the moderate churchmen in a wider and long-standing Protestant battle against the whole direction of post-Tridentine Catholic thought. As H. R. McAdoo pointed out some years ago, the Roman Catholic Church in the period after Trent, and in particular the Jesuit Order, tended to separate moral and ascetic theology into independent categories, with the result being that instead of one all-inclusive program for preparing souls for eternal salvation, "two distinct sciences emerged, the one occupied with the legality or illegality of human acts, the other concerned with spiritual progress and holiness."[5] For Anglicans who confidently claimed apostolic and early church practice for their position, such an arbitrary separation of moral and ascetic teaching could only result in a situation where the whole spiritual tone of Christian practice was measurably lowered, where rigorous training in Christian holiness was superseded by legalistic concern over the lawfulness or necessity of specific actions. The Catholic emphasis on compulsory confession and the sufficiency of penance highlighted this juristic bias within the Roman communion. Such a split between the minimum demands of right conduct—religion at the cheapest rate—and the deeper cultivation of exacting Christian virtues, where every action is informed and regulated by the spirit of holiness, was for Anglicans a cynical and irresponsible abandonment of religious edification and guidance towards salvation. Even English Calvinists, as John Morgan has reminded us, incorporated into predestinarian theology a call for inner repentance and instruction with the express purpose of leading the individual to saving faith.[6]

In addition to their sharp rebuttal of Catholic legalism, seventeenth-century Anglicans were also convinced that the Puritan concern with theological precision and with the anagogical sense of Scripture, while laudable in correcting many of the interpretive abuses introduced by Rome, had contributed not a little to the ongoing fragmentation of Reformed Christianity and in particular to the outbreak of civil war in England. Those who saw God as an angry and arbitrary master, one who delights in the ruin of the majority of his creatures, were for Anglicans most likely to treat their neighbors in a similar fashion "since all religion inclines men to imitate the God whom they worship."[7] In his popular *Parable of the Pilgrim* (1663), Patrick's traveler is shocked at the divisiveness among those "holy" men who would guide him to Jerusalem, "for there was no sin in those days like moderation, and no virtue comparable to a furious and headlong zeal." The pilgrim's modest and conciliatory guide was held in contempt by his peers and thought to be "no friend of truth, because he is no great stickler about the questions that have vexed our unhappy days."[8] The Puritan formula for the realization of the godly community—a doctrinal orthodoxy which embraced predestination and the primacy of the elect—had succeeded only in undermining the basis of social and political order by impeaching both the ideas and the actions of the unregenerate.

A theology built upon the twin axes of predestination and unqualified human depravity had, it seemed, demonstrated its incapacity to nourish a sense of God's love which should be reflected in man's earthly passage. The jurist Matthew Hale was only one who deeply regretted that disputes over doctrinal matters had increased men's fancies with useless speculations "instead of filling their hearts with the true and genuine effects of Christian religion."[9] For Hale and his fellow Anglicans—and for moderate Nonconformists—the larger tragedy for an increasingly fratricidal Protestant community lay in the fact that theological exclusiveness invariably obscured important areas of broader agreement which would have furthered that divine love. Baxter summed up this attitude when he observed that of the four groups contending for power in the church—Erastian, Episcopal, Presbyterian, and Independent—"each one had some truths in peculiar, which the others overlookt" and "all of them had so much truth in common among them, as would have made these Kingdoms happy, if it had been unanimously and soberly reduced to practice, by prudent and charitable Men."[10] "Knowledge and Practice," insisted John Moore, "how much soever they may differ in our Notions of them, are in Christian Religion but Two Terms importing the same matter."[11] This animus toward those who would make right belief the core of religion to the neglect of practical reform remained a fixture of Latitudinarian belief. "There is no fundamental Doctrine of Christianity," Moore wrote, "but an Obligation naturally flows from it to some Instance or other of a good Life." Prudent practice seemed to be the only logical means of rescuing the Protestant cause from the degenerative and anarchic grip of its own first principle: the priesthood of all believers. And that practice had to be built upon those few saving truths in Scripture which were above all textual and hermeneutical difficulties.[12]

The aim of practical divinity for Anglicans, then, was to bring sinners to heaven by building upon the remnants of God's image in man here on earth, to encourage them in the direction of Christian perfection, and to further the power of the Spirit within each person by reminding them that Christ died to free them from slavery to sin. Like their predecessors among the sixteenth-century humanists, Anglicans turned from the medieval concentration on the contemplative and insisted instead that man's justification depended largely on his behavior in this life. This was to preach works as Christ and the apostles did, said Chillingworth; "it is to preach the necessity of them, which no good Protestant, no good Christian ever denied; but it is not to preach the merit of them, which is the error of the papists."[13] Their ethics were not dissimilar to those contained in a work like More's *Utopia*, where a man's felicity was the product of a virtuous life—one lived according to nature or the precepts of reason.[14] "Points of Speculation and benefit are otherwise good and useful for us in their season," wrote John Cosin, "but points of duty and practice are more behaveful for us all."[15] The bishop of Durham, whose own unhappy exile during the years of Cromwell's rule had steeled him against all pretenders to theological purity, found common cause with the Latitudinarians on the need for a reorientation of the place of the church in the community after 1660. Nor was Cosin the only Restoration bishop to call for a theology where the necessary articles of belief were clear and their validation through practice essential. As early as 1639, only one year after the publication of Chillingworth's *Religion of Protestants*, Robert Sanderson had written that "it would be safe for us (for the avoiding of Errors and Contentions, and consequently in order to those two most precious things, Truth and Peace) to contain ourselves within the bounds of Sobriety, without wading too far into abstruse, curious and useless speculations." The most necessary truths, he said in language later to be employed by the Latitudinarians, "and such as sufficed to bring our fore-fathers (in the Primitive and succeeding times) to heaven, are so clearly revealed in Scripture, and have been so universally and constantly consented unto by the Christian Church in a continued succession of times; as that to doubt of them must needs argue a spirit of Pride and Singularity at least, if not also Strife and Contradiction." No man can claim the assistance of grace who will not strive to please his Eternal Father.[16] For Bishop Brian Duppa, prayer was unavailing without such striving, "For what an impudence were it to expect pardon for those sins which I am yet so far pleased with, as I am not resolved to leave."[17] Sancroft laconically summed up the whole direction of Caroline theology when he stated that "the life of Religion is Doing."[18] Men who expect the crown of righteousness must learn to exhibit justice and exercise charity in their own lives, reintroducing themselves to a form of humanism which had been sadly eclipsed by the more extreme forms of Reformed thought during the course of the sixteenth century.

In rebuilding the church after a decade of neglect, the call to practical reform, a theology which impressed upon its audience the need to demonstrate the strength of their belief seemed essential, and all alternatives to this work were studiously avoided. The mystical strain which characterized the teaching of the Cambridge Platonists, for example, was a luxury that their Latitudinarian disciples could not afford to indulge. The speculations of the cloister and the college were ill suited to the demands of the busy urban parish, and concerns unique to Platonism, like the effort to identify a spiritual principle in nature in order to confound atheists, seemed remote from the workaday tasks of boosting attendance at daily services and catechizing a new generation in a faith backed by reason. "'Tis True," wrote John Wilkins with respect to speculative theology, be it Puritan or Platonic, "subtle notions and questions are more the fashion of the times, than these moral duties . . . but they are withal the disease of the times."[19] The Latitudinarians joined their clerical counterparts within the church in the task of treating that disease, fully aware of the impediments which lay before them. For the moderate churchmen, practical theology represented an opportunity to restore the fabric of a living faith which had for too long been distracted by speculation, dogmatic precision, and a species of religious hatred not to be rivaled by the bloodiest of national and imperial conflicts.

The work of restoration was no simple task, however. Latitudinarian "moral preaching" was not designed to lower the standards of moral action in order to accommodate the selfish values of a rising commercial elite, for, as we have seen, their picture of human nature buttressed an experiential conviction that moral reform was "contrary to the Practice of this degenerate World" and that the reform-minded Christian "doth embark on a most difficult, and dreadful warfare."[20] The depth of man's depravity remained an enormous barrier to practical reform, and the responsibility of the clergy in this undertaking at times seemed daunting. "'Tis little we can do," Glanvill wrote in a particularly disconsolate moment, "to make the world wiser or better; it is too wise, too conceited to be taught; and too bad in practice, by us, to be amended."[21] While the Dissenter and Catholic complacently put their trust in the promise of unmerited free grace and the idle show of ceremony respectively, the chief responsibility of the Anglican was "to govern within, and not to make Laws for the World without us."[22]

The actual work of moral reform for the Latitudinarians was a lifelong undertaking of such rigor that few, in the end, could be counted upon to remain steadfast. "To be good for a while," wrote Patrick, "after we have fasted, confessed our sins, and prayed, will not quite turn away his wrath, though it may defer it." The demand was much more exacting for the serious Christian, for God expected no less than "an eternal divorce between us and our sins, and that we seek him with our whole heart, so as to continue in well-doing."[23] Hezekiah Burton warned that when our repentance falls short of an intense hatred of the offence committed, "'tis not a thorough change of his Mind, 'tis no Repentance to Life." According to Burton, the truly penitent sinner can never think of his affront to God without inward grief and shame, "which is not done away by the greatest assurance which men have of God's mercy, but rather increased" as time elapses. And as long as the soul of man entertains a fondness for one sin "it is incapable of pardon."[24] The precepts of Christianity may not be grievous, Tillotson indicated in an address of the same title, "yet it is fair to let men know, that they are not thus easy." In a sermon of 1681 which Evelyn described as "a tirrible & severe discourse, shewing how it concerned sinners to serious repentance," Tillotson stressed the dimensions of the task facing his generation: "Considering the propension of our depraved nature, the progress of virtue and goodness is up the hill, in which we not only move hardly and heavily, but are easily rolled back: but by wickedness and vice we move downwards; which, as it is much quicker and easier, so it is harder for us to stop in that course, and infinitely more difficult to return from it."[25] Not many of the fashionable parishioners at Saint Lawrence Jewry could have found comfort in such words. The Latitudinarian belief that the duties of religion were not burdensome for the truly spiritual man was designed to draw sinners to what these churchmen saw as the true test of religious conviction. Genuine love for God, as Tillotson preached, completely transformed our understanding of otherwise onerous responsibilities and made us eager to cross our most powerful inclinations in the service of our maker. "Did but the love of God rule in our hearts," he said, "and the severest parts of religion would become easy."[26] The confidence of the Puritan elect, their refusal to accept that the chosen few might fall from grace, was for the Latitudinarian the unpardonable sin of men who would forfeit their own salvation in the imperious process of denying it to others.

Some contemporary scholars have seen in the Latitudinarian concern with morality elements of a calculating hedonism where the sinner reluctantly conforms to the dictates of God's eternal law simply out of a fear of punishment and a selfish desire for reward. A cursory glance at the titles to some of Tillotson's sermons—"The Unprofitableness of Sin in this Life," "The Advantages of an Early Piety," "The Nature and Benefit of Consideration"—together with his observation that in doing our duty "we directly promote our own happiness, and in serving God do most effectually serve our own interest," illustrates a temper that is thought to be normative for the Latitudinarians. But if the appeal to self-interest was widely employed by the moderate churchmen, they were certainly not alone among Anglicans in this regard, and a study of Tillotson's printed sermons indicates that the symbolic leader of the moderate churchmen just as frequently admonished his parishioners to discount self-interest and "look beyond things present and sensible, unto things which are not seen and eternal . . . and refer all the things of this short and dying life to that state which will shortly begin, but never have an end." [27] John Hales had maintained that it was the unfortunate fact of man's corruption which made the lure of reward necessary, while the Sheldonian bishops saw nothing problematic in mankind's striving to please God in anticipation of the benefits to be received. Sanderson went so far as to link self-interest with wisdom in one sermon, suggesting that by seeking God's glory we always promote our own. [28] But there was, nevertheless, an otherworldly strain within Anglicanism which directed attention away from the needs of the penitent sinner and focused instead on the value of works without reference to man. The non-juror George Hickes expressed this point of view when he wrote that unless our services proceed from a principle of real love and inward holiness "and a perfect Resignation of the Soul, to the divine Will," they would not be received by a merciful God in the spirit of reconciliation. We must first be transformed after the likeness of God, argued Hickes, and the divine life must be active within our souls. [29] The Platonist Henry More also expressed the essence of this Anglican strain when he indicated that to love God simply because He loves us is no better than juvenile self-love. But to esteem God "because he is simply Good, and simply and unconfinedly to imitate his Goodness, makes a Man truly Religious." [30]

In June of 1699 Edward Fowler, in the process of controverting the charge that the Latitudinarians preached a minimal, self-interested moralism, outlined a position identical to the one taken by the non-juror Hickes. Addressing members of the Societies for the Reformation of Manners (men who might, one suspects, feel very good about their chances for salvation on the basis of their works), Fowler insisted that whatever service we are employed in without consideration of the divine law cannot constitute obedience to God. He drew a firm distinction between our engaging in some action simply out of respect for God's command, "as when a Man obeys God from a slavish Dread of Him, as the poor Americans worship the Devil," and doing it in a selfless effort to glorify our maker, "when his Moral Perfections do shine in our selves." We exalt and celebrate God, Fowler told his audience, when we most resemble his qualities out of a love "not considered merely as good to us or ours, but chiefly as infinitely good in Himself," that is, without reference to our own situation or prospects or "in regard of any Advantage that he can reap thereby." Here was a definition of living Christianity sharply at odds with the sort of worldly preaching which is too often associated with the moderate church movement, a picture of faith stripped of base utility and one not very far distant from the Platonist view of self-renouncing devotion in a world where the "candle of the Lord" illuminates the mind of the believer.[31] For the Latitudinarians, the goodness of an action depended entirely upon the motive which inspired it.[32] Since God has an absolute claim upon our lives, and knowing that every power we possess is dependent upon his will, opportunities for expressing that power were to be engaged by every person for the purpose of forming a closer union with the divine.

Stillingfleet echoed Fowler's view of mankind's relationship with God, preaching that only a uniquely contrite person would find God willing to accept his repentance. "A truly spiritual Mind," he said, "is one that is possessed with the Love of God above all, and that values other things, as they tend to the Enjoyment of Him." Nothing less than a "Supreme transcendent Degree of Love" was required to free a man from the grip of an otherwise carnal mind. The Latitudinarians were normally very wary of stressing the spiritual component of the faith, not out of any animus towards Platonism, but due to the dangerous pretensions made on its behalf by some Dissenters. Notions about mystical union, spiritual raptures, and religious exaltation could not qualify as the genuine promptings of the Holy Spirit for men who had witnessed the abuses of such claims during the 1640s and 1650s. In the opinion of Stillingfleet, a spiritual mind "is such a one as is not only convinced of the Reality of Spiritual things; but of their Excellency and Desirableness, above any others that can be offer'd to our Choice." A mind purged of all desire for base material pleasures, he said, moves "toward the Divine Nature, by a gradual Participation of it" whereby it is fit for "a perpetual Conversation with Divine and Spiritual Objects."[33] This special participation in the divine nature is a long way from calculating hedonism and bespeaks a sensitive recognition on the part of the moderate churchmen of the importance of an otherworldly temper for the genuine Christian.

In maintaining that the work of reform was a lifelong commitment, the Latitudinarians endorsed a broader seventeenth-century

Anglican position regarding the problem of differentiating between specific sinful actions. Distinctions between mortal and venial sin had been made in the early Catholic Church in order to separate offences which required public penance and absolution from those lesser sins capable of pardon under more lenient terms. Throughout the patristic period, the test for determining the category appropriate for particular sins had been an objective one, but during the course of the Middle Ages a new and more subjective evaluation had emerged which was based on the degree to which the sin in question had been committed with knowledge and consent. This criterion, in order to prove effective, depended very much upon the honesty of the offender and the skill and diligence of the priest; thus the room for abuse was enormous. Most Church of England divines, while acknowledging that some sins by their nature were more heinous than others, remained deeply suspicious of a casuistry where a benignant confessor would be free to extend the limits of venial sin beyond all reasonable bounds.[34] The Catholic distinction between mortal and venial sin was, for Anglicans, another example of Catholic laxity and authoritarian legalism.[35] In this instance Anglicans, including the Latitudinarians, looked upon sin from the perspective of its inherent nature rather than in terms of its effects upon man, concluding that since all sinful behavior was a direct repudiation of God's will, every instance of disobedience deserved eternal punishment. The post-Tridentine papacy had condemned the notion that no sin of its own nature could be considered venial, but Anglicans argued throughout the seventeenth century that to accept any distinction between acts of disobedience would only result in the encouragement of vicious habits and undermine the entire process of repentance. Sins of infirmity—those committed in error or in moments of spiritual weakness—were, for practical pastoral purposes, acknowledged by the Church of England, but these were still considered deadly. Given such a severe position, one where no sin can consist with the love of God, repentance for the Anglican divine was confirmed as a continual process rather than as a set of separate occasional acts to be performed only as required. Latitudinarians may have stressed the loving and forgiving qualities of God in their sermons, but the reception of His grace was not to be achieved without constant attention to the imperatives of strictest Christian morality and reform.

Their suspicion of temporal motives and selfish opportunism, together with a reluctance to distinguish between "venial" and "mortal" sins, raises another important issue which has for some time tarnished the image of the Latitudinarians in the minds of contemporary scholars. Margaret Jacob has argued that the Latitudinarians utilized the mechanical model of Newtonian science in order to support a particular social outlook which would be favorable to the established church, and that their natural theology was designed to liberate an acquisitive, capitalist impulse which was already developing in the late seventeenth century.[36] Others have also pointed to the popularity of the Latitudinarian preachers with London's fashionable community, assuming that their influence was due to a theology which required little from its practitioners. There is no question that the social and political outlook of the Latitudinarians did not differ in any substantial measure from that of their High-Church counterparts. All believed in the need for strong government and preached nonresistance to authority. The idea of a rigid hierarchy may have been crumbling in the heavens during the final decades of the seventeenth century, but its application in the social sphere was still firmly embraced by all churchmen.[37]

It is true that the London-based Latitude-men most often preached in churches frequented by affluent members of the business and legal communities, but these recent indictments of their message from the pulpit fail to appreciate the fact that in virtually all of the discussions of money contained in the homiletic literature of the period, the Latitudinarians more often than not excoriated the business ethic as being antithetical to the chief duty of man: his pursuit of eternal happiness under the aegis of divine grace. They refused to consider the world of economic activity as an autonomous sphere of human behavior, one completely outside the purview of a universal moral law whose contents were made plain by the representatives of the official church. Their gainsaying the values of the marketplace may have placed them at odds with the chief prejudices of their parishioners, but their rational defense of what was essentially a medieval frame of reference towards the ethical implications of business nevertheless endeared them to their loyal congregations. "Men are generally by inordinate Desires of earthly things chained to this World," Burton explained, "as slaves to their Gallies, and are tugging hard at the Direction of their Master, Pride, or Covetousness, or Sensuality." While in this impoverished condition, the soul of man can make no progress toward real happiness, but "is more and more deprest and sunk down into Brutishness."[38] Such persons may make their weekly obeisance to religion, "but Mammon is adored by them in their whole life," and whatever conceits they may entertain about their service to God, "Lovers of Money" would remain outside the compass of divine grace, "in a state opposite to Religion, that teaches us to give God and Spiritual things the chief of our affections."[39] Without a genuine contempt for the present world, Patrick believed, "all the advice that can be given will signify little to secure us in the true religion." He told his parishioners at Saint Paul's, Covent Garden, that their concern with riches, honors, and preferment "blinds their judgment, bribes their affections, corrupts their consciences, and carries them into the foulest dotages."[40] During the plague year in London, few of Patrick's wealthy auditors had embraced that degree of contempt for the things of this world to keep them from fleeing their less fortunate neighbors, but Patrick refused to leave despite the importunities of friends, patiently burying the scores of dead and comforting the grief stricken with assurances of the inexplicable providence of God.[41]

For the Latitudinarians, the economic "virtues" were of value to man only when he placed them at the service of his maker. After caring for our basic requirements, advised Barrow, men are obliged by God to supply their neighbor.[42] Our goods, our wealth, and our estates are not, properly speaking, our own, for we hold them in trust from God and are enjoined to use them for the relief of the less fortunate. "We ourselves are naturally mere slaves and vassals to him [God]: as we can never be our own, (masters of ourselves, of our lives, of our liberties) so cannot we ever properly be owners of any thing; there are no possible means by which we can acquire any absolute title to the least mite."[43] The man who ignores charity is not simply misguided or avaricious, said Barrow, but "must be either a mere atheist, disbelieving the existence of God, or an epicurean, in his heart denying God's providence over human affairs."[44] Each of the Latitudinarians had a deep-rooted suspicion of the capitalist ethic, and they spared no opportunity to condemn the man of inordinate worldly ambition. If such a man would only take the time to examine his station with respect to God, he would discover that he was every bit as impoverished as the pauper in the street. As recalcitrant sinners we are every day contracting debts which we can never hope to repay; thus all of us "from prince to peasant, live merely upon alms, and are most really in condition beggers."[45] The moral component of the Latitudinarian message, which had originally been designed to check the pretensions of predestinarian enthusiasts and Antinomians, was by the end of the century increasingly employed to dispute the smug complacency of newly affluent London congregations.

Obviously, the underlying weakness in this and in all pleas for a new set of values that would translate into action involved the problem of utilizing rational entreaties with individuals already firmly under the control of the very vices which the Latitudinarians hoped to eradicate. Barrow acknowledged that "the will of men sometimes may be so depraved, that dissolute persons wantonly and heedlessly may scoff at and seem to disparage goodness," but he was, in the end, comforted by the faith that "the understanding of men can hardly be so corrupted, that piety, charity, justice, temperance, meekness, can in good earnest considerately by any man be disallowed."[46] I use the word "faith" here deliberately, because by the admission of the Latitudinarians themselves, there was precious little empirical evidence to support such a claim. In fact their sermons repeatedly emphasized the obverse about man. Yet the moderate churchmen continued to insist that they could somehow realize effective reform even when those most in need of it were contentedly deaf to appeals based on reason. Barrow once criticized the ancient philosophers who sought to make the practice of virtue its own reward. Most men, he confessed, will not "cross the bent of their natural inclinations, forfeit their present ease [or] wave occasions of getting to themselves profit" as long as moral behavior did not entail some tangible reward.[47] Given the Latitudinarians' broader picture of human nature, their own rational weapon for the reform of society seemed every bit as deficient as the classical alternative, in terms of both strategy and attractiveness. Barrow himself admitted that "plain reason is deemed a dull and heavy thing," and in his own age, where "the mental appetite of men is become like the corporeal, and cannot relish any food without some piquant sauce," one might be required to use wit and raillery to gain the attention of an increasingly indifferent generation.[48] If, as so many have claimed, there is in the Latitudinarian movement an optimism about mankind that is missing in the work of their predecessors, it is to be found most clearly in their exaggerated estimation of the power of innate principles to assist in the rehabilitation of the Christian sinner. Locke's death warrant for innatism, although angrily contested by contemporaries who worried about its implications for morality, was, in retrospect, delivered just in time.

Perhaps the most awkward challenge facing the official clergy after 1660 involved balancing their deep-seated reservations about "enthusiasm" in the pulpit with the need to make a dramatic and enduring impression upon an often apathetic audience. Much has been written about the development of the "plain style" during the Restoration, the cultivation of sermons unembellished by metaphor and displays of patristic and classical learning and combined with a habit of delivery designed to reach the common man. Since their theology was meant for people and not for scholars and churchmen, its nature was basically occasional, and its focus was the pulpit.[49] These important adjustments to traditional oratory, while developed partly in response to the clear, descriptive language of the new science, were intended chiefly to broaden the appeal of Christ's message by demonstrating its compatibility with the dictates of plain reason and good sense; the Church of England, it was thought, could best enhance its appeal by presenting its case in an unambiguous, reasonable, and forthright manner.[50] This approach, after all, had been that of the apostles, "a company of plain and illiterate men, most of them destitute of the advantage of education." Saint Paul in particular had been first and foremost "a gospel preacher" inspired by God to teach only "what men might understand, and what they ought to believe and practice, in a plain, unaffected, and convincing manner."[51] The earliest teachers designed to instruct the generality of men, said Barrow, and "would not use words otherwise than according to their most common and familiar acceptation."[52] Stillingfleet told the clergy of his diocese that only by preaching in a plain style and stressing the punishments awaiting sinners would the message of the gospel reach the new commercial classes. "Stupid and senseless People," he confided to the men under his direction, "whose Minds are wholly sunk into the Affairs of the World, buying, and selling, and getting gain," were unlikely to respond to a more elevated and intellectually taxing approach.[53]

But despite all efforts to clarify the import of Scripture by adopting the requirements of the plain style, Anglicans found themselves having to contend with the disturbing fact that many Nonconformist ministers continued to elicit strong support by exploiting the emotions of their audience. The effective use of nonrational factors in religious experience, and the continuing popularity of preachers who condemned the proponents of rational religion, placed the Latitudinarians in an unenviable position, one where a modicum of compromise with "enthusiastic" preaching became unavoidable lest the influence of the church continue to decline. Joseph Glanvill, writing in the 1670s, was appalled at the general contempt in which ministers of the Anglican Church were held outside London. Perhaps, as Jackson Cope suggests, these sentiments were the sad reflections of a man who, tied to the capital by friends and intellectual interests, was forced to suffer the bleak life of the provinces for many years, but others within the church certainly shared his concerns.[54] Glanvill thought that part of the solution to the problem of the clergy's poor reputation lay in restoring some of the "zeal" which the moderate clergy had recently downplayed in the interests of preaching the virtues of a rational religion in a plain style. He worried that the moderate skepticism of Anglicans aided Dissenters whose willingness to provide final answers to all religious questions would appeal to a popular mind craving certainty but unwilling to undergo the necessary intellectual quest themselves. Taught that the use of reason is a "low, carnal thing," indolent man will only too eagerly turn to pretended illuminations for an anchor and guide in faith.[55] For those simple parishioners unaccustomed to the new, more modest style in the pulpit, the result could often be a church filled with a wealth of "toying, talking, gazing, [and] laughing."[56] In Simon Patrick's numerous directions to the clergy of Ely, one finds the bishop deeply disturbed over the decline in attendance at daily services; but like Glanvill he refused to throw the entire fault on the supposed indifference of the layman, "for it is to be feared that we have been to blame also, in not admonishing them of their duty." Even Muslims, he suggested, are more conscientious about daily worship than Englishmen, "which is a public witness against us, that we are degenerated from our first principles, and by degrees grown cold and remiss in our religion."[57]

Bishop Stillingfleet commented on the same general contempt of the clergy in the 1690s—and proposed a solution not unlike Glanvill's. Stillingfleet thought that moderate Anglicans who employed the plain style were at a distinct disadvantage when set against Catholic and Dissenting preachers since they "can neither comply with the People in Gestures, and Phrases, and Enthusiastic Heats, nor Superstitious Devotions and Priest-Craft." Moderate churchmen may have the weapons of reason, Scripture, and antiquity on their side, mused Stillingfleet, "but these are dry and insipid things to the common people, unless some arts be used to recommend them." He directed the clergy of his own diocese of Worcester to be wary of appealing to "the fancies of People" while in the pulpit, but he suggested none-theless that "we ought to do what we can to excite their affections."[58] He had given an example of such preaching as early as 1672 when, speaking before a Whitehall audience on the subject of God's final judgment, he began with the Latitudinarian commonplace that all arguments for the faith must work upon the reason and understand-ing of the listener. He then proceeded to violate the spirit of this precept by launching into a description of our condition on the day of judgment which mirrored the harshest strictures of Calvinist divinity. Our mirth, warned Stillingfleet, will be "turned into bitter howlings" and our ease "into a bed of flames." And such a lot, he promised, "the greatest part of the World will fall into when that terrible day of the Lord shall come." He reminded his audience of the astonishment all expressed during the Great Fire but asked what they would do "to see the Earth vomit and cast forth fire every where about us, and the Sea boil and swell and froth like water in a seething pot . . . and to see no light in the Heavens, but what the flashings of lightning give?" Here, surely, in language which anticipates the terrifying sermons of the eighteenth-century New England preacher Jonathan Edwards, was a stark acknowledgment of the power and efficacy of the Puri-tan pulpit and evidence of the search for a compromise between the rationalism of the plain style and the imperatives of engaging oratory.[59]

To his credit, Stillingfleet was unwilling to place the blame for the declining spiritual stock of the established church on the calculated hostility or simple indifference of parishioners, nor did he attribute much of the crisis to the rise of Deism and general religious skepti-cism. Rather, his charges to the clergy of Worcester repeatedly stress the need to begin with critical self-analysis and reform. Opposing both the legal right to pluralism which some clergy enjoyed and the right of lay patrons to set the terms by which clergy would hold their tenure, Stillingfleet demanded that his parish churches be staffed by competent incumbents who were committed, especially after the passage of the Toleration Act, to challenging the appeal of Dissent by the example of their ministry, "by out-doing them in those things which make them most popular."[60] Stillingfleet fully acknowledged the limits of the appeal to reason which formed the cornerstone of Latitudinarian thought, and he was flexible enough to counsel a grass-roots approach to the ministry: "If they [Dissenters] gain upon the People by an Appearance of more than ordinary Zeal for the good of Souls, I would have you go beyond them in a true and hearty Concernment for them; not in irregular Heats and Passions, but in the Meekness of Wisdom, in a calm and sedate Temper; in doing good even to them who most despitefully reproach you."[61] The clergy were to redouble their efforts in the area of catechizing children because of parental indifference, offer communion on a more regular basis in order to remind each person of Christ's special sacrifice, address the needs of the sick and infirm, and steer a difficult middle path when in the pulpit between extemporaneous preaching on common themes and elaborate exegesis of difficult concepts, remembering always to adapt their message to "common understandings."[62] The plain style had to be combined with a sympathetic concern for the emotional needs of each individual; the gospel of reason would do little to restore the credibility of the church if the message delivered from the pulpit ignored the world outside the intellect.

We have already mentioned how the whole program of practical moral reform was to a significant degree predicated upon the success of Christian education and how an essentially Augustinian view of human nature tempered the more sanguine estimates of man's ability to transcend his innate inclination to the practice of evil.[63] The popular image of the tabula rasa, adopted by others within the Latitudinarian circle, did not imply the type of radical environmentalism that has so often been associated with Locke's theory.[64] With the publication of *Some Thoughts Concerning Education* in 1693, Locke seemed to be using the empirical method which he had advocated in his earlier *Essay Concerning Human Understanding* in order to overturn the traditional Christian picture of man's nature in the aftermath of the Fall. But while suggesting at the outset of *Some Thoughts* that education was the arbiter of an individual's character, Locke went on to qualify sharply these positive statements by explaining that the child at birth, while possessing no store of innate ideas, was faced with a host of innate passions, dispositions, and destructive drives, all of which made the job of the educator one of extensive remediation as well as instruction. He shared with his moderate church friends the conviction that children must be raised from the level of their natural desires—the hypertrophy of irrational passions and appetites— to the plane of right reason and moral action by the force of extended tuition and example. Both parents and clergy, each in their own way, were responsible for the proper training of youth, and it was believed that the guardian who failed in this charge would be exposed to the full wrath of God's eternal justice.[65]

The negligence of parents in the education of their children was a particularly resonant theme in the sermons of the Latitudinarians. Stillingfleet was infuriated by the fact that most parents, irrespective of their material circumstances, would not hesitate to have their children instructed on how to gain an estate while completely disregarding their education into the principles of the faith.[66] Because of the depravity of human nature, the untoward example of parents had much greater force on the child's early development than did the fruit of Christian training.[67] "There is a softness in the Temper of Youth," John Moore warned, "and they are yielding to the Impressions of Vice, which act directly upon the Senses; but the Influences of Virtue enter more hardly, whose Excellencies can only be discerned by some Thought and Consideration, of which they are impatient."[68] Fowler placed the blame for the gross ignorance of English Christians squarely on the shoulders of irresponsible adults who failed to catechize their children properly. Good preaching, whether employing the new plain style or not, would be ineffectual unless the congregation had some rudimentary understanding of the Scriptures beforehand.[69] Patrick worked to stem some of this ignorance through his many catechisms and manuals of family prayer. In *The Devout Christian*, for example, Patrick built upon the Book of Common Prayer in offering specially focused devotions for each day of the week, for the death of a friend or child, for pregnant women, good harvests, war, sickness, storms, long journeys, and a variety of more mundane matters. Each was carefully crafted to remind the subject of mankind's complete dependence on God's mercy and grace in all of life's circumstances, and the texts were composed in a simple language designed to appeal to the broadest possible audience.[70] Patrick informed the clergy of Ely diocese that in catechizing children, they should "teach them the meaning, and make them understand the weight of every word" by holding fifteen-minute sessions every day during the long summer evenings. This would not only bring more people into church for regular services but, in the long run, help the parishioners better understand the contents of the Sunday sermon.[71]

A similar recognition of the importance of Christian education inspired Tenison to open a school for indigent children and a library for the use of clergy residing in the parish of Saint Martin-in-the-

Fields. By 1688 he was working with Dr. Kennet, vicar of Saint Paul's, Covent Garden, to improve and expand the scheme, and in April of 1688 the school, now under the direction of two teachers, found a permanent home in the basement of Tenison's Free Library. According to the statutes, the children were to be "instructed in the Principles of Church Religion, and care taken that their manners be formed accordingly."[72] Tenison would later found schools in Saint James's parish and, after his elevation to Canterbury, a school for poor girls at Lambeth and another at Croyden. By 1704 there were fifty-three boys at the Saint James's parish school, thirty-six of whom were educated without charge. "Our Lusts and Appetites," he preached in 1694 before assuming his duties as archbishop, "till Reason and Grace subdue them, are strong and impetuous. Our Mind is, generally speaking, overgrown very early with the Prejudices and Indiscretions of Youth; we are first accustomed to Folly and Vanity, before we are acquainted with Christian Piety."[73] His work on behalf of education in London was inspired by a recognition of the deep impress made upon human nature by the sin of Adam and a frank acknowledgment that the future of the church's mission in an increasingly secular environment was contingent upon the success of efforts to demonstrate to the young the incapacity of that environment to guarantee lasting happiness.

The program of practical reform advocated by the Latitudinarians was, by most accounts, a failure in its impact on English society during the last years of the seventeenth century. If action was in fact the natural corollary of saving faith, then Calvin's observations regarding the number of the elect were not unduly parsimonious. Looking back on the last year of Stuart rule from the vantage point of 1690, Edward Fowler observed with some fondness how Protestants who had for so long differed in opinion at last came together in mutual charity for a common cause. But as the final decade of the century began, "the old Nick-names and Terms of Reproach are now revived, but never did the Differing Parties make less Conscience of Defaming and most Shamefully Belying one another."[74] The compulsory retreat of English Puritanism as a political force after 1660, together with the eclipse of Calvinist theology, had done very little to moderate the extremes of bitterness occasioned by religious differences. The failure to reconcile an official policy of active persecution of dissent with a more general call for a living, active faith, posed an insuperable obstacle to the success of the moderate church ideal.

When a majority of its proponents within the church could not adhere to a theological position built around the idea of moral reform, then there was scant hope that it would win the allegiance of significant numbers within the wider community of English Protestants.

Some supporters of the ideal, like Barrow, might put on a brave face and admit "that things never have gone there as the wisest judge, or the best men desire." It was clear to the Latitude-men that reasonable Christians would acknowledge the futility of prolonged doctrinal disputes over nonessentials, that the claims of enthusiasts to special Revelation should be avoided, and that faith, if it were to avoid the contumacy of blaming God for the sins of men, must always issue in moral action. The difficulty, of course, involved educating men into the exercise of reason—reforming their natures—whereby both the contents of their duty would become apparent and the motives to obedience compelling. In the end Barrow may have been correct to assert that good men "are an Elect" in this world, "culled out of a great lump of those, who either reject religion, or embrace it only in verbal profession or formal show."[75] But such an admission of the limits of moral reform, if it was anywhere near being accurate, would have made much of the moral preaching of the Latitudinarians quite beside the point, a supernumerary work taken on by men who lacked either the vision or perhaps the courage to admit the cogency of Calvin's disquieting prospect.

The elevation of John Tillotson to the see of Canterbury in May 1691 not only was an important episode in the protracted struggle between the non-juring clergy and the revolutionary government of William and Mary but also represented the temporary ascendency of the Latitudinarian wing of the church after the fall of James II. For in the wake of Sancroft's refusal to recognize the legitimacy of the new political order, five sitting bishops followed their primate into oblivion, two more had died before the deprivation took effect, and one had followed James into exile. During the first three years of his reign, the new king was able to nominate a full sixteen of the twenty-six bishops, and, in the estimate of F. G. James, William clearly favored the moderate churchmen "both because he approved of their greater tolerance towards Dissenters and because he thought them more trustworthy politically."[1] In addition to Tillotson, other prominent figures received preferment in the wake of the events of 1688—Stillingfleet to Worcester, Burnet to Salisbury, Fowler to Gloucester, Moore to Norwich, Grove to Chichester, and Patrick first to Chichester and subsequently to Ely—leading some to believe that a new era of comprehension and toleration lay at hand.[2] But this shift in the leadership structure notwithstanding, the Church of England after the expulsion of the last Stuart king was plagued by numerous sharp divisions which would make the tenure of the new moderate church bishops both frustrating and unproductive, with the Church of England losing its monopoly over the spiritual life of the nation and becoming entangled in the rage of party. The rise of Deism and anti-trinitarianism, the end of clerical censorship of theological books, the achievement of a partial toleration, high taxes on the clergy in a war economy, and the experience of painful schism all placed enormous strain on the church after the revolution. If, as one recent historian has averred, the church by 1689 "had lost the intellectual, moral and spiritual authority it had acquired by 1603," then the task facing the Latitudinarian bishops, despite their sudden empowerment, could not have been more problematic, their chances for success less likely.[3]

If theology be the science which treats of God in the largest sense— his attributes, his intentions, his relation to the universe and to man— then it is difficult to see where the Latitudinarians had any particular reform goal to pursue after 1689. As we have seen, their soteriology, their perspective on grace, their affirmation of revelation and particular providence, and, at the core of all of these, their picture of human nature since the fall of Adam, remained consistent with the point of view held by their supposedly more orthodox critics. What divided them from those critics was their unwillingness to be dogmatic about matters of form and ceremony peculiar to the Church of England, a wish to maintain a dialogue with men who differed from them on these matters, a refusal to consistently attribute all religious error to sinful pride and obstinacy, and, as Burnet indicated, an advocacy of "great freedom both in philosophy and divinity."[4] For the Latitudinarians, the personal relationship between a believer and God took precedence over the external requirements of worship mandated by any single communion, regardless of how historically appropriate such practices might be. Although sensitive to the need for an ordered liturgy and a learned, disciplined clergy, especially in light of the excesses of the radical sects during the Civil War and Interregnum, the Latitudinarians attempted to remain faithful to what might with some justice be considered the central principle of Reformed Christianity: the solitary responsibility of the sinner before God. They would not distract from the salience of this obligation by closing the door to moderate Nonconformists whose theology coincided with that espoused by Anglicans. With this in mind, the work towards a comprehension was rekindled in the aftermath of the Revolution of 1688.

The London Latitudinarians—Tillotson, Patrick, Stillingfleet, Moore and Tenison—had been instrumental in convincing Sancroft during May 1688 that some overture to moderate Dissenters was necessary in the face of James's Declaration of Indulgence. Presbyterians, Congregationalists, and Baptists had, by and large, resisted the blandishments of a disingenuous monarch and remained loyal to the parliamentary cause. Now, more than at any other time since 1660, it was thought, Protestants had stood together in a united front against the Catholic menace, and it was time for the official church to recognize the services of dissent in preserving the reformed faith. It was this same group of clergymen who solicited the opinions of their London brethren on the question of reading the offending declaration in church.

After the trial of the seven bishops, Sancroft began to treat with Dissenters and cooperated with the Latitudinarians in a plan for a bill of comprehension to be introduced in a future session of Parliament.[5] In a set of instructions to the bishops in July 1688, the archbishop exhorted the clergy to have "a very tender regard to our brethren, the Protestant Dissenters, that upon occasion offered they visit them at their houses, and receive them kindly at their own."[6] But Sancroft's proposals for comprehension and toleration were discussed solely within the context of James II remaining as king. The archbishop, after all, had been a staunch supporter of James's cause during the Exclusion Crisis, and as a member of the king's new ecclesiastical commission after 1681, he had made recommendations for places in the church on the basis of the candidates' political loyalty to the then duke of York.[7] Until very late in the day, after most observers had recognized James's obtuse designs for what they were, Sancroft continued to hope against hope that the king would recognize the error of his tolerationist ways and reconstruct an alliance with his loyal servants within the established church. With the flight of James on 11 December, however, the whole political foundation upon which Sancroft had consented to discussion with Dissenters was swiftly overturned. The archbishop ended his activities on behalf of reform, and at a meeting in Stillingfleet's London house on 14 January 1689, Patrick, Lloyd, Tillotson, Sharp, and Tenison took it upon themselves to draw up a bill for comprehension which would be introduced in the Lords as soon as it proved feasible.[8]

As G. V. Bennett has shown, the London moderates were able to exercise a significant measure of influence on the church policy of William III through their close connection with Daniel Finch, earl of Nottingham. Nottingham, who was chosen secretary of state by the new king, had for some time supported a policy of greater comprehension for moderate Dissenters. The king himself desired a much more extensive reform, calling for toleration for Jews, Catholics, and Dissenters as well as the abolition of the sacramental test for office-holders.[9] On 27 February 1689, Nottingham received the approval of William III to introduce a bill into the House of Lords "for uniting their Majesties' Protestant subjects." This bill, together with another "for exempting their Majesties' Protestant subjects, dissenting from the Church of England, from the penalties of certain laws" received second readings on 14 March before being assigned to a select committee chaired by Nottingham. But William, who much like his predecessor had little real sympathy for the church he had been chosen to defend, then proceeded to alarm the conservative Anglican squir-archy by his announcement to both Houses on 16 March that he was in favor of repealing the Test Act for all Protestants, a request which would have abruptly ended the Anglican monopoly on political power.[10] Thoroughly alarmed at this apparent attempt by a Calvinist monarch to undercut the interests of an established church which had long been the bulwark of the monarchical principle, 150 M.P.s met at the Devil's Tavern in Fleet Street to condemn William's position, and the Parliament bluntly refused to go along with the king's desire to abolish the sacramental test for officeholders. Tories in the Commons, who had already cooperated with Whigs over the constitutional settlement, now prepared themselves to resist all substantive concessions in the religious arena. Two bills for comprehension, one originating in the Lords and the other in Commons, were vigorously debated and then dropped, while the separate bill for tolerating dissent outside the church received approval only after the king assured Parliament that he was committed to the support and defense of the established religion.[11]

Since Nottingham and his clerical allies had envisioned the two bills as a package on the assumption that a broad comprehension would make the Toleration Bill applicable for only a tiny minority, an alternative strategy was deemed essential. After the failure of Parliament to accept the principle of rapprochement with Dissenters, William attempted to mend fences with Anglican M.P.s and suggested that the matter of comprehension be taken up in Convocation, a body which had not met since 1664. Tillotson, who had been appointed clerk of the closet earlier in April, insisted that to introduce such a broadly defined concept into a body still deeply split over the wisdom of extending the boundaries of admission to the church would lead only to interminable wrangling. Better to appoint a special commission to hammer out the proposal, he advised, before submitting it to a vote in Convocation.[12] A warrant for such a commission, composed of ten bishops and twenty other clergy and empowered to consider revisions in liturgy, canons, courts, and church discipline, was issued on 4 September, and delegates met from 10 October until 18 November. There was considerable difficulty at the conference, however, as certain members questioned its legality and withdrew after the early sessions, while others believed that further concessions would only be interpreted by "peevish" Dissenters as an admission on the part of the church that it had always been in the wrong.[13] The final proposal was drafted without consulting the Dissenters, and the hope was that moderate Presbyterians would accept the terms without first suggesting revisions. When Convocation met on 21 November, however, Dr. William Jane, who had walked out of the commission after the third day, was elected prolucutor of the Lower House over the court-sponsored candidate Tillotson.[14] It was a short and noisy session, for the opposition to the comprehension scheme was well organized. William quickly recognized the futility of pursuing the issue and adjourned the body on 14 December 1689, before the matter of revising the liturgy was even discussed; he would not allow it to meet again until 1701.

Since the Toleration Bill was originally designed for a tiny number of extreme sectaries, while the companion Comprehension Bill had been proposed in order to attract moderate Dissenters to the church, the terms of the act which was approved by Parliament were exceptionally grudging in nature. Many rank and file Anglicans looked upon it as a temporary concession to be withdrawn when circumstances seemed more propitious.[15] And as the act was in no respect the product of advancing skepticism or an enlightened recognition of the futility of persecution, it did not proclaim a state of general toleration, but merely exempted non-Anglican Trinitarian Protestants from the penalties of the Clarendon Code, which was not officially withdrawn. It precluded the participation of Dissenters from the civil and educational life of the nation, required that all meeting-houses be registered with a bishop or at the appropriate quarter session, and mandated that dissenting ministers agree to the doctrinal provisions of the Thirty-nine Articles. In essence the act was just another form of special indulgence, and High Church Tories were never satisfied with its modest provisions.[16] For one thing, the practice of occasional conformity, whereby Dissenters maintained public positions by nominal adherence to the Anglican rite of Holy Communion, infuriated defenders of the Establishment who repeatedly witnessed this circumvention of the Test Act. Incidents like the one in 1697, when the lord mayor of London, Sir Humphrey Edwin, twice attended an afternoon service at a dissenting congregation after worshiping as an Anglican in the morning, certainly exacerbated tensions.[17] In 1702, disgruntled High Church politicians, infuriated by William III's practice of abetting those who engaged in this studied contempt for the Holy Sacrament—what the intemperate Henry Sacheverell called "a religious piece of hypocrisy as even no heathen government would have endured"—introduced legislation designed to curb the practice, while moderates like Burnet found themselves on the defensive, pleading the case of charity for the violators.[18]

More importantly, the extension of toleration to an estimated half a million persons, together with the eclipse of Convocation during the 1690s, inadvertently enabled a sizable minority of Englishmen to escape the disciplinary power of the national church, destroying forever the centuries-old notion that the church represented the touchstone of moral authority in a society committed to a single conception of temporal and transcendent good.[19] However much that ideal may have been contravened in the expanding commercial environment of the late seventeenth century, none of the Latitudinarians ever accepted the premise that a separate code of thought and action might be applicable in the daily affairs of men, one wholly outside the purview of the church or under the competence of another, rival communion. Although the Toleration Act retained the old laws regarding attendance at services on Sunday, such a mandate was difficult to enforce once the principle of uniformity was abandoned. In growing towns such as Birmingham, Manchester, Leeds, and Liverpool, for example, attendance at church services plummeted.[20] The act dramatically stripped the national church of any pretense to represent the spiritual welfare of all of England's inhabitants. But while this legislative abandonment of coercion and tacit acknowledgment of the validity of honest differences in interpreting God's word may have pleased the Latitudinarians (given their commitment to a religious perspective where the individual's relationship with God, rather than the rigor of form and ceremony, constituted the core of faith), the surrender of their own church's special mandate which the rejection of the Comprehension Bill signaled was a matter of deep regret. The Latitudinarians' preference for an Erastian solution to the problem of dissent, with a liberal theology within the state church rather than diversity through exclusion, now had to be abandoned in favor of their friend John Locke's new secular model of politics.[21]

In the aftermath of this important failure to realize a comprehension, there were still those, like Burnet, who hoped for another opportunity to push a bill through Parliament, who continued to believe that a child born into the English nation should be considered a member of the English church.[22] But the hostility of an emerging High Church party, together with the recognition that any concessions would be interpreted by the non-jurors as a further betrayal of the church, made such a political solution unlikely. England would enter the eighteenth century with a liberty of worship that far exceeded anything achieved in most of Western Europe, and although the church remained the principal agent of the state in the countryside, teaching obedience and condemning radical politics,[23] the consequences of that liberty for the life of the church could not have been more unfortunate, as the group of moderate churchmen patronized by Nottingham and the king found themselves increasingly estranged from the sensibilities—and the prejudices—of the simple country parson and the politically powerful Anglican squirarchy, both of whom equated Latitudinarianism with the eclipse of church authority and influence.[24]

From the point of view of moderate Dissenters, however, the failure of the 1689 Comprehension Bill did not disappoint them as much as previous efforts had. Members of a younger generation did not share the hopes of Baxter and Bates for a united Protestant community; they were quite prepared to strike out on a separate existence and expressed no special desire to be a part of a church which had persecuted them for so long. Familiar appeals like those of John Moore, who after the revolution wrote that the Church of England retained only a few rites and ceremonies in order to preserve decency and order in worship, now had little impact on men who found no compelling reason to abandon their distinct church orders, their settled ministries, and their academies dedicated to training future ministers and productive laymen.[25] Developing, in the words of Professor Hill, a "more utilitarian, more critical, more democratic culture," the Dissenters adjusted quickly to their new status, focusing their talents on trade and industry and ultimately losing much of the religious zeal of their forefathers.[26] Some twenty-five hundred licenses were issued under Article 19 of the Toleration Act between

1691 and 1710, and while most of these were for existing congregations who were simply establishing more permanent quarters, many
High Churchmen interpreted the fact that meetinghouses soon out-
numbered Anglican parish churches in London as a serious challenge to the future integrity of the Anglican communion.[27] That the
"fanaticism of the sects" remained a fear of High Churchmen after
1689 is testified by the Sacheverell episode beginning in 1702. The
fear was misplaced, of course, but as Geoffrey Holmes has written,
"men are not objective about their fears; and there was just enough
substance to this one in the years after 1688."[28] As the eighteenth century dawned, the dichotomy between "church" and "chapel" became
more pronounced as differing traditions of worship highlighted the
failure, and perhaps the impracticality, of the comprehension idea.[29]
And as the Church of England increasingly interpreted its liturgical and governmental borrowings from early church formularies as
a positive strength, Presbyterians, Congregationalists, and Baptists
reaffirmed their biblical mandate for a very different form of worship. "Things indifferent" for the Latitudinarian divines—use of the
surplice, signing of the cross in baptism, use of the ring in marriage, kneeling for Holy Communion, even the architectural style of
churches—quietly became the indispensible marks of an Anglican
adherence to ancient tradition and a parallel disdain for innovation.[30]

Hoping to further the cause of comprehension by working closely
with the court, the moderate churchmen's very political trustworthi-
ness would cause them many problems after the revolution. Between
the Restoration and the departure of James II, there had been a host
of important issues dividing the Anglican communion, but a basic
set of similar objectives—countering the Catholic menace, checking
radical dissent, decrying resistance to royal authority, extending the
spiritual influence of the church—had bound the disparate parties
together in a larger, if at times uncomfortable, union. But the need
to justify their desertion of the long-held Anglican principle of obedience to hereditary monarchy (no matter how distasteful a particular monarch might be) created for the moderate churchmen serious
casuistical difficulties. In a church which since 1660 had advanced
the idea of personal monarchy and authoritarian government, Tillotson had been one of the more vocal supporters of hereditary right
and nonresistance, viewing all duly constituted political authority
as unimpeachable, and his letters to the condemned Lord Russell
in 1683 provided prime examples of that belief, even "if our reli-

gion and rights should be invaded."[31] Such unequivocal statements would haunt his tenure as primate, as angry non-jurors pointed to the inconsistency of Tillotson's words with his opportunistic support for the usurper, his abandonment of the principle of deference and inviolable hierarchy for the sake of uncanonical preferment.[32]

It appeared to many ejected ministers that Tillotson and his colleagues were once again playing the old game of profitable compromise with illegitimate regimes, just as they had under Cromwell's regicide gang in the 1650s. Tillotson's employment of the doctrine of "divine right by Providence" may have appeared plausible to the moderate church clergy who accepted preferment under the new government, but to those who remained loyal to the Stuart claim, the idea smacked of sheer hypocrisy and an abusive interpretation of particular providence. The experience of Puritans who had justified their earlier political success in similar terms remained all too clear in the collective memory of such men.[33] One of the central messages from the pulpit for the previous three decades, after all, had to be impaired in order to accommodate the de facto rule of William of Orange, a revolution lacking genuine moral authority given the church's strong identification with the restored Stuart monarchy. And while a sympathetic House of Lords in the spring of 1690 sought to delete the requirement that all clerical incumbents take an oath to the new monarchy, an Erastian Commons insisted upon the loyalty test for all who received either civil or ecclesiastical preferment from the Crown.[34]

For the first generation of non-jurors, men who had in many cases lived through the period of Puritan control without taking the required oaths, the ultimate effect of the Latitudinarian compromise with principle would be to produce a further decline in the church's autonomy from the encroaching designs of the state. The state enjoyed no better security, wrote Charles Leslie, than when the people were taught to obey for the sake of conscience by men who have won their respect and esteem. But "when they see Bishops made by the Court, they are apt to imagine that they speak to them the Court-language. . . ."[35] Around four hundred of the inferior clergy declined to speak the language of the court in 1690, choosing instead to follow Sancroft's path into an unwanted schism. Their small numbers, together with their internal disputes, belied their influence as powerful critics of the church under Tillotson's stewardship, and their presence as the living conscience of the old ways contributed in no small part to the failure of the Latitudinarians to achieve a comprehension after 1689.[36]

William first mentioned the primacy to Tillotson in September of 1689 and pressed it upon him again in February of 1690, but Tillotson, doubtless realizing the burden of the task facing the next primate, begged the monarch to excuse him the dubious honor of overseeing the exit of Sancroft and his supporters.[37] Educated at Cambridge and ejected from his fellowship at Clare College by Peter Gunning in 1660, Tillotson, as we have seen, had behind him a distinguished career in the pulpits of London's churches, serving both as preacher at Lincoln's Inn and as Tuesday lecturer at Saint Lawrence Jewry since 1663.[38] He had also served as a chaplain to Charles II, was appointed dean of Canterbury in 1672, and finally had received the honor of dean of Saint Paul's soon after the revolution. It was, by all measures, a remarkable rise for the son of a Yorkshire cloth worker, but Tillotson also carried with him a number of serious liabilities, none of which troubled his closest rival for the primacy, Bishop Henry Compton of London. Whereas Compton, the most implacable of James's clerical opponents and the only senior church official to sign the invitation to William, had enjoyed a long and successful career as bishop of a busy diocese, Tillotson's extensive contacts with London Dissenters and with Socinians like the philanthropist Thomas Firmin (Tillotson acted as godfather to Firmin's son in 1665) presented clear targets for non-juring critics.[39] High Church ideals were deliberately inculcated at the universities after the Restoration, and the movement unquestionably gained force in response to the growth of Socinianism and Deism in the 1690s. To select an archbishop who counted among his friends men who openly promoted heterodox views seemed inexcusable to a younger generation of conservative parish clergy, men who were, generally speaking, better educated, more prosperous, and from a higher social class than their earlier seventeenth-century counterparts.[40]

In ill health and dreading the inevitable outcry against his appointment, Tillotson was consecrated on Whitsunday at Saint Mary-le-Bow church and took possession of Lambeth in November 1691. As anticipated, he immediately became the target of attack for all those who opposed the new government. Condemned as a schismatic, Socinian, Deist, Arian, atheist, abettor of Dissent, and ecclesiastical interloper, he took little constructive action towards reform before his death in 1694 and certainly nothing toward reviving the idea of a comprehension or lessening the parliamentary burdens of the bishops.[41] The Latitudinarian emphasis upon the importance of pastoral care would continue to receive derisory observation as long as bishops were obliged to spend a large part of each year addressing affairs of state in Westminster.[42] Attendance upon court and Parliament was nothing new, of course, as the Caroline predecessors to the Latitudinarian bishops had generally spent most of their time in the capital, but while residence in London afforded the bishops direct influence over political decisions affecting the welfare of the church, the new practice of annual parliamentary sessions and the emergence of bitter party struggles invariably took their toll on the administrative and, more importantly, the spiritual life of each respective diocese. In such an environment, conscientious fulfillment of episcopal visitations, confirmations, and ordinations placed an enormous burden upon the time and physical energies of an already overcommitted bench. "The attendance on parliaments," complained Burnet, "is a great distraction, and puts us to a great charge, besides calling us off half the year from doing our duty."[43] And even in those cases, like Burnet's, where a moderate church bishop was particularly conscientious in working to influence the quality of spiritual life in the parishes, the word of the local parson—who identified with his parishioners, worked alongside them, and in many cases lived with them longer than most could remember—was of far greater moment than the injunctions of a peripatetic representative of Tillotson's church.[44]

Tillotson's unwillingness to press for the revival of Convocation and his preference for the employment of royal injunctions as a mechanism for governing the church enraged High Churchmen who interpreted these trends as a capitulation to secular authority. The popularity of Atterbury's catalogue of ills facing the Establishment, published during the primacy of Tillotson's successor under the title *A Letter to a Convocation Man*, attested to the depth of dissatisfaction at this apparent sycophancy on the part of the new leadership.[45] "The Church in Danger" became the central rallying cry of all those who objected to the moderate leadership of the 1690s, a leadership which had overseen a serious decline in attendance at Anglican services, the expansion of Dissenting congregations (in both wealth and numbers), and the continuing encroachments of irreligion and Deism. As Michael Hunter has recently observed, at a time when "It was widely believed that the fabric of society depended on a philosophical and theological consensus, the acceptance of unorthodox viewpoints indicated a willingness to put at risk the fragile peace and stability of English society."[46] Even Burnet admitted that "It became a common topic of discourse to treat all matters of religion as the contrivances of priests to bring the world into a blind submission to them," while the High Churchman Humphrey Prideaux observed that many defend toleration "to separate from all manner of worship to perfect irreligion."[47]

As Deism and atheism gained adherents among the upper classes and open debate over the nature of Christ both shocked and challenged the clerical community, an apparently insensitive Tillotson continued to cultivate his friendships with the likes of the heterodox Thomas Firmin and John Locke.[48] With the prospect of any future convocation turning into a bitter stalemate, with his deprived predecessor living in quiet dignity in East Anglia, making plans to perpetuate the "true" episcopate and conferring his own archiepiscopal powers to a successor, and with large numbers of humble parish clergy in sympathy with the non-jurors, Tillotson had little room to formulate, much less to implement, a program of renewal for the church which included concessions to Dissenters. He survived Sancroft by only twelve months, and, characteristically, was attended by his non-juring friend Robert Nelson during the last days of his life. Only in the eighteenth century, when his preaching, "simple, elegant, candid, clear and rational" according to Bishop Warburton, became the model for many within the Anglican community, did Tillotson win a place as an important figure in the homiletic tradition of the church.[49] His advocacy of the plain style in the pulpit survived the political controversies which surrounded his primacy, but his theological orthodoxy met with an altogether different fate, eventually overshadowed and obscured by his controversial associations and his alliance to the new political order.[50]

When Tillotson died in November 1694, both Burnet and the queen pressed the king to nominate Stillingfleet for the post, but William decided to select another member of the London clergy who had been so pivotal in rallying opposition to James during 1688. The choice of Thomas Tenison meant that the church would be led by an accomplished administrator rather than a scholar, preacher, or theological polemicist. During his brief tenure as bishop of Lincoln (1692–94) he had exhibited an efficiency in organizing his diocese and a commitment to parish visitations which epitomized the Latitudinarian ideal of practical religion, and he would continue this activity while in residence at Canterbury.[51] A participant at the commission appointed by William to draw up terms for a comprehension in 1689, Tenison was deeply disappointed by its failure in Convocation. But while he never attempted to overturn Parliament's settlement of the issue directly, as archbishop Tenison worked to achieve by leniency what had been lost through the inaction of Parliament. Throughout his primacy he refused to take measures against occasional conformists, thus allowing politically active Dissenters to maintain their civil equality despite High Church opposition.[52]

Noted especially for his charitable work as vicar of Saint Martin-in-the-Fields from 1680 until the revolution, Tenison recognized that if the church in the 1690s was to have a voice in shaping the religious character of the nation, it must do so without relying upon the state for support.[53] The voluntary idea, designed to make the church more spiritually effective in the community, reached its height under his tenure, with Thomas Bray's Society for Promoting Christian Knowledge (1698) and the Society for the Propagation of the Gospel (1701) being the two best-known efforts to extend the word. The idea of lay religious societies had probably begun with Anthony Horneck in the 1670s when he organized a group of artisans and mechanics into a voluntary association which met on a regular basis for devotion and the organization of charity, while Thomas Firmin's efforts to coordinate poor relief and provide employment for London's destitute encouraged more systematic endeavors.[54] Expanding to some sixteen groups by the mid-1690s, small-scale charitable groups provided a model for the more ambitious efforts sponsored by lawyers, businessmen, and civic authorities.

The charity schools established by the Society for Promoting Christian Knowledge provided a modicum of training in reading and writing for some two thousand poor children in fifty-four London schools by 1704. The problem of poor relief in the city had taken on a new urgency after the Revolution of 1688, as economic crisis resulting from the effects of an unusually cold winter and the outbreak of war against France in 1690 resulted in widespread hardship for the laboring poor.[55] Tenison, as founder of a charity school in his own parish of Saint Martin's in 1683, eagerly encouraged the expansion of these educational projects, and he continued to found institutions of his own after becoming archbishop. Like most of his more moderate colleagues, Tenison identified the origins of atheism not with "the arguments of a sound Mind in a sober Temper, but in a sensual Disposition, which inclines Men to seek out for colors, whereby they may deceive themselves into an opinion of the safety of living in a course that pleases them."[56] Such philanthropy, of course, barely touched the estimated one-half of the population of England and Wales which, according to the statistician Gregory King, was earning insufficient income to maintain themselves.[57] In the country there was considerable resistance to charity schools, as many ministers viewed the establishment of the institutions as a critical reflection on their own efforts to catechize and discipline through informal, personal channels. Nevertheless, bishops like Patrick and Burnet encouraged their clergy to support the charity school concept and to begin subscriptions for schools in the parishes.[58]

More than anything else, it was the growth of the dependent poor and the visible affront of abandoned and neglected children in the capital which spurred men to action in the 1690s.[59] The schools were founded chiefly to provide the social discipline which was no longer being inculcated by family and church, to train up a God-fearing generation who understood and accepted the propriety of social order and degree.[60] As the new king indicated to Bishop Compton of London, "we must earnestly desire, and shall endeavour a general reformation of the lives and manners of all our subjects, as being that which must establish our throne, and secure to our people their religion, happiness, and peace, all of which seem to be in great danger at this time, by reason of that overflowing of vice, which is too notorious."[61] Only through instruction in the rudiments of the Protestant faith would children be able to resist the attractions of Rome and the comfortable alternative of Deism. The subscription that supporters of the charity schools signed reads like a frank acknowledgment of the failure of the church to fulfill its educative function. It was plain to "common observation," the subscription declares, "that the growth of Vice and Debauchery is greatly owing to the gross ignorance of the principles of the Christian Religion, especially among the poorer sort."[62] The training—basic reading and penmanship with perhaps a little arithmetic—was designed not to develop an autonomous individual, one capable of evaluating one's faith critically, for example, but rather to fit the child for a particular place in the economic order and to prevent future social upheaval. For the middle-class supporters of the schools, "It was beyond the range of their mentality to conceive that the poor were poor because society was an ill-regulated machine, or that the body politic was, as a whole responsible for the disease which attacked it."[63] The charity schools were designed not to end the all-too-common practice of child labor but to prepare their charges for a more constructive role within the existing social and economic hierarchy. The inequalities of wealth in late seventeenth-century London were accepted by the subscribers as the decree of God. Still, the charity school approach to the problem of vice and the reform of manners had much to commend it when compared with both the scheme for children's workhouses suggested by the philosopher John Locke for the Board of Trade in 1696 and the less than gentle methods of the Societies for the Reformation of Manners, which freely utilized the sanction of the civil law to enforce morality. The system of lay informants integral to the "success" of these groups, together with incidents of notorious abuse of the legal system, disturbed many who resented such officious intrusions into their affairs, and their questionable tactics probably had little impact on the conscience of the offender, but even Tenison heartily endorsed such activities in lieu of any effective legal alternative.[64]

Had the non-juring schism been the sole problem facing moderates within the church after 1689, Tillotson's brief stewardship might have been more productive. But just as the unfortunate division within the church was frustrating any hopes for greater comprehension, the explosive Deist quarrel of the 1690s called the entire tradition of Anglican rationalism into question. Against the background of a growing debate over the earliest forms of human behavior and the rational components of all pre-Christian religious systems, the English Deists took advantage of the expiration of the Licensing Act in 1695 to attack the church and its clergy with relative impunity, providing hostile non-jurors with sufficient ammunition to link the Latitudinarian divines with a movement whose express purpose was to cashier the mysteries of the faith and enthrone frail human reason in the seat of divine wisdom.[65] The rationalism of the Latitudinarians was now correlated with the irrepressible arrogance of the Deists and anti-trinitarians, and Tillotson's Church of England would find itself constantly on the defensive against a host of determined critics from both ends of the religious spectrum.[66] In the event, their work of pious exhortation, of instructing an increasingly indifferent people in the requirements of the faith, was made more difficult if not altogether impracticable.

As Leslie Stephen observed more than a century ago, the numerous geographical, historical, and astronomical discoveries of the

seventeenth century challenged Christians to defend their own special revelation as normative for all mankind. The Bible chronology
itself, if accepted literally, was beginning to jar uncomfortably with
the evidence of natural philosophy and the expanding knowledge of
other world civilizations. As Christianity was slowly recognized for
the minority religion that it was, as the particular nature of a revelation recorded in a dead language came to trouble many interpreters,
and as the finite universe of the medieval mind gradually gave way to
the vast expanses of a Newtonian cosmos governed by a few uniform
laws, the search for universal moral and religious principles, common
guideposts which transcended the limits of time and circumstance,
began to accelerate.[67] The solution to conflicting interpretations of
Scripture that had been proposed by Lord Herbert of Cherbury during the 1620s and reiterated by his disciple Charles Blount (1654–93)
seemed to take on added urgency at the end of the century, as differences among Christians were compounded by the fact that millions
who had never heard God's word, much less the contemporary conflicts over its meaning, seemed to live their lives according to the
highest standards preached by Christians. For Herbert and Blount,
God's inherent goodness meant that the means to salvation were
available to all men and women; thus no single set of beliefs could
be uniquely salvific.[68] Perhaps the example of the Greeks, upholding
the rule of reason and individual dignity in a pre-Christian setting,
was no aberration after all; perhaps there were common principles
of morality and goodness to be arrived at without the interference
of a clerical estate, principles which surpassed culturally conditioned
systems of belief.[69]

In 1696, a youthful John Toland published his *Christianity Not Mysterious* with the immodest intention of substituting a universally valid
natural theology for the ambiguities of Scripture, that source of re-
proachable imprecision which Toland, like the moderate churchmen,
was convinced had contributed so much to the religious violence of
the seventeenth century.[70] The book was presented as a nuisance by
the grand jury of Middlesex and ordered to be burnt by the parliament in Dublin, but the author confidently refused to abandon his
cause. "I hope to make it appear that the use of reason is not so dangerous in religion as it is commonly represented," he wrote in the
preface of what was to become one of the first important texts in
the Deist controversy, a request that seemed very much in keeping
with the spirit of Anglican rationalism.[71] Confident that the law of

nature was synonymous with reason and that the propriety of reason's mandate would be acknowledged by all sensible men, Toland
took angry exception to divines who would tell us "we must adore
what we cannot comprehend."[72]

The English Deists of the closing decade of the seventeenth century, although difficult to identify with a consistent school of thought,
consciously adopted many of the characteristics of the moderate
church position: a skeptical temper which called into question the authority of conflicting churches, a belief that reason could not contra-
dict revelation, a plain and popular style of exposition, and a focus
on moral behavior as the principal measure of piety. Indeed some of
the Deists saw their own religious perspective as a logical outgrowth
of the Anglican rationalism sponsored by the Latitudinarians. Their
effusive praise of their unsuspecting mentors—including Toland's
misleading quotation from Tillotson on the title page of *Christianity
Not Mysterious* and his facile attempt to link his own views with the
epistemological ideas of John Locke—was clearly designed to blunt
the anticipated criticism of their radical departure from orthodoxy.[73]
Rejecting Saint Thomas's conviction that "certain things that are true
about God wholly surpass the capability of human reason," Deism
challenged Anglicans to reconsider their century-old appropriation
of reason for the defense of traditional faith and placed the Latitudinarians in the awkward position of dissociating their own rational
theology from the newly discovered religion of nature.[74] For whatever their purported adherence to the values of the rationalist tradition, and despite their repeated protests that theirs was an effort to
restore the substance of the primitive faith, the Deists' understanding
of the competence of reason and their employment of skepticism
when evaluating revealed truths went far beyond anything allowed
by the moderate church divines. Peter Gay was correct when he suggested that the relation of Deism to its predecessors was a dialectical
one, both intimate and remote. They eagerly "learned what they
could and then rejected their preceptors," and while they may have
taken one step beyond Anglican rationalism, "the step they took was
across an unbridgeable abyss."[75]

There are numerous points at which the Deists turned to account
the theological rationalism preached by the moderate churchmen,
but at the heart of all their religious convictions was a special view
of human nature which the Latitudinarians simply could not share.
Rejecting the whole concept of a historic Fall resulting in the taint of

original sin, seeing no radical defect at the center of man's being, and convinced that evil was exclusively the product of bad environment, the Deists thought that achieving moral excellence was not only possible without the assistance of grace, but also a matter of relatively moderate exertion. According to Dryden, who shared the rationalism of the Latitudinarians, the Deist would tolerate no limits placed upon mankind's freedom and power:

> Thus Man by his own strength to Heaven wou'd soar:
> And wou'd not be Oblig'd to God for more.[76]

Such a perspective allowed the Deist to pretermit the role of Christ as Redeemer, for there was really no need for pardon through divine sacrifice when everyone could merit salvation through obedience to the moral law. The entire drama of Christ's suffering and death was, for Deism, reduced to a mere story of the life of one exceptionally good man. The feeling of sin, the need for grace, and the uncertainty of salvation were noteworthy only by their absence from a universe devoid of mystery thanks partly to the popularization of the new philosophy.[77]

Because their view of man's nature was abstract and unhistorical, the Deists blithely ignored the power of evil in human life and embraced an unaffected optimism about the human condition and the capacity of man to follow his own best interests. Rejecting the authority of monk, priest, and pastor, the efficacy of ceremony and sacrament, and the redeeming work of Christ as superficial accretions to primitive religion, they turned to ill-defined "nature" as their guide. Even revelation became redundant, for the divine word, when stripped of its multiple contradictions and absurdities, served merely to confirm the truths established through natural reason. According to Deism, God would not communicate his message to a primitive and superstitious people like the Jews of the Old Testament, nor would he violate his own perfect laws through direct providential action. When Toland declared that "there is nothing in the Gospel contrary to reason, nor above it," he was effectively reducing God's wisdom to the unbecoming level of human intelligence, making man the sole instrument of his own renewal. And in demanding that our assent should follow only clear and unequivocal demonstration, he was rejecting the sort of mitigated skepticism which had served the Latitudinarians so effectively throughout the Restoration period. Stillingfleet had observed this tendency as early as 1677, when he complained that the

Deists lacked "a great part of judgment and Understanding, to know the proportion and fitness of evidence to the Nature of the thing to be proved." If we follow the Deist principle and fail to proceed with belief or action until all possible objections are met, then our lives will come to a standstill, and we must even refuse to accept that the soul or the world of extended matter exists.[78] The Deists' ignorance of life's complexities, their insensitivity to any human dimension beyond the purely rational, their substitution of intellectual instruction for the support of grace, and their dogmatic insistence upon absolute certainty in matters of belief debilitated the inherent richness of religious experience and transformed personal devotion into a matter of simple ethics.

Toland, who enjoyed a slight acquaintance with John Locke, borrowed freely from the philosopher's *Essay Concerning Human Understanding* in defining reason as a discursive faculty and in discussing the origin of ideas.[79] Claiming the support of Locke's theory of ideas, Toland flatly rejected the historic Christian claim that reason is in some measure corrupt and depraved in every man. "Reason taken for the Principle of Discourse in us," he wrote, "or more particularly for that Faculty every one of us has of judging of his Ideas according to their Agreement or Disagreement, and so of loving what seems good unto him, and hating what he thinks evil: Reason, I say, in this Sense is whole and entire in every one whose Organs are not accidentally indispos'd."[80] Men may not always make a right use of this faculty, they might indulge their inclinations and frame wrong conceptions of things, but these are errors subject to gentle remediation. "There is no Defect in our Understandings but those of our own Creation," he intoned, for every person is capable of moral perfection through the reform of bad habits, and the failure to realize the life of reason cannot detract from the truth of this Pelagian principle.[81]

Toland had conveniently published *Christianity Not Mysterious* one year after Locke had entered the field of religious speculation with his *Reasonableness of Christianity* (1695). According to Locke, he had completed his small exercise with "some hope of doing some service to decaying piety, and mistaken and slandered Christianity."[82] The publication of the book, so clearly reflecting the values of the Latitudinarian divines, represented both a familiarity with the earlier works of Chillingworth, Hales, and Taylor and the culmination of a long friendship with some of the moderate churchmen. After moving from Oxford to London in 1667 in order to join the household of Anthony Ashley Cooper, Locke had made the acquaintance of Benjamin Whichcote, who had been offered the curacy of Saint Lawrence Jewry following the appointment of John Wilkins to the see of Chester. During the 1670s, Locke frequented the Lombard Street home of Thomas Firmin and, joined there by moderate clerics like Tillotson, Whichcote, and Edward Fowler, was introduced to the idea of the minimal creed and the conviction that conduct lay at the heart of Christianity.[83] Toward the end of his life, Locke would recommend the sermons of Tillotson, Whichcote, and Isaac Barrow as "masterpieces" of instruction in morality, works of spirituality and edification most in harmony with the message of Christ.[84] The philosopher endorsed the moderate skepticism of the Latitudinarians, affirming that an absolute rule of faith was unnecessary and that probable knowledge was sufficient to confirm the validity of Christian revelation. More importantly, he also accepted their picture of man's fallen nature in the wake of Adam's sin and the need for unmerited grace. Whereas Tillotson could preach with confidence that the minds of young Christians were "naturally inclin'd to that which is evil," Locke would write in the 1680s that sinful man must in charity "pray god for the assistance of his spirit for the enlightening of our understandings and subduing our corruption soe we may perform unto him a reasonable and acceptable service and shew our faith by our works."[85] Tillotson's unexpected death in 1694 left Locke "scarcely anyone whom I can freely consult about theological uncertainties."[86] The philosopher's own encounter with the Deist challenge serves to further illuminate the depth of the chasm which distinguished the Latitudinarians from their supposed intellectual heirs.

In the *Essay Concerning Human Understanding*, as we have previously observed, Locke had forcefully repudiated the concept of innate ideas which had undergirded the fixed moral order posited by Anglicans. He faced a torrent of criticism for suggesting that all our ideas, including ideas of God and morality, were products of experience, the result of sense impressions, and the reflection of the mind upon the ideas gathered from environment. But Locke firmly accepted the Anglican position that reason is our only reliable guide in distinguishing between genuine revelation and the fantasy of the enthusiast. Reason may be weak and subject to error, he acknowledged, but it remains the best compass we have to the truths of revelation and indeed to all truths above our grasp. Like the Latitudinarians, faith for Locke meant a settled assent built "upon the credit of the proposer as coming from God in some extraordinary way of communication."[87] And it was our reason which determined whether or not this testimony was satisfactory. To abandon this God-given guide would be to invite every form of religious excess and absurd claims to special inspiration, what Locke described as "the conceits of a warmed and overweaning brain."[88] But unlike Toland, Locke was careful not to limit knowledge to things that reason could grasp or that our senses could experience directly. Some truths, and the truths of revelation especially, were forever above the reach of limited human reason, albeit never contradictory to it: "Reason is natural revelation, whereby the eternal Father of Light and Fountain of all knowledge, communicates to mankind that portion of truth which he has laid within the reach of their natural faculties. Revelation is natural reason enlarged by a new set of discoveries communicated by God directly, which reason vouches the truth of by the testimony and proofs it gives that they come from God."[89] This crucial qualification, this Latitudinarian axiom, Toland and his Deist contemporaries could not accept, for to include as part of Christianity elements which the human mind could not fully understand was to open the door to arbitrary authority and interpretive confusion. Anthony Collins, another Deist who befriended Locke during the philosopher's final years, agreed wholeheartedly with Toland's position, while Locke's recognition of the limits of human understanding and mankind's pressing need for a supplementary guide to conduct was something which both "disciples" found convenient to disregard.[90]

In his *Reasonableness of Christianity*, a book which is often given credit for inaugurating the Deist critique of revealed religion, Locke accepted the plenary inspiration of the Bible but turned aside the surfeit of critical commentary in order to read the New Testament without prepossession. The simple message which emerged for Locke, the single creedal imperative which would qualify one as a believing Christian, was the acknowledgment of Jesus as Messiah. This, said Locke, "is all that is required to be believed by those who acknowledge but one eternal and invisible God."[91] And while such a bold exegesis might provide plausible grounds for Toland's claim of intellectual kinship, Locke, who had seen Toland's manuscript two years before its publication, was quick to point out that belief in Christ perforce involved belief in all that the Messiah had taught us, including the necessity of redemption from sin.[92] At the beginning of *The Reasonableness of Christianity*, Locke took issue with Deists who thought that there was no redemption necessary "and so made Jesus Christ nothing but the restorer and preacher of pure natural religion; thereby doing violence to the whole tenor of the New Testament."[93] Confident that no man could fulfill the law and claim righteousness for himself, Locke wrote that it was our faith in Christ as redeemer which alone supplies the defect in our attempts at righteousness, defects which are inevitable because of our incapacity to obey since the Fall.[94] Any suggestion that the minimal creed obviated the call for gratuitous pardon through the sacrifice of Christ met with an immediate denial on the part of Locke, who later compared his own view of the Messiah with that of his late friend Tillotson.[95]

Deists like Toland confused Locke's epistemology with his anthropology, believing that by his rejection of innate knowledge Locke was denying that man had a particular nature—good or bad—at birth and thus any need for a redeemer in the person of Christ. Locke's own experience of man's inveterate sinfulness, however, an experience he shared with his Latitudinarian friends, was the central assumption which informed *The Reasonableness of Christianity*. At the same time that he equated the duties of faith with the rule of reason, he iterated the pressing need for revelation due to the practical limits of reason in most men and of their consequent failure to follow its dictates. Locke's insistence that religion must be tested by reason, then, did not mean that he advocated the natural religion of the Deists or even that he gave precedence to "Nature" over revelation. While the works of nature, "in every part of them, sufficiently evidence a Deity," he said, "yet the world made so little use of their reason, that they saw him not, where, even by the impressions of himself, he was easy to be found."[96] According to Locke, the knowledge of morality "makes but a slow progress, and little advance in the world" because of the passions, interests, and vices of men.[97] Since the greatest part of mankind cannot know, they must accept, through belief, the plain rules of morality delivered in Scripture.[98] And he was resigned to the fact that unassisted human reason had largely failed men in the business of morality, had "never from unquestionable principles, by clear deductions, made out an entire body of the law of nature."[99] There could be no more direct rejection of the essential Deist position than this statement, and it was only by a process of careful selection that any other message could be extracted from *The Reasonableness of Christianity*.

As we have seen, Locke, like his Latitudinarian friends, insisted that reason must judge the validity of revelation and exhorted men to test all claims to special inspiration. But it is perhaps worth recalling in this context that the one virtue he praised most about the earliest apostles was their "implicit trust" in Christ, their believing him to be the Messiah, and their innocence from skepticism. They were "a company of poor, ignorant, illiterate men" who, unlike those of greater knowledge, were not to be found prying into Christ's designs, questioning his motives, or prematurely revealing his identity as Messiah.[100] Locke saw these trusting men, who kept Christ's commands and humbly obeyed their commission, as embodying the highest quality of obedience by virtue of their simple faith in God's power to save and to forgive. In fact he wondered whether Saint Paul, "by his learning, parts, and warmer temper," was not better fitted to be an apostle after the conclusion of Christ's ministry, when an open proclamation of his real nature was desired.[101] The first apostles only came to understand the full nature of Christ's kingdom and message for mankind with the assistance of the Holy Spirit.[102] An independent mind and the right to free inquiry were consistently championed by Locke, but he nonetheless reserved his deepest respect for those persons who placed their faith before their ambitious intellect, a characteristic not to be found within Deist circles.

Deism would continue to ignite the passions of contending parties well into the Augustan Age, reaching its height with the publication in 1730 of Matthew Tindal's *Christianity As Old As Creation*, a work which includes repeated references to Tillotson's sermons, and calling forth a number of rejoinders by ambitious clerics who sought preferment through theological controversy. By their assaults on the authority of the institutional church and their refusal to countenance miracle, mystery, or particular providence, the Deists represented the outermost limits of a rationalist theology built around the idea of finding constructive alternatives to the incessant feuding within the family of English Protestants. Later apologists for the tradition of Anglican rationalism like William Law and Bishop Butler would be more successful than the Latitudinarians in pointing up the inadequacy of reason to solve the larger mysteries of life—the relation of soul to body, the origin of evil, the nature of wisdom and goodness— and the presumption involved in the Deist restriction of divine reason to the level of its insignificant human counterpart.[103] But that later effort to refute Deism in no respect diminishes the significance of the gulf which separated the first generation of Deists from an embattled

Latitudinarian bench. The moderate church apologists for a more reasonable faith could still find comfort and direction in the majesty of God, the incomprehensibility of his full nature, the transcendence of his power and will, the generosity of his forgiveness. These singular attributes were diminished to the purview of the human compass by works like *Christianity Not Mysterious*, while the labor of Deism's principal spokesmen to link their world of clear ideas and pellucid moral precepts with the official leaders of the church secured for the Latitudinarians an undeserved place in the history of ideas. The Deist campaign may have been brief, and Burke may have been correct in writing its epitaph in 1790, but it was, nevertheless, an influential campaign which has, among other things, effectively defined our historical understanding of the Latitudinarians, overshadowing their deep commitment to a point of view very much in harmony with the temper of the seventeenth century and quite out of keeping with the ruling assumptions of the eighteenth.

CONCLUSION

The dissimilarity of opinion on matters of doctrine, ecclesiology, and discipline which Paul Elmer More once noted as a central characteristic of seventeenth-century Anglican writers doubtless owed something to the fact that there was no English Luther or Calvin to whom contending parties could reference their appeal.[1] Boasting of no master except the Word of God in Scripture, which everyone agreed "containeth all things necessary to salvation,"[2] English Protestants in the years before the Civil War discovered through the crucible of experience that the errors of the human mind, together with the inescapable depravity of each sinful inquirer, left little room for consensus over the substance and intendment of crucial passages in Holy Writ. As in the rest of Europe during the first half of that bellicose century, recourse to arms had failed to inaugurate the rule of the godly, and in the aftermath of war and the failed Puritan experiment in government, the previously derided "middle way" of searching out the fundamentals of the faith while exercising moderation and restraint—the voice of sixteenth-century humanists like Erasmus and Colet—received a serious if much-belated hearing. Reclaiming reason as a valid epistemological tool in the study of Scripture and incorporating what they believed to be the best of church tradition into a nondogmatic model of a comprehensive Protestant communion, the Latitude-men sought to salvage the vision of a unified national church despite the failure of men to reconcile their understanding of the written word in Scripture. Their defense of the Church of England as the model best fitted to further the interests of a single Christian community was, paradoxically, largely the product of their adiaphorism, where rites and actions not strictly forbidden by Scripture can and should be adopted in the interest of good order and worship. The logic employed against Calvinist theologians by Richard Hooker in the late sixteenth century, then, continued to play a not-insignificant role in the thought of the moderate churchmen. In fact, the men of latitude viewed themselves as the heirs of a genuine Catholic tradition first articulated by Hooker, and their pastoral activities, together with their preaching after 1660, were designed to build upon the work of that great apologist.

Unlike the majority of the clerical establishment after 1660, however, the Latitudinarians were genuinely interested in pursuing a dialogue with Dissenters, hoping that moderates like Baxter would eventually come to see that by conforming to the established church they would compromise neither their theology nor their self-respect. In this search for a comprehension, punctuated by disappointments in Parliament, royal prevarication and deceit, High Church opposition, periodic impatience with and insensitivity towards their dissenting opposites, and, of greatest moment, a desire to restore a Christian ideal of temporal society where the church would speak with a single voice on matters of behavior in this world pursuant to one's fortune in the next, the Latitudinarian divines set themselves apart from the rest of the episcopally ordained clergy. This latter goal, what Paul Johnson has described as a "compulsory society of faith," was premised on a picture of mankind which held little confidence in the ability of heterogeneous communions to arrive at a common Christian pattern of life.[3] The emergence of the church as a voluntary association, made possible by the Toleration Act, was a development neither anticipated nor welcomed by the bishops who were charged with respecting its mandate during the course of the 1690s. The prospect of English Christians going their separate ways was, perhaps, the least palatable aspect of their tenure on the episcopal bench.

It is also obvious that the moderates were motivated in their search for a comprehension by a variety of motives, and some of these—a commonplace fear of Catholicism, a desire to maintain the existing social and political order, and an all-too-human ambition to enhance one's own power and prestige, be it individual or institutional—were hardly laudable. Still, despite these very real shortcomings, the initiative in efforts to end those divisions which had proved so destructive of human life in the recent past were taken almost exclusively by a small group of individuals who have, ironically, most often been remembered for undermining the faith which they had ostensibly set out to fortify. Given the assumptions and the prejudices of their day— the widespread impatience to crush dissent after 1660, the bland association of Nonconformity with sedition, and a reflexive Erastianism which, under the fourth Stuart monarch, became an intolerable dilemma—the Latitudinarian disposition to respect at least the theological sincerity of the moderate Dissenters held considerable value for an inchoate ecumenism. At the end of our period Henry Saceverell could write in derision that the moderate might profess himself to be a Church of England man, "yet he has that tender regard to weak brethren, that upon occasion he can see the inside of a conventicle, be of any synagogue but that of Satan and can show more signs of devotion at the heat and rapture of an extempore cant than at the flat forms of the undignified liturgy."[4] Such intemperate remarks, although clearly designed to stir up High Church antipathy against the Latitudinarian episcopate, unwittingly acknowledged that the Latitudinarian search for a comprehensive church was exceptional even in defeat.

To link these moderate divines with the rational theology of the Enlightenment, however, is to overlook the particular context in which they wrote and preached. For if the effort to distinguish between the constitutive and the accessory—the essentials of the faith and the practices borne of convention and convenience—lay at the core of the theology espoused by the men labeled Latitudinarians, then the efforts of the moderates must be evaluated in light of a tradition begun by Hooker at the close of the Elizabethan period. If opposition to both Catholic and radical Protestant infallibilists (the one upholding the pretensions of the papacy and the other insisting upon the transparency of Scripture) be a hallmark of Latitudinarian thought, then one must associate almost every seventeenth-century Anglican apologist with this movement in ideas. If the appeal to reason be a measure of an affinity with Deism, then the moderate churchmen can no more be identified as the sole progenitors of that hostile force than the medieval successors to Aquinas. And if a preference for the practical aspects of Christianity can be associated with the rise of moralism and the consequent erosion of interest in the mystery of salvation, then the entire seventeenth-century established church must inevitably be included in the indictment. The new sect of Latitude-men, as Patrick had petitioned as early as 1662, did "sincerely embrace all the Articles of Doctrine held forth by the Church, they cheerfully use and approve her Liturgy and Ceremonies, they cordially love and obey her government." Even their interest in the new philosophy, which some interpreted as a preference for mechanistic explanations of reality, was designed from the start to maintain the credit of the church with the gentry, to "free religion from scorn and contempt." Most importantly, the term of reproach which was attached to them for their unwillingness "to knock people on the head because they are not of our Church" could not attenuate the fact that the moderate churchmen shared with their most vociferous detractors a picture of man's estate which forever precluded any possibility of eternal happiness without the benefaction of the supernatural, without the extenuation of Christ's final act of obedience to the undeserving whole of humanity.[5]

During the course of the Enlightenment, the religious impulse which had for centuries been integral to the spiritual and psychological equipoise of educated men would gradually retreat from its privileged position at the apex of intellectual pursuit. In its place a reawakened interest in the temporal and the contingent, in man's environment and in ameliorating both his physical and his social condition, signaled the eclipse of the ecclesiastical world and all its ancilliary concerns. At the same time, the age-old picture of reason as the mirror of the divine mind—where the finite participates in the nature of the eternal and is permitted to know certain essential truths a priori—began to give way before a new and more modest understanding of intellect, one where function replaced being, where reason was viewed as an acquisition, an energy or force which enables one to know through the data of experience.[6] The absentee creator of the Deists, a God who had made the world but lived apart from it, content to observe its operation in accordance with fixed laws, seemed admirably designed to complement the popularized version of the Newtonian universe, while the epistemological innovations associated with Locke's *Essay Concerning Human Understanding* freed the eighteenth century to look anew at the pessimistic anthropological assumptions associated with historic Christianity. For many, a practical ethics would now stand proudly in the place of theology, the life of reason would become a sound substitute for the chronic distempers occasioned by the multiple ambiguities of Scripture. The numinous came to be equated with intellectual immaturity and the deceit of men and institutions interested only in perpetuating the religious vassalage of the majority, while the sense of empowerment associated with natural theology emboldened not a few to place all trust in the sufficiency of the reasoning faculty. It would take nothing less than the radical empiricism of David Hume before the exposure of reason as simply the most recent version of "faith" was placed in a clear, albeit disturbing, light.

With this alternative picture of man's potential in a world devoid of mystery, the Latitudinarians, we have suggested, had very little to do. Despite their enthusiasm for the new philosophy, they continued to view the world and everything in it as the free creation, *ex nihilo*, of a transcendent, omnipotent, yet loving God who, although a spiritual being, is capable of being comprehended by man. Because there is a divinely ordained order to creation, man is graciously fitted to understand something of that masterwork through scientific inquiry. But the God of the Latitude-men was not precluded from direct intervention in his creation. The active sovereignty of God, the immediate and constant presence of a spiritual being whose concern for the eternal welfare of man was evidenced in his acts of encouragement and retribution, remained a cornerstone of Latitudinarian thought notwithstanding the popularity of the mechanical model articulated by the proponents of the new science. God's sustaining force, at once transcendent and immanent, was in fact most clearly exhibited in the orderly disposition of physical creation. The habit of anthropomorphism, so prominent a part of the medieval world picture, continued to afford eschatological comfort and spiritual security to a generation buffeted by the growth of religious heterodoxy and the fear of atheism. A host of images derived from human relationships was used by the moderate churchmen to detail God's character, and each of them implied a pattern of love for mankind which exceeded all hope of full reciprocation on the part of finite beings. There was never any effort to equate the image of the divine with human excellence when employing descriptive language appropriate for man, only an unpretentious desire to communicate some small sense of the nature and power of the Eternal Father in terms that every Christian could understand.

The Latitudinarians accepted an orthodox theodicy where the problem of evil was attributed to man's voluntary repudiation of God's love, his refusal to accept what he was meant to be, what one twentieth-century author has called an act of self-will "which constitutes an utter falseness to its true creaturely position."[7] They saw sin not as belonging to separate individuals, as was the wont of anti-

Augustinians from the fifth-century to the late seventeenth-century Deists, but rather as a fundamental characteristic of the entire human race, a radical corruption of the will which ultimately manifests itself in particular acts of disobedience. Rejecting the possibility of an independent force for evil in a world created good, the moderate churchmen, like Saint Augustine, interpreted all evil as the disordering or privation of a mutable good which could only be remedied through the intervention of Christ.[8] Without a doctrine of sin and a theory of human depravity, of course, Christianity simply would not have made sense to thinking men and women in the seventeenth century.[9] The acceptance of the fact that all men have fallen short of the standard set for them is at the heart of the Christian story, where sin is not simply the fortuitous product of habit but the symptom of an inward disease which alienates us from our maker. For the moderate churchmen, as for all Anglicans, the fall of man in Adam had placed the meaning of free will in an entirely new and more restrictive light, one where freedom to choose the good and the power to pursue it flowed from the blessings of the supreme sacrifice, where all necessary soteriological resources lay outside the purview of human nature.

According to the popular sermons of the moderate churchmen, it was only through the intervention of Christ that men had passed out of darkness and into the possibility of eternal life. Article X of the Thirty-nine Articles had emphatically denied man's power to do good works without the grace of God by Christ. All human merit was precluded in the moderate church vision of salvation, although works remained a sign of God's grace active within the saved man. The new life in Christ was only proved by the changed conduct of sinners who now lived according to the precepts of the Gospel; thus the Latitudinarians took seriously Christ's repeated references to reward and recompense based on behavior in this life.[10] Believing that the fundamental demand made by Christ on those who sought to participate in God's glory was that they should repent, the Latitudinarians could not in good conscience divorce their piety from simple moral obligations.[11] For all Anglicans and particularly for the Latitudinarians, the point of Christ's redemption was that men might become good before God—not that they might merit salvation but that a gracious God might respond as if our actions had contained some inherent value—and no view of the Atonement would satisfy which did not transform men into the very likeness of Christ.[12] The English descendants of Calvin, it was thought, had failed to affirm that primary desideratum of the faith and in their negligence had contributed not a little to the lamentable state of contemporary Protestantism, divided, as it was, into hostile camps and serving as testimony to the strength of the Catholic position on the need for order from above lest there be theological chaos from below.

By seeking out the fundamentals of the faith, by defending the power of God-given reason in settling religious questions, the Latitudinarians doubtless contributed to an intellectual climate in which men hoped to settle their religious differences through the aid of natural theology alone. What was a useful support of revelation in the sermons of clerics who had experienced civil war and religious hatred became in the pamphlets of younger men a facile solution to the evil which, according to the Christian story, lay at the heart of the human dilemma. Archbishop Tillotson, like all his predecessors at Canterbury, did not believe that this evil could be excised here in our earthly state. Men like Toland emphatically disagreed, and whatever fate may have befallen Deism as a credible body of thought by the mid-eighteenth century, it was Toland's anthropology, not Tillotson's, which became the common possession of that more confident period. During the course of what for the sake of convenience has been labeled the "Age of Englightenment," autonomy replaced the arbitrariness of divine grace and spiritual dependence in the minds of those who felt that the mystery of religion had too often been a force for ill in the world. And the theological vision of the Latitude-men, the protracted search for unity without coercion anchored in a traditional picture of mankind's sorrow without Christ, gradually became as friendless as the message contained in Augustine's *City of God,* as unwelcome as the memory of those two hundred African bishops who, meeting in the city of Carthage in 418, formally condemned the heretical teaching of a British ascetic and reformer named Pelagius.

NOTES

Introduction

1. Margaret Jacob, *The Newtonians and the English Revolution* (Ithaca: Cornell University Press, 1976), has discussed the social and political outlook of the Latitudinarians in connection with the new science, but their theology has not been closely examined. Norman Sykes, *From Sheldon to Secker: Aspects of English Church History, 1660–1768* (Cambridge: Cambridge University Press, 1959), 146, stresses the wide diversity of opinion which Latitudinarianism covered, thus making generalizations difficult. Jacob, *Newtonians*, 29, concurs with this assessment. Sir George Clark, *The Later Stuarts, 1660–1714*, 2d ed. (Oxford: Clarendon Press, 1961), 33, thought that the Latitudinarians "were outside the mainstream of Anglican theology," while more recently John Spurr, "Latitudinarianism and the Restoration Church," *The Historical Journal* 31, no. 1 (1988): 61–82, takes the opposite view and questions the whole notion of a distinctive Latitudinarian group within Anglicanism after 1660.

2. Edward A. George, *Seventeenth-Century Men of Latitude* (New York: Scribner's, 1908); William E. H. Lecky, *A History of England in the Eighteenth Century* (London: Longmans, Green, and Co., 1888), 1:84–85. John Tulloch, *Rational Theology and Christian Philosophy in the Seventeenth Century* (Edinburgh: Blackwood, 1872), 1:76, believed that late seventeenth-century Anglican divinity was "rationalist to the core." Tulloch was primarily interested in the background to the Latitudinarians. Macaulay, *History of England from the Accession of James II* (London: Longmans, Green, Reader, & Dyer, 1873), 1:163, identified Latitudinarianism with "constitutional principles of government" and argued, incorrectly, that the Latitude-men would have granted toleration to all Protestant sects. See also M. W. Robinson, *A History of the Church of England*, 2d ed. (London: Longmans, Green, and Co., 1933), 374. Mark Pattison's work is an important exception to this nineteenth-century Whig bias. See his "Tendencies of Religious Thought in England, 1688–1750" in *Essays*, ed. Henry Nettleship (Oxford: Clarendon Press, 1889), 2:42–118.

3. Cragg, *Reason and Authority in the Eighteenth Century* (Cambridge: Cambridge University Press, 1970), 60. See the same author's *The Church in the Age of Reason*

(London: Pelican, 1980), 72, and *From Puritanism to the Age of Reason* (Cambridge: Cambridge University Press, 1950), 29. Mark Pattison, *Essays*, 2:42, described the last two decades of the century as "an age destitute of depth or earnestness," while Cragg, *Reason and Authority*, 20, 29, has described "the unabashed hedonism of this complacent period which acknowledged few limits," an age where there "was no longer any deep concern with the doctrine of grace." See also C. F. Allison, *The Rise of Moralism: The Proclamation of the Gospel from Hooker to Baxter* (New York: Seabury Press, 1966), 150; Arthur M. Wilson, "The Enlightenment Came First to England," in Stephen Baxter, ed., *England's Rise to Greatness* (Berkeley: University of California Press, 1983), 5; C. John Somerville, *Popular Religion in Restoration England* (Gainesville: University of Florida Press, 1976), 73; id., "The Anti-Puritan Work Ethic," *Journal of British Studies* 20, no. 2 (1981): 79, where many important Anglican leaders are seen to advocate "a bookkeeper's approach to virtue."

4. Quoting Cragg, *Reason and Authority*, 60.
5. Davies, *Worship and Theology in England from Andrewes to Baxter and Foxe, 1603–1690* (Princeton: Princeton University Press, 1975), 183–84. Davies first stated this criticism in *Worship and Theology in England from Watts and Wesley to Maurice, 1690–1850* (Princeton: Princeton University Press, 1961), 56. See also Irene Simon, ed., *Three Restoration Divines: Barrow, South, Tillotson* (Paris, 1967), Introduction; Dewey D. Wallace, *Puritans and Predestination: Grace in English Protestant Theology, 1525–1695* (Chapel Hill: University of North Carolina Press, 1982), 171; Jackson Cope, *Joseph Glanvill: Anglican Apologist* (St. Louis: Washington University Press, 1956), 85–86; Richard E. Sullivan, *John Toland and the Deist Controversy* (Cambridge: Harvard University Press, 1982), 55. Frank Manuel, *The Religion of Isaac Newton* (Oxford: Oxford University Press, 1974), 116, speaks of Anglican preachers who "soothed self-satisfied parishioners with rationalist reassurances that their faith did not require too much of them, that its burdens were not oppressive."
6. Basil Willey, *The Seventeenth-Century Background*, (London: Chatto and Windus, 1934), 133–69, contains a typically sympathetic treatment of the Platonists. In his introduction to *The Cambridge Platonists* (New York: Oxford University Press, 1968), 9, Cragg writes that the Latitudinarians "lacked the subtle sense of spiritual truth, the mystical awareness of an eternal order, which marked the older generation of Cambridge men." See also Sykes, *Sheldon to Secker*, 150–51. Much of the reason for the popularity of the Platonists has to do with their never having won enemies as pulpit preachers and active figures in the life of the church. They remained, by and large, behind the walls of the academy throughout their careers (Whichcote was the most prominent exception.)
7. Cragg, *Church in the Age of Reason*, 158. Christopher Hill, "Sin and Society," in *The Collected Essays of Christopher Hill* (Amherst: University of Massachusetts Press, 1985–86), 2:132, says that the Latitudinarians gradually took control of the church. Cf. Hill, *Some Intellectual Consequences of the English Revolution* (Madison: University of Wisconsin Press, 1980), 69.
8. While the term "Latitudinarian" was used throughout the eighteenth and nineteenth centuries to describe churchmen who emphasized an individual interpretation of Scripture, this study seeks to examine its original seventeenth-century context. John Gascoigne, *Cambridge in the Age of Enlightenment: Science, Religion and Politics from the Restoration to the French Revolution* (Cambridge: Cambridge Univer-

sity Press, 1989), traces the Latitudinarian tradition into the eighteenth-century church.

9. On the first two problems, Geoffrey Holmes, *Politics, Religion and Society in England, 1679–1742* (London: Hambledon Press, 1986), 187, writes that "The first half of the seventeenth century in England bequeathed two extremely powerful phobias to the second half of the century. And circumstances conspired to make these phobias stronger than ever between 1670 and 1700. One was the fear of Popery; the other was the fear of Puritan fanaticism, of a Second Coming of the Saints."

10. Gordon Rupp, *Religion in England, 1688–1791* (Oxford: Oxford University Press, 1986), 37, 41. H. R. McAdoo, *The Spirit of Anglicanism: A Survey of Anglican Theological Method in the Seventeenth Century* (London: Adam and Charles Black, 1965), 174; Louis Bredvold, *The Intellectual Milieu of John Dryden* (Ann Arbor: University of Michigan Press, 1934), 80, and Howard Schultz, *Milton and Forbidden Knowledge* (New York: Modern Language Association, 1955), 171, like Rupp, are more sympathetic toward the method employed by the moderate churchmen and are more appreciative of their seriousness. G. R. Cragg, in *Reason and Authority*, 61, does acknowledge some of the positive contributions of the Latitudinarians in the late seventeenth century, but the thrust of his argument is highly critical. Roland Stromberg, *Religious Liberalism in Eighteenth-Century England* (Oxford: Clarendon Press, 1954), 1–2, argues that the hostile eighteenth-century critique of Latitudinarianism was in large part a product of the Methodist movement.

11. For a discussion of this tradition and its transmission to England, see Margo Todd, *Christian Humanism and the Puritan Social Order* (Cambridge: Cambridge University Press, 1987), chapters 2 and 3.

12. Alan C. Clifford, *Atonement and Justification: English Evangelical Theology, 1640–1790* (Oxford: Clarendon Press, 1990), 41, 43; Spurr, "Latitudinarianism," 61–82; Gerard Reedy, S.J., *The Bible and Reason: Anglicans and Scripture in Late Seventeenth-Century England* (Philadelphia: University of Pennsylvania Press, 1985), 11.

13. Quoting Basil Willey, *The Eighteenth-Century Background* (Boston: Beacon Press, 1961), 3.

14. Diversity of opinion among Anglican writers was one of the hallmarks of a church which acknowledged no single theologian or authority as the arbiter of disputes. One must search for direction rather than finality within the Anglican communion. See Paul Elmer More and Frank Leslie Cross, eds., *Anglicanism: The Thought and Practice of the Church of England, Illustrated from the Religious Literature of the Seventeenth Century* (London: Society for Promoting Christian Knowledge, 1935), xx. Puritans could also combine a "general unity of purpose" with disagreements over specific issues. See John Morgan, *Godly Learning: Puritan Attitudes Towards Reason, Learning and Education, 1560–1640* (Cambridge: Cambridge University Press, 1986), 2.

15. R. Buick Knox, "Bishops in the Pulpit in the Seventeenth Century: Continuity and Change," in Knox, ed., *Reformation, Conformity and Dissent: Essays in Honor of Geoffrey Nuttall* (London: Epworth Press, 1977), 92–112, has identified the correspondence between the teaching of bishops throughout the course of the seventeenth century in a number of areas, suggesting that Latitudinarians like Tillotson were much closer to their pre–Civil War episcopal counterparts than they were to late seventeenth-century Deists.

16. See, for example, Pepys, *Diary*, ed. Robert Latham and William Matthews (Berkeley: University of California Press, 1970–1983), 2:167, 190.
17. R. H. Tawney's argument that the attitude described here had been abandoned by the latter half of the seventeenth century stands in need of revision. See *Religion and the Rise of Capitalism* (Gloucester, Mass.: Peter Smith, 1962).
18. Quoting Thomas Wood, *English Casuistical Divinity During the Seventeenth Century* (London: Society for Promoting Christian Knowledge, 1952), xii.

1 : The Origins of Latitudinarianism

1. Simon Patrick, *A Brief Account of the New Sect of Latitude-Men* (1662), ed. T. A. Birrell (Los Angeles: University of California Press, 1963), 4–5. Birrell notes that authorship of the pamphlet has been questioned but provides evidence which indicates that the work belonged to Patrick. Cf. Gascoigne, *Cambridge in the Age of Enlightenment*, 40–41; Rupp, *Religion in England*, 29.
2. On the reaction at Cambridge, see John Gascoigne, "Politics, Patronage and Newtonianism: The Cambridge Example," *The Historical Journal* 27, no. 1 (1984): 4–7; id., *Cambridge in the Age of Enlightenment*, 29–35; Marjorie Nicholson, "Christ's College and the Latitude Men," *Modern Philology* 27 (1929): 35–53, and Gilbert Burnet, *Supplement to Burnet's History*, ed. H. C. Foxcroft (Oxford: Clarendon Press, 1902), 464. On Tillotson, see Clifford, *Atonement and Justification*, 36.
3. Patrick, *Brief Account*, 5. He subsequently stated his preference for "liberty of conscience" as long as a man leads "the most unblameable life." Ibid., 11. More confirms their loyalty to church and state. See Marjorie Nicholson, ed., *The Conway Letters* (New Haven: Yale University Press, 1930), 230.
4. *Brief Account*, 9. Glanvill supported Patrick's claim here. See Jackson Cope, "The Cupri-Cosmits: Glanvill on Latitudinarian Anti-Enthusiasm," *Huntington Library Quarterly* 17, no. 3 (1954): 171. We will return to this important theme in chapter 3.
5. *Brief Account*, 10–11. Joseph Glanvill's thinly disguised story of life for the moderate churchmen at Oxford during the Interregnum is similar to Patrick's description of Cambridge. See Glanvill, "Anti-Fanatical Religion, and Free Philosophy," in *Essays on Several Important Subjects in Philosophy and Religion* (London: John Baker, 1676).
6. Baxter noted that the Latitudinarians were "mostly Cambridge men" (*Reliquiae Baxterianae*, ed. Matthew Sylvester [London: T. Parkhurst, 1697], part 2, 386), while Henry More, writing to Lady Conway in 1665, said that "they push hard at the latitude men as they call them." (*Conway Letters*, 243). See also Gilbert Burnet, *Supplement to Burnet's History*, 463–64.
7. Spurr, "Latitudinarianism," 62–64.
8. David Lloyd, *Wonders No Miracles* (1661), quoted in Spurr, "Latitudinarianism," 63.
9. Kenneth E. Kirk, *The Vision of God: The Christian Doctrine of the Summum Bonum* (London: Longmans, 1931), 330–35.
10. On the relationship between the northern humanists and reformed Christianity, see Alister McGrath, *The Intellectual Origins of the European Reformation* (Oxford: Basil Blackwell, 1987), 41–68. Cf. Hugh Trevor-Roper, "The Religious Origins of the Enlightenment," in *Religion, the Reformation and Social Change* (London: Macmillan, 1972), 219; C. Sydney Carter, *The English Church and the Reformation* (London: Longmans, 1915), 9–17, and Carlos M. W. Eire, *War Against the Idols: The*

Reformation of Worship from Erasmus to Calvin (Cambridge: Cambridge University Press, 1986), 45–53.

11. Robert Hoopes, *Right Reason in the English Renaissance* (Cambridge: Harvard University Press, 1962), 107–21. Cf. George Tavard, *Holy Writ or Holy Church* (New York: Harper and Brothers, 1955), 80–110; Myron P. Gilmore, *The World of Humanism* (New York: Harper Torchbooks, 1962), 204–28; H. Wheeler Robinson, *The Christian Doctrine of Man* (Edinburgh: T. & T. Clark, 1947), 215–28; Sydney Cave, *The Christian Estimate of Man* (London: Duckworth, 1944), 126–56; John T. McDonough, "The Essential Luther," in John C. Olin, ed., *Luther, Erasmus and the Reformation* (New York: Fordham University Press, 1969), 59–66. On the English humanists, see Fritz Caspari, *Humanism and the Social Order in Tudor England* (Chicago: University of Chicago Press, 1954); Todd, *Christian Humanism*, chapter 2.

12. James K. McConica, *English Humanists and Reformation Politics* (Oxford: Clarendon Press, 1965), 26; Tulloch, *Rational Theology*, 1:2–3; Richard Popkin, *The History of Scepticism from Erasmus to Spinoza* (London: University of California Press, 1979), chapter 1. On biblical criticism and religious radicalism in the seventeenth century, see Christopher Hill, *The World Turned Upside Down* (New York: Viking, 1972), 208–15.

13. Erasmus-Luther, *Discourse on Free Will*, trans. and ed. Ernst F. Winter (New York: Frederick Ungar Publishing, 1961), 7, 100. Luther defined his assertion as "a constant adhering to and affirming of your position, avowing and defending it, and invincibly persevering in it. . . . Far be it from us Christians to be sceptics and academics." Ibid., 100–101.

14. Popkin, *History of Scepticism*, 19, 33; Henry G. Van Leeuwen, *The Problem of Certainty in English Thought, 1630–1690* (The Hague: Martinus Nijhoff, 1963); C. B. Schmitt, "The Rediscovery of Ancient Scepticism in Modern Times" in Myles Burnyeat, ed., *The Sceptical Tradition* (Berkeley: University of California Press, 1983), 225–42.

15. Percival Chubb, ed., and John Florio, trans., *Essays of Montaigne* (London: Walter Scott, n.d.), 79. During the Restoration, Montaigne's reputation reached its peak in England, while the works of Pierre Charron were also translated into English. Bredvold, *Intellectual Milieu*, 47. See also Perseved Smith, *The Social Background of the Reformation* (New York: Collier Books, 1967), 166–69; Don Cameron Allen, *Doubt's Boundless Sea: Scepticism and Faith in the Renaissance* (Baltimore: Johns Hopkins University Press, 1964), 79–97, and Terence Penelhum, *God and Scepticism: A Study in Scepticism and Fideism* (Dordrecht, Holland: D. Reidel Co., 1983), 22–25.

16. Schmitt, "Rediscovery of Scepticism," 228; Bredvold, *Intellectual Milieu*, 17–18.

17. Hooker, *Laws of Ecclesiastical Polity* (Oxford: Oxford University Press, 1875), book 1, chapter 2, 5–6. On Hooker's opponents, see Robert K. Faulkner, *Richard Hooker and the Politics of a Christian England* (Berkeley: University of California Press, 1981), 13–58.

18. Peter Lake, *Anglicans and Puritans?: Presbyterian and English Conformist Thought from Whitgift to Hooker* (London: Unwin Hyman, 1988), 151.

19. John S. Marshall, *Hooker and the Anglican Tradition* (London: Adam and Charles Black, 1963), provides a good analysis of Hooker's thought. See also Peter Munz, *The Place of Hooker in the History of Thought* (London: Routledge and Kegan Paul, 1952), 29–67, for a discussion of Hooker's borrowings from Aquinas; and Hoopes,

168 : Notes to Pages 17–20

Right Reason, 123–45. The emphasis on pastoral care would provide a centerpiece of later Latitudinarian thought.

20. Lake, *Anglicans and Puritans?*, 196.

21. *Laws*, book 5, chapter 6, 2. See also, Bernard M. G. Reardon, *Religious Thought in the Reformation* (New York: Longmans, 1981), 282. On Hooker's view of the Church of England's ties with Rome, see Conrad Russell, *Origins of the English Civil War* (Oxford: Clarendon Press, 1990), 96–97; and Paul Avis, *Anglicanism and the Christian Church* (Edinburgh: T. & T. Clark, 1989), 51, who writes that Hooker "was unswayed by the understandable anti-papal paranoia of a time when Roman Catholicism stood for treason as well as heresy."

22. Carl Bangs, "Arminius and the Reformation," *Church History* 30 (June 1961): 158–63, and id., *Arminius: A Study in the Dutch Reformation* (Nashville: University of Tennessee Press, 1971). See also R. T. Kendall, *Calvin and English Calvinism* (Oxford: Oxford University Press, 1979), 141–50; Arthur C. McGiffert, *Protestant Thought Before Kant* (London: Duckworth, 1911), 188–89, and A. W. Harrison, *Arminianism* (London, 1937). Laud quoted in L. J. Reeve, *Charles I and the Road to Personal Rule* (Cambridge: Cambridge University Press, 1989), 64, n. 38. As Reeve points out, Laud's Arminianism was clericalist in nature, and he certainly objected to enhancing the power of the laity through individual interpretation of Scripture.

23. Grotius, *The Truth of the Christian Religion* (London: Richard Royston, 1680), 81, 94. The book was originally published in Dutch in 1622. The Latitudinarian Simon Patrick would translate the work into English in 1680, adding his own final chapter which concluded with a long quote from Erasmus on the virtues of ignoring nonessential doctrines.

24. Willey, *Seventeenth-Century Background*, 121–32, places Herbert within context. See also Popkin, *History of Scepticism*, 151–57; R. D. Bedford, *The Defence of Truth: Herbert of Cherbury and the Seventeenth Century* (Manchester: University of Manchester Press, 1979); John M. Robertson, *A Short History of Freethought* (London: Watts and Co., 1915), 2:69–71; Harold R. Hutcheson, ed. and trans., *Lord Herbert of Cherbury's De Religione Laici* (New Haven: Yale University Press, 1944), 17–20.

25. Lord Herbert, *De Veritate*, quoted in Willey, 126.

26. On the English background to the Synod, see Nicholas Tyacke, *Anti-Calvinists: The Rise of English Arminianism* (Oxford: Clarendon Press, 1986), 87–93.

27. Alan P. F. Snell, *The Great Debate: Calvinism, Arminianism and Salvation* (Worthing, England: H. E. Walter, 1982), 14.

28. Hales was chaplain to Sir Dudley Carelton, English ambassador to The Hague, and it was in this capacity that he was in attendance at Dort. James H. Elson, *John Hales of Eton* (Morningside Heights, N.Y.: King's Crown Press, 1948), 15; Kendall, *Calvin and English Calvinism*, 149–50.

29. Hales, "A Tract Concerning Schism and Schismatics," in *The Works of the Ever Memorable Mr. John Hales of Eton* (Glasgow: Robert and Andrew Foulis, 1765), 1:125.

30. The split between Puritans and Anglicans prior to Laud's rise to power had been chiefly over matters of church government, not theological issues. The Arminian challenge upset the Calvinist theological position of the church. See Tyacke, *Anti-Calvinists*. On Laud and Arminianism, see Charles Carlton, *Archbishop William Laud* (New York: Routledge and Kegan Paul, 1987), 11–13, 39–40.

31. Hugh Trevor-Roper, "The Great Tew Circle," in *Catholics, Anglicans and Puritans: Seventeenth-Century Essays* (Chicago: University of Chicago Press, 1988), 166–230; B. M. H. Wormald, *Clarendon* (Cambridge: Cambridge University Press, 1951), 240–82. See also G. R. Cragg, *Freedom and Authority: A Study of English Thought in the Early Seventeenth Century* (Philadelphia: Westminster Press, 1975), chapter 9; K. Weber, *Lucius Cary: Viscount Falkland* (New York: Columbia University Press, 1940), chapter 4. Aubrey, in *Brief Lives*, ed. Oliver L. Dick (Ann Arbor: University of Michigan Press, 1957), describes various members of the group. Cf. Clarendon, *History of the Rebellion and Civil Wars in England*, ed. W. D. MacRay (Oxford: Clarendon Press, 1888), 3:179–89.

32. See the thorough discussion in Barbara Shapiro, *Probability and Certainty in Seventeenth-Century England* (Princeton: Princeton University Press, 1983), 74–118, and H. Van Leeuwen, *Problem of Certainty*, 13–48. On John Wilkins's skepticism, see M. Jamie Ferreira, *Scepticism and Reasonable Doubt* (Oxford: Clarendon Press, 1986), 10–31.

33. Lucius Cary, *Discourse of the Infallibility of the Church of Rome* (London: R. Royston, 1651). The work was published in 1645 without a preface. Henry Hammond was responsible for the 1646 text of the same work.

34. Chillingworth, *The Religion of Protestants a Safe Way to Salvation* (1638) in *Works* (Oxford: Oxford University Press, 1838). Robert R. Orr, *Reason and Authority: The Thought of William Chillingworth* (Oxford: Clarendon Press, 1967); Cragg, *Freedom and Authority*, 248–63. Aubrey, *Brief Lives*, 64, says that Chillingworth became familiar with the writings of Sextus Empiricus while a student.

35. Lucius Cary, *Discourse of the Infallibility of the Church of Rome*, 11.

36. Aubrey, *Brief Lives*, 64; Trevor-Roper, "Great Tew Circle," 187.

37. For wartime developments, see G. E. Aylmer, *Rebellion or Revolution?: England 1640–1660* (Oxford: Oxford University Press, 1986), 47–77.

38. Wilkins, *Sermons Preach'd Upon Several Occasions* (London: Richard Chiswell, 1701), 174, 183 (first published 1682).

39. Shapiro, *John Wilkins: An Intellectual Biography* (Los Angeles: University of California Press, 1969), 64–65, 67.

40. Hammond, *A Practical Catechism* (London: M. Flesher, 1684; first published 1644), 3; Burnet, *A Discourse of Pastoral Care* (London: Richard Chiswell, 1692), 82, 84. On Hammond's career, see John W. Packer, *The Transformation of Anglicanism, 1643–1660* (Manchester: University of Manchester Press, 1969). Trevor-Roper, "Great Tew Circle," 219–20, and Avis, *Anglicanism and the Christian Church*, 87, both call Hammond the intellectual heir of Falkland and Chillingworth. Patrick consulted with Hammond before receiving episcopal ordination in 1658, while Isaac Barrow was another protégé. See P. H. Osmond, *Isaac Barrow: His Life and Time* (London: Society for Promoting Christian Knowledge, 1944).

41. Burnet, *A History of My Own Time* (Oxford: University Press, 1833), 1:322; Packer, 197–98. Hammond embraced the common sense epistemology, grounding the truth of Christianity on the strength of the evidence provided by Scripture. See *Of the Reasonableness of the Christian Religion* (London: Miles Flesher, 1684; first published 1650).

42. C. J. Stranks, *The Life and Writings of Jeremy Taylor* (London: Society for Promoting Christian Knowledge, 1952), 63–76. Cf. H. Trevor Hughs, *The Piety of Jeremy Taylor*

(London: Macmillan, 1960), 17–44; Frank Livingston Huntley, *Jeremy Taylor and the Great Rebellion* (Ann Arbor: University of Michigan Press, 1970), 31–55; Richard Symonds, *Alternative Saints: The Post-Reformation British People* (London: Macmillan, 1988), 101–10, and, more generally, F. R. Boton, *The Caroline Tradition in the Church of Ireland* (London: Society for Promoting Christian Knowledge, 1958).

43. Taylor, *A Discourse of the Liberty of Prophesying*, in *The Whole Works of the Right Reverend Jeremy Taylor*, ed. Reginald Heber (London: Ogle, Duncan, and Co., 1822), 7:ccccii.

44. Ibid., 8:99.

45. Ibid., 7:440–41.

46. Sheldon had opposed Laud's attempt to award Taylor with an Oxford Fellowship in 1635, while Taylor's view of original sin outlined in *Unam Necessarium* alienated Bishop Brian Duppa. Stranks, *Life and Writings*, 43, 142.

47. Glanvill, *The Vanity of Dogmatising*, ed. Stephen Medcalf (Hove, England: Harvester Press, 1970), 142–43. According to Louis Locke, *Tillotson: A Study in Seventeenth-Century Literature* (Copenhagen: Rosenkilde and Bagger, 1954), 17, Tillotson's father was a Calvinist. Fowler's father and brother were both Nonconformists after 1662, and Fowler himself did not conform until 1664.

48. See, for example, Frederick J. Powicke, *The Cambridge Platonists* (London: J. M. Dent, 1924); G. R. Cragg, ed., *The Cambridge Platonists* (New York: Oxford University Press, 1968); C. A. Patrides, ed., *The Cambridge Platonists* (Cambridge: Cambridge University Press, 1971); Winthrop K. Jordon, *The Development of Religious Toleration in England* (Gloucester, Mass.: Peter Smith, 1965), 4:94–136.

49. *The Autobiography of Simon Patrick*, in *Works*, ed. Alexander Napier (Oxford: Oxford University Press, 1858), 9:419–21. As a child Patrick feared the harsh implications of predestinarian theology. He wrote that upon hearing of predestination as a boy, he resolved "that if that were true, I would never marry; because most, if not all of my children, might be damned." Ibid., 9:410.

50. Patrick, "Sermon Preached at the Funeral of Mr. John Smith," in *Works*, 7:472.

51. Christ is able, said More, "through the Power of the Spirit to raise us also up to Newness of Life." *Exposition of the Grand Mystery of Godliness* in *The Theological Works of Henry More* (London: Joseph Downing, 1708), 269.

52. See Phillip Harth, *Context of Dryden's Thought* (Chicago: University of Chicago Press, 1968), 115–16.

53. Sir Walter Mildmay's Puritan institution was, ironically, the training ground for many who rejected Puritanism by the mid-seventeenth century. On Whichcote, see J. D. Roberts, *From Puritanism to Platonism in Seventeenth-Century England* (The Hague: Martinus Nijhoff, 1968), chapter 1.

54. Samuel Salter, ed., *Eight Letters of Dr. Anthony Tuckney, and Dr. Benjamin Whichcote* (London: J. Payne, 1753), 38–39.

55. Salter, ed., *Eight Letters*, 8, 100, 127. This theme was no aberration in Whichcote's theology. Compare Whichcote, *Moral and Religious Aphorisms*, ed. Samuel Salter (London: J. Payne, 1753), #43, where he writes that "Only Mad men and Fools are pleased with Themselves: no Wise man is Good enough for his own Satisfaction." See also Cudworth, "The Christian's Victory," in *The Works of Ralph Cudworth* (Oxford: D. A. Talboys, 1829), 4:370, 371, 373, and Henry More, *Explanation of the Grand Mystery of Godliness*, in *Works*, 91.

56. *Eight Letters*, 58.

57. Tillotson, "Sermon Preached at the Funeral of Benjamin Whichcote," in *Works*, ed. Thomas Birch (London: J. F. Dove, 1820), 1:372. Whichcote was ejected from the provostship of King's at the Restoration. See Roberts, *From Puritanism to Platonism*, 9.

58. More, *Explication of Grand Mystery*, 37. Cf. Whichcote's sermon before the House of Commons on 4 February 1673 in *Works* (Aberdeen, Scotland: J. Chalmers, 1751), 4:132.

59. Cudworth, "The Christian's Victory," in *Works*, 4:376. More, *An Account of Virtue* (London: Benjamin Tooke, 1690), 6, wrote that "all pravity is repugnant to human nature."

60. Whichcote, "The Difference of Times, with Respect to Religion," in *Works*, 1:45. Cf. More, *Select Sermons*, in John Wesley, ed., *A Christian Library* (London: J. Kershaw, 1819–27), 23:142.

61. Sykes, *From Sheldon to Secker*, 145.

62. More, *Collection of Aphorisms*, 4.

63. David Clarkson, "Of Original Sin," in *Sermons and Discourses on Several Divine Subjects* (London: Thomas Parkhurst, 1696), 7.

64. Whichcote, "The Difference of Times, with Respect to Religion," in *Works*, 1:37.

65. The representative sermon belongs to Cudworth, who, preaching before the House of Commons on 31 March 1647, attacked the presumption of those who would place the search for signs of "election" before the work of moral reform. See, in particular, Cudworth, *Works*, 4:300.

66. Robert Todd Carroll, *The Common Sense Philosophy of Religion of Bishop Edward Stillingfleet* (The Hague: Martinus Nijhoff, 1975), 14, 15. See also James Nankivell, *Edward Stillingfleet, Bishop of Worcester, 1689–1699* (Worcester, England: Ebenezer Baylis, 1946), 1–2, and Richard Popkin, "The Philosophy of Bishop Stillingfleet," *Journal of the History of Philosophy* 9 (1971): 303–19. There is no modern biography of Stillingfleet.

67. Edward Stillingfleet, *Irenicum: A Weapon-Salve for the Church's Wounds*, in *Works* (London, 1707–10), 2:148–49, 155–56, 254. Baxter thought highly of Stillingfleet's book, especially the argument that prelacy, though lawful, is not necessary. *Reliquiae*, Part 2, 388. John Spurr has pointed out that Stillingfleet's intention in the *Irenicum* was to demonstrate that Presbyterianism was not *jure divino*. Spurr, "Latitudinarianism," 74. C. E. Whiting, *Studies in English Puritanism from the Restoration to the Revolution, 1660–1688* (London: Frank Cass and Co., 1931), 479, dates the work to the 1650s. John Marshall, "The Ecclesiology of the Latitude-men: Stillingfleet, Tillotson and Hobbism," *Journal of Ecclesiastical History* 36, no. 3 (1985): 410, reminds us that Stillingfleet was addressing the troublesome issue of individual conscience in this work and that given the inevitable differences between men's minds, uniformity of practice, while desirable, was hardly practicable. The Erastianism of Stillingfleet and (more particularly) Tillotson was in response to the perceived connection between the claims of conscience and the late Civil War.

68. Burnet, *History*, 1:336.

69. Geoffrey F. Nuttall and Owen Chadwick, ed., *From Uniformity to Unity, 1662–1962* (London: Society for Promoting Christian Knowledge, 1962), 4–9.

70. *Brief Account*, 12–13. Norman Sykes, *The Church of England and Non-Episcopal*

Churches in the Sixteenth and Seventeenth Centuries (London: Society for Promoting Christian Knowledge, 1948), 15, disagrees, arguing that the Latitudinarians, because of their indifference to matters of church polity, were unrepresentative of the Anglican tradition.

71. *Brief Account*, 8.
72. Ibid., 9.

2 : *The Restoration Church and the Limits of Reform*

1. R. A. Beddard, "The Restoration Church," in J. R. Jones, ed., *The Restored Monarchy, 1660–1688* (Totawa, N.J.: Rowman and Littlefield, 1979), 155–59, discusses the serious miscalculation made by Charles and Clarendon here. Eager to rebuild the bond between church and state which had existed prior to the Civil War, Cavalier gentlemen viewed any concession to Dissenters as the opening wedge of a movement to undermine both religion and magistry. Ronald Hutton, *The Restoration: A Political and Religious History of England and Wales, 1658–1667* (Oxford: Oxford University Press, 1987), 143–44; Paul Seaward, *The Cavalier Parliament and the Reconstruction of the Old Regime, 1661–1667* (Cambridge: Cambridge University Press, 1989), 162–95; A. O. Whiteman, "The Restoration of the Church of England," in Geoffrey Nuttall and Owen Chadwick, ed., *From Uniformity to Unity* (London: Society for Promoting Christian Knowledge, 1962), 19–88; Paul H. Hardacre, "The Genesis of the Declaration of Breda, 1657–1660," *Journal of Church and State* 15, no. 1 (1973): 65–82; George R. Abernathy, *The English Presbyterians and the Stuart Restoration, 1648–1663*, Transactions of the American Philosophical Society, vol. 55, pt. 2 (Philadelphia: The Society, 1965), provide the details. Robert S. Bosher, *The Making of the Restoration Settlement* (London: Dacre Press, 1957), argues that Charles and Clarendon were from the outset dishonest with the Presbyterians, seeking to fully restore the rights and prerogatives of the pre–Civil War church, but I. M. Green, *The Re-establishment of the Church of England, 1660–1663* (Oxford: Oxford University Press, 1978), disputes this interpretation. The declaration is printed in A. Browning, ed., *English Historical Documents, 1660–1714* (New York: Oxford University Press, 1953), 8:58.
2. Whiteman, "Restoration," 22–23.
3. Michael R. Watts, *The Dissenters: From the Reformation to the French Revolution* (Oxford: Clarendon Press, 1978), 220–21; Beddard, "Restoration Church," 161, says that Charles struggled against Cavalier demands for more than a year before capitulating to their call for a return to the old episcopal order. Macaulay, *History*, 1:83, and John Stoughton, *History of Religion in England, from the Opening of the Long Parliament to the End of the Eighteenth Century* (London: Hodder and Stoughton, 1881), 3:73–74, offer critical nineteenth-century assessments of Charles's character.
4. Charles issued his first detailed call for comprehension in October 1660, calling on bishops to exercise their authority with the advice and consent of their presbyteries, advocating a revision of the prayer book, promising to waive minor points of ceremony in any future settlement and to excuse subscription to canonical obedience as a condition of ordination. Brought before Parliament in the form of a bill on 6 November, it was defeated in Commons. For details see Roger Thomas,

"Comprehension and Indulgence," in *From Uniformity to Unity*, 192–94; Leopold von Ranke, *A History of England, Principally in the Seventeenth Century* (Oxford: Clarendon Press, 1875) 3:352–54; Hutton, *The Restoration*, 184. Leading Presbyterians were offered bishoprics at this point, but only Reynolds accepted. Baxter feared that Parliament would not ratify the king's declaration, and, in the event, he was correct. *Reliquiae*, Part 2, 281–82.

5. Spurr, "Latitudinarianism," 62–63; Barbara Shapiro, *John Wilkins*, 148–50; Clifford, *Justification and Atonement*, 10. On the petitions of sequestered clergy, see Green, *Re-establishment*, 37–60.

6. H. Tyler Blethen, "Episcopacy and Stability in Restoration England," *Historical Magazine of the Protestant Episcopal Church* 46, no. 2 (1977): 209–14. Seward, *Cavalier Parliament*, 62–66, argues that uncompromising Anglicans exercised a disproportionate amount of influence in Parliament and did not reflect the more moderate position of most gentry. On the decline of deference among the poor after 1660, see David Underdown, *Revel, Riot, and Rebellion: Popular Politics and Culture in England, 1603–1660* (Oxford: Oxford University Press, 1988), 271–91.

7. David L. Edwards, *Christian England: From the Reformation to the Eighteenth Century* (Grand Rapids, Mich.: William B. Eerdmans, 1983), 427–28. For an overview of one of these uncompromising churchmen, see H. A. Lloyd Jukes, "Peter Gunning, 1613–1684: Scholar, Churchman, Controversialist," in C. W. Dugmore and Charles Duggan, ed., *Studies in Church History*, vol. 1 (London: Thomas Nelson, 1964), 222–32.

8. For treatment of Anglicans during Interregnum, see W. K. Jordon, *Development of Religious Toleration*, vol. 3; Bosher, *Making of Restoration Settlement*, chapter 1; Whiteman, "Restoration," 29–35. Evelyn describes Juxon's infirmity at the coronation ceremony. *The Diary of John Evelyn*, ed. E. S. de Beer (Oxford: Clarendon Press, 1955), 3:282. On Sheldon, see Victor D. Sutch, *Gilbert Sheldon, Architect of Anglican Survival* (The Hague: Martinus Nijhoff, 1973), 64–65, 94; R. A. Beddard, "Sheldon and Anglican Recovery," *Historical Journal* 19 (1976): 1005–17. According to Pepys (4 June 1663), Juxon was respected by most within the church. On Sheldon, Pepys wrote (3 September 1662) "The bishop of London is now one of the most powerful men in England with the King." *Diary*, 3:186.

9. Burnet, *History*, 1:320; J. H. Overton, *Life in the English Church, 1660–1714* (London: Longmans, 1885), 19–20, and J. R. Jones, *Country and Court: England, 1658–1714* (Cambridge: Harvard University Press, 1979), 145–49; Whiteman, "Restoration," 58; Bosher, *Making of Restoration Settlement*, 29, and Edwards, *Christian England*, 429–30, defend Sheldon as a constructive leader of the church despite his implacable hostility towards Dissenters.

10. Burnet, *An Exposition of the Thirty-Nine Articles of the Church of England* (London: R. Roberts, 1699), iv–v, praised Hammond for his just temper in managing controversies. Baxter, who had serious differences with Hammond before 1660 "took the Death of Dr. Hammond . . . for a great loss; for his Piety and Wisdom would sure have hindred much of the Violence which after followed." *Reliquiae*, Part 2, 208. See also, Davies, *Worship and Theology, 1603–1690*, 363–73.

11. Gerald R. Cragg, *Puritanism in the Period of the Great Persecution* (New York: Russell and Russell, 1971), 6; Thomas J. Fawcett, *The Liturgy of Comprehension, 1689* (Southend-on-Sea, England: Alcuin Club, 1973), 3–4; Norman Sykes, *Church and*

State in England in the Eighteenth Century (New York: Octagon Books, 1975), 10–11; Stoughton, *Religion in England*, 3:177, 181.

12. W. C. Abbot, "English Conspiracy and Dissent, 1660–1674," *American Historical Review* 14 (1908–9): 503–28; James Sutherland, *English Literature of the Late Seventeenth Century* (Oxford: Oxford University Press, 1969), 297–99.

13. Baxter was singularly deficient in the art of negotiating, and his humorless personality offended many at the conference. See George Clark, *The Later Stuarts, 1660–1714*, 2d ed. (Oxford: Clarendon Press, 1961), 20; Whiteman, "Restoration," 77–78; Fawcett, *Liturgy of Comprehension*, 4. The Presbyterian demands for revision were similar to the ones tabled at the beginning of the century during the Hampton Court Conference.

14. Ronald Hutton, *Charles the Second* (Oxford: Clarendon Press, 1989), 180–81. Some six hundred alterations were made in the Book of Common Prayer. For details, see Stoughton, *Religion in England*, 3:217; Clark, *Later Stuarts*, 21–25. The election to the Parliament of 1662 would be the last for eighteen years, thus making chances for legislative reform remote.

15. Commons also burned the covenant and restored bishops to the House of Lords. In November 1661, after the failure of the Savoy Conference, the Corporation Act was passed, which effectively excluded Dissenters from any form of government service, thereby stripping Presbyterians of their influence in the towns. J. R. Jones, *Country and Court*, 143; Barry Coward, *The Stuart Age* (London: Longmans, 1980), 250; J. P. Kenyon, ed., *The Stuart Constitution* (Cambridge: Cambridge University Press, 1966), 363.

16. Hutton, *The English Church: From the Accession of Charles I to the Death of Anne* (London: Macmillan, 1913), 187. See also Horton Davies, *The English Free Churches* (London: Oxford University Press, 1963), 91, and Leopold von Ranke, *History of England*, 3:368–75, who stresses Charles's financial difficulties in his acceptance of the Act of Uniformity.

17. Robert South, "Religion the Best Reason of State," in *Sermons Preached Upon Several Occasions* (Oxford: Clarendon Press, 1823), 1:99.

18. For the full text, see Andrew Browning, ed., *English Historical Documents, 1660–1714*, 377–82. Burnet, *History*, 1:336, says that he was told by some of the bishops that many clergy had subscribed before they had even seen the act. A. G. Matthews, *Calamy Revised* (Oxford: Clarendon Press, 1934), xii–xiii, estimates that 1,000 lost their places by the act, while another 760 had been ejected between 1660 and 1662. About one-tenth of all clergy in England and Wales lost their livings, while the percentage in London was much higher, with one-third of the ministers affected. Hutton, *Restoration*, 176–77. The king sought to delay the implementation of the act, but he was vigorously opposed by the episcopal bench. See William Simon, *The Restoration Episcopate* (New York: Bookman Associates, 1965), 95. For the first time, the Church of England removed itself from its connection with other reformed churches by refusing to accept ordination outside the Anglican rite.

19. M. W. Patterson, *A History of the Church of England* (London: Longmans, 1933), 360. Macaulay observed how by 1685 only two sons of peers were bishops, arguing that noble families no longer viewed an ecclesiastical career as the best avenue of advancement for their intellectually superior offspring. *History*, 1:159–60.

20. John Miller, "James II and Toleration," in Eveline Cruickshanks, ed., *By Force or By Default? The Revolution of 1688* (Edinburgh: John Donald, 1989), 11. On pluralism, see Sykes, *Church and State*, 14–16.

21. G. V. Bennett, *The Tory Crisis in Church and State: The Career of Francis Atterbury* (Oxford: Clarendon Press, 1975), 295.

22. Ibid.

23. Barrow, "Of Obedience to Our Spiritual Guides and Governors," in *The Theological Works of Isaac Barrow*, ed. A. Napier (Cambridge: Cambridge University Press, 1859), 4:8. Using the criteria of social stability and religious peace as touchstones, Barrow asked Dissenters whether the objections against obedience to the church were so clear as the commands which enjoin them. More to the point, he wanted to know whether the inconveniences of adhering to the Church of England are so grievous "as are the mischiefs which spring from disobedience." Ibid., 45. See also id., "Of a Peaceable Temper and Carriage," 2:430.

24. Somerville, *Popular Religion*, 31, uses the figure of 5 percent. Tim Harris, *London Crowds in the Reign of Charles II* (Cambridge: Cambridge University Press, 1987), 66, says that 15 to 20 percent of the London population could be ranked among Dissenters. Browning, ed., *English Historical Documents*, 8:413–16. S. A. Peyton, "The Religious Census of 1676," *English Historical Review* 48 (1933): 99–104. John Morrill, "The Church in England, 1642–1649," in Morrill, ed., *Reactions to the English Civil War, 1642–1649* (New York: St. Martin's Press, 1982), 89–114, discusses the popularity of Anglicanism during the 1640s.

25. Whiteman, "Restoration," 48; John Hunt, *Religious Thought in England* (London: Strahen and Co., 1871), 1:278; and Bosher, *Making of Restoration Settlement*, 26–27, all describe the obscurity and inactivity of the bishops during the Interregnum.

26. Claire Cross, *English Church and People, 1450–1660* (Atlantic Highlands, N.J.: Humanities Press, 1976), 233; John H. Pruett, *The Parish Clergy Under the Later Stuarts: The Leicestershire Experience* (Urbana: University of Illinois Press, 1978), 17, 23; John Redwood, *Reason, Ridicule and Religion: The Age of Enlightenment in England, 1660–1750* (London: Thames and Hudson, 1976), 18–20; Trevor-Roper, "Great Tew," 215–16.

27. Norman Sykes, *From Sheldon to Secker: Aspects of English Church History, 1660–1768* (Cambridge: Cambridge University Press, 1959), 1–35; Overton, *Life in the English Church*, 159–76; Hutton, *The Restoration*, 143, 172, 177; Simon, *Restoration Episcopate*, 35–38; Jones, *Country and Court*, 149; A. O. Whiteman, "The Episcopate of Dr. Seth Ward, Bishop of Exeter" (D. Phil thesis, Oxford University, 1951), 63–64.

28. Redwood, *Reason, Ridicule and Religion*, 18. Evelyn, *Diary*, 3:60 (15 February 1652); 3:153 (8 July 1655). Evelyn explained that he "frequently stayd at home to Catechize & Instruct my Familie, those exercises universally ceasing in the parish churches." *Diary*, 3:160 (21 September 1655).

29. Sprat, *Sermons Preached on Several Occasions* (London: Charles Brome, 1697), 31.

30. Hutton, *Restoration*, 173–74. On episcopal appointments, see Bosher, *Making of Restoration Settlement*, 180–84; Sykes, *Sheldon to Secker*, 6.

31. See Burnet's complaints in *Supplement to Burnet's History*, 505–6; Cross, *Church and People*, 227.

32. Hutton, *Charles the Second*, 152–53. The plan for suffragan bishops had first been

proposed by Ussher before the outbreak of the Civil War, but the king, despite his recommendation, was the first to insist upon the primacy of the bishop's political function. Bosher, *Making of the Restoration Settlement*, 237.

33. Baxter thought such an insensitive position was at the very heart of Latitudinarianism. The Latitudinarians, while "abhoring at first the Imposition of these little things," did not think them to be "great enough to stick at when imposed." *Reliquiae*, Part 2, 386.

34. Baxter, *Reliquiae*, Part 2, 386; Shapiro, *John Wilkins*, 152.

35. The following information is drawn from Gascoigne, *Cambridge in the Age of Enlightenment*, 48–51. See also Peter Earle, *The Making of the English Middle Class* (Berkeley: University of California Press, 1989), 63–65, for a description of the London clergy.

36. Pepys, *Diary*, 3:165, did not think very highly of Wilkins's ability as a preacher. Evelyn, *Diary*, 3:165, was satisfied with his pulpit style, however. Shapiro, *John Wilkins*, 153, attributes the pragmatic focus of Latitudinarian reform, as distinguished from the more mystical orientation of Cambridge Platonism, to Wilkins's influence.

37. Robert Nelson, "Address to Persons of Quality and Estate," quoted in G. F. A. Best, *Temporal Pillars: Queen Anne's Bounty, the Ecclesiastical Commissioners, and the Church of England* (Cambridge: Cambridge University Press, 1964), 14. Macaulay exaggerated the ignorance of the rural clergy, as C. E. Whiting, *Studies in English Puritanism*, 404–9, and Sykes, *From Sheldon to Secker*, 11–12, make clear.

38. Cragg, *Church in the Age of Reason*, 123–28, discusses conditions into the early eighteenth century. Cf. Bennett, *Tory Crisis in Church and State*, 15.

39. Pepys, *Diary*, 3:271, 8:364, describes criticism of the bishops. See Harris, *London Crowds*, 81; Thomas, "Comprehension and Indulgence," 195–96. Evelyn, *Diary*, 3:419, indicates that Sheldon remained at Lambeth.

40. Seaward, *Cavalier Parliament*, 192; Stoughton, *Religion in England*, 3:332–33, 355–56. Hutton, *Restoration*, 232, indicates that at least nineteen Anglican churchmen remained in the city. One-third of London's ministers had been expelled under the terms of the Act of Uniformity in 1662. Ibid., 177. Baxter, *Reliquiae*, Part 3, 19, said that many Anglican divines, having lost their maintenance after the fire, left the city. "Yet at the same time it happily also fell out that the Parish Churches, that were left standing, had the best and ablest of the Conformists in them." He mentions Stillingfleet, Tillotson, Patrick, and Whichcote in this context.

41. Cragg, *Puritanism in the Age of Persecution*, 13–15.

42. Sykes, *From Sheldon to Secker*, 70.

43. Seaward, *Cavalier Parliament*, 67–68; Pepys, *Diary*, 8:584–85, 593; Burnet, *History*, 1:474; Harris, *London Crowds*, 80; Hutton, *Restoration*, 197; Simon, *Restoration Episcopate*, 47. Charles had called upon the bishops to support the impeachment motion against Clarendon in 1667, but they refused. Ibid., 98.

44. Thomas, "Comprehension and Indulgence," 197–98. The 1667 bill would have recognized Presbyterian orders while use of the surplice, the sign of the cross, and kneeling at the sacrament would become discretionary. See Fawcett, *Liturgy of Comprehension*, 6–7; John Spurr, "The Church of England, Comprehension, and the Toleration Act of 1689," *English Historical Review* 104 (1989): 933.

45. Burnet, *History*, 1:476. Pepys thought Wilkins "a mighty rising man . . . as being a Latitudinarian and the Duke of Buckingham his great friend." *Diary*, 9:485.

46. Pepys, *Diary*, 8:584–85 (21 December 1667). See also Douglas R. Lacey, *Dissent and Parliamentary Politics in England, 1661–1689* (New Brunswick: Rutgers University Press, 1969), 55–56; Maurice Lee, Jr., *The Cabal* (Urbana: University of Illinois Press, 1965), 173–75.

47. Shapiro, *Wilkins*, 171–72; Fawcett, *Liturgy of Comprehension*, 7. Objections to these requirements had become traditional, having been urged throughout the reign of Elizabeth and embodied in the 1603 Millenary Petition. See Stoughton, *Religion in England*, 3:103. Wilkins knew Burton at Cambridge when the latter was a fellow at Magdalene. According to Wood, *Athenae Oxoniensis*, ed. P. Bliss (1813–20), 4:513, Wilkins, who was master of Trinity, formed a club to promote comprehension which met regularly at Burton's chamber.

48. Walter G. Simon, "Comprehension in the Age of Charles II," *Church History* 31, no. 3 (1962); 440–47; Shapiro, *John Wilkins*, 169–74; Sutch, *Gilbert Sheldon*, 107–12; Lacey, *Dissent and Parliamentary Politics*, 56–58; Sykes, *Sheldon to Secker*, 72–73.

49. Quoting Pepys, *Diary*, 9:60 (10 February 1688); Gilbert Burnet, *The Life and Death of Sir Matthew Hale* in *The Works, Moral and Religious, of Sir Matthew Hale*, ed. T. Thirlwall (London: H. D. Symonds, 1805), 1:33. See also Edmond Heward, *Matthew Hale* (London: Robert Hale, 1972), 101. Charles II quoted in Sykes, *Sheldon to Secker*, 73; Thomas Birch, *Life of John Tillotson*, in *Works*, 1:xxviii–xix.

50. Wilkins opposed the Conventicle Act in the Lords, angering Sheldon and Gunning. Simon, *Restoration Episcopate*, 81. On the London riots, see Harris, *London Crowds*, 82–91. On Parliament's response to Wilkins and the Comprehension Bill, see Thomas, "Comprehension and Indulgence," 200–203. On the new repression of 1669–70, see Richard Ashcraft, *Revolutionary Politics and Locke's Two Treatises of Government* (Princeton: Princeton University Press, 1986), 23–31. Tillotson preached at Wilkins's consecration on 15 November 1668, while an unenthusiastic Sheldon officiated. See Evelyn, *Diary*, 3:517.

51. Patrick, *A Friendly Debate*, in *Works*, 5:280.

52. *Friendly Debate*, 5:291. Glanvill, *The Various Methods of Satan's Policy Detected*, in Anthony Horneck, ed., *Some Discourses, Sermons and Remains of the Reverend Mr. Jos. Glanvill* (London: Henry Mortluck, 1681), 376–90, attributed sectarian insolence, free grace for the elect, and claims to spiritual illumination to the work of Satan.

53. Sheldon subsequently assisted Patrick's brother in procuring the position of preacher for the Charterhouse and was instrumental in securing a prebendary at Westminster for Patrick in 1672. Patrick later dedicated his *Witness to Christianity* (1675) to Sheldon. See *The Autobiography of Symon Patrick* (Oxford: J. H. Parker, 1839), 60, 66, 68, 77.

54. Baxter, *Reliquiae*, Part 3, 40. Cf. Burnet's critical observations in *History*, 1:190.

55. *Reliquiae*, Part 3, 20; Burnet, *History*, 1:476.

56. Spurr, "Church of England," 940–41, 942.

57. F. Bate, *The Declaration of Indulgence*, chapter 5; R. A. Beddard, "Vincent Alsop and the Emancipation of Restoration Dissent," *Journal of Ecclesiastical History* 24 (1973): 161–84; Lacey, *Dissent and Parliamentary Politics*, 70.

58. Hutton, *Charles the Second*, 194, 198; Coward, *Stuart Age*, 251–52; Beddard, "The

Restoration Church," 163–64; Jones, *Country and Court*, 150–51.

59. Text in Kenyon, ed., *Stuart Constitution*, 407. For details and motives behind the Indulgence, see John Miller, *Popery and Politics in England, 1660–1688* (Cambridge: Cambridge University Press, 1973), 116–17; Lee, *The Cabal*, 186–201. The consensus on the limits of the crown's right to dispense with laws is discussed by J. R. Western, *Monarchy and Revolution: The English State in the 1680s* (Totawa, N.J.: Rowman and Littlefield, 1972), 15–16.

60. Burnet, *History*, 2:4–10; Hutton, *Charles the Second*, 285, stresses the king's reluctance to make the declaration and argues that his advisors (Ashely, Buckingham, James, Clifford, Arlington, and Lauderdale) pushed the measure upon him.

61. Sykes, *Sheldon to Secker*, 75–76. James refused to take the test, although he continued to exercise influence informally. John Miller, *James II: A Study in Kingship* (Hove, England: Wayland Publishers, 1977), 69, 70.

62. Jones, *Court and Country*, 185–86; Lacey, *Dissent and Parliamentary Politics*, 71–72; Miller, *Popery and Politics*, 122–23. Danby ordered the confiscation of two-thirds of all recusants' estates, but the machinery needed to enforce such an order was not available. Kenyon, ed., *Stuart Constitution*, 450.

63. Tim Harris, *London Crowds*, 64–65; Seaward, *Cavalier Parliament*, 60; Watts, *Dissenters*, 244–49; Cragg, *Puritanism in the Period of Persecution*, 18. Anthony Flether, "The Enforcement of the Conventicle Acts, 1664–1679" in W. J. Shields, ed., *Persecution and Toleration* (N.p.: The Ecclesiastical History Society Studies in Church History, 1984), 237. Economic prosperity was one of the arguments used by the Crown in advancing the idea of indulgence. Jones, *Country and Court*, 154.

64. Sykes, 75–77; Cragg, *Puritanism in the Period of Persecution*, 20, notes that Stillingfleet, in *The Unreasonableness of Separation*, 23, dated the beginning of Nonconformity from the year 1672. Cf. Keith Feiling, *A History of the Tory Party, 1640–1714* (Oxford: Clarendon Press, 1924), 132–33.

65. Thomas, "Comprehension and Indulgence," 211–13; Western, *Monarchy and Revolution*, 181; Spurr, "Church of England," 935; Fawcett, *Liturgy of Comprehension*, 9.

66. Harris, *London Crowds*, 70–71; F. Bate, *Declaration of Indulgence*, 109–10; Stoughton, *Religion in England*, 3:431–33; Sykes, *Sheldon to Secker*, 77–78.

67. Miller, *Popery and Politics*; chapters 7 and 8 provide the best coverage.

68. The origins of Charles's sympathy for English Catholics is discussed by Green, *Reestablishment of the Church of England*, 26. On suspicion of the Stuart monarchs, see John Kenyon, *The Popish Plot* (London: Heinemann, 1972), 8–10.

69. Sykes, *Sheldon to Secker*, 78–79; Spurr, "Church of England," 936; Stoughton, *Religion in England*, 3:429–30, suggests that Morley's desire to reach accommodation with the Presbyterians as a check against Catholicism was his motive in entertaining Baxter's plans.

70. Thomas, "Comprehension and Indulgence," 219, suggests that Hale may have been involved.

71. Baxter *Reliquiae*, 1, Part 3, 156–57; Birch, *Life of Tillotson*, (London, 1753), 44.

72. Croft published *The Naked Truth or the True State of the Primitive Church* in 1675. He would dispose of the surplice, kneeling at communion, bowing at the altar, the cross in baptism, and the ring in marriage.

73. Burnet, *A Modest Survey of the Most Considerable Things in a Discourse Lately Published, Entitled Naked Truth* (London: Moses Pitt, 1676), 3:292.

74. H. Horwitz, "Protestant Reconciliation in the Exclusion Crisis," *Journal of Ecclesiastical History* 15, no. 2 (1964): 204.

75. Kenyon, *The Popish Plot*, 3; W. A. Speck, *Reluctant Revolutionaries* (Oxford: Oxford University Press, 1988), 168.

76. Patrick, "A Sermon Preached Before the Lord Mayor, 22 October 1680," in *Works*, 8:149.

77. Thomas, "Comprehension and Indulgence," 225–26.

78. John Miller, *James II*, 111; Sykes, *Sheldon to Secker*, 83. On fears of another civil war, see Speck, *Reluctant Revolutionaries*, 37.

79. R. A. Beddard, "The Commission for Ecclesiastical Promotions, 1681–4: an instrument of Tory Reaction," *Historical Journal* 10 (1967): 11–40; Western, *Monarchy and Revolution*, 185; Mark Goldie, "Sir Peter Pett, Sceptical Toryism and the Science of Toleration in the 1680s," in *Persecution and Toleration*, 247–88.

80. Some four hundred meeting houses were affected, while 3,800 arrests took place for breaches of the penal laws. Speck, *Reluctant Revolutionaries*, 173.

81. Speck, *Reluctant Revolutionaries*, 39, 45; Western, *Monarchy and Revolution*, 46–81; Miller, *James II*, 112–13. Id., "The Crown and the Borough Charters in the Reign of Charles II," *English Historical Review* 100 (1985): 53–84, describes the role of local Tory officials in the surrender of borough charters.

82. Miller, *James II*, 120; Speck, *Reluctant Revolutionaries*, 42–43; Bennett, "Conflict in the Church," 158; Burnet, *History*, 3:6.

83. Compton of London was suspended for refusing to silence the clergyman John Sharp. Miller, *James II*, 154; id., *Popery and Politics*, 209, 210. Cf. J. R. Jones, *The Revolution of 1688 in England* (New York: Norton, 1972), chapter 5.

84. Whig historians have accepted the argument that James was using Catholicism to further absolutism. Miller, *Popery and Politics*, 196–202, disputes this connection.

85. During 1685 and 1686, Dissenters had been vigorously persecuted under the Conventicle Act. Miller, *Popery and Politics*, 205, 208. James also purged municipal officeholders as a preliminary to managing later Parliamentary elections. Jones, *Court and Country*, 236.

86. Bennett, "Conflict in the Church," 155–56.

87. Birch, *Life of Tillotson* (London, 1753), 102–4; Kenyon, ed., *Stuart Constitution*, 381.

88. Spurr, "Church of England," 937–38; Halifax, in his 1687 *Letter to a Dissenter*, told Nonconformists that they "were to be hugged now, only that you may be the better squeezed at another time." Quoted in Western, *Monarchy and Revolution*, 227.

89. See George Every, *The High Church Party* (London, 1956), chapter 2; G. M. Trevelyan, *England Under the Stuarts* (New York: G. P. Putnam's Sons, 1946), 362.

90. Quoted in Speck, *Reluctant Revolutionaries*, 183.

91. Jones, *Country and Court*, 244; Miller, *James II*, 171–72; Speck, *Reluctant Revolutionaries*, 183; Thomas, "Comprehension," 232. James deplored the consequences of the Edict of Nantes and believed that Catholicism could advance in England through peaceful conversion.

92. Roger Thomas, "The Seven Bishops and Their Petition, 18 May 1688," *Journal of Ecclesiastical History* 12, no. 1 (1961): 56–70.

93. Text in Kenyon, ed., *Stuart Constitution*, 441–42.

94. Miller, *James II*, 185; R. Thomas, "Seven Bishops and Their Petition," 65–66; G. V. Bennett, "The Seven Bishops: A Reconsideration," in D. Baker, ed., *Religious*

Motivation (Studies in Church History 15, 1978), 267–87.

95. Patrick, *Autobiography*, in *Works*, 9:510; Stoughton, *Religion in England*, 4:138.
96. Western, *Monarchy and Revolution*, 231–32.
97. John Carswell, *The Descent on England* (New York: John Day, 1969), 142–51; Kenyon, ed., *Stuart Constitution*, 424.
98. Western, *Monarchy and Revolution*, 271–72; Jones, *Revolution of 1688*, 262–64.
99. Quoting Jones, *Court and Country*, 251.
100. Lucille Pinkham, *William III and the Respectable Revolution* (Hamden, Conn.: Archon Books, 1969), 3, argued that William coveted the crown as early as 1686, but Speck, *Reluctant Revolutionaries*, 75, places the decision in early 1688.

3 : Assessing Adam's Bequest

1. Patrick Collinson, *The Elizabethan Puritan Movement* (London: Cape, 1967); id., *The Religion of Protestants* (Oxford: Clarendon Press, 1982); Peter Lake, "Calvinism and the English Church," *Past and Present* 114 (1987): 32–76, and William Haller, *The Rise of Puritanism* (New York: Columbia University Press, 1938), discuss the Puritan outlook.
2. John Morgan, *Godly Learning: Puritan Attitudes towards Reason, Learning, and Education, 1560–1640* (Cambridge: Cambridge University Press, 1986), 23; Hershal Baker, *The Wars of Truth: Studies in the Decay of Christian Humanism in the Earlier Seventeenth Century* (Gloucester, Mass.: Peter Smith, 1969), 25. According to Baker, 37, Calvin's picture of the natural man was so harsh "that it is possible to write the intellectual history of seventeenth-century England in terms of the efforts to mitigate and modify his strictures on human dignity." Cf. Ernst Cassirer, *The Philosophy of the Enlightenment* (Princeton: Princeton University Press, 1979), 140.
3. Calvin, *Institutes of the Christian Religion*, trans. John Allen (Philadelphia: Westminster Press, 1936), 1: book 2, chapter 2, sections I, X.
4. Quoting John Bunyan, *A Defence of the Doctrine of Justification, By Faith in Jesus Christ* (London: Francis Smith, 1672), 3. On the Calvinist view overall, see Edmund Morgan, *Visible Saints: The History of a Puritan Idea* (New York: New York University Press, 1963), 67; John Coolidge, *The Pauline Renaissance in England: Puritanism and the Bible* (Oxford: Clarendon Press, 1970).
5. Cragg, *Reason and Authority*, 10, argues that the growing emphasis on reason in religion led to a fundamental reassessment of man's inherent capacities. On the resurgence of sin, see Christopher Hill, "Sin and Society," in *Essays*, 2:117-40.
6. See chapters 4 and 5.
7. Grove, *A Vindication of the Conforming Clergy* (London: Walter Kettilby, 1676), 24.
8. Nicholas Tyacke, *Anti-Calvinists*; id., "The Rise of Arminianism Reconsidered," *Past and Present* 115 (1987): 201–29; J. F. H. New, *Anglican and Puritan: The Basis of Their Opposition, 1558–1640* (Stanford, Calif.: Stanford University Press, 1964), 13; Saint Augustine, *City of God*, trans. John Healey (London: J. M. Dent, 1945), 2: book 13, chapter 14, book 14, chapter 1; Charles and Catherine George, *The Protestant Mind of the English Reformation, 1570–1640* (Princeton: Princeton University Press, 1961), 43, 54, 65–66.
9. Patrick, *The Devout Christian*, in *Works* 2:304, 305. Compare Tillotson, "Concerning the Divinity of Our Blessed Saviour," in *Works*, 3:301.

10. William Barclay, *The Mind of St. Paul* (New York: Harper and Row, 1958), 184. Cf. Aquinas, *Summa Contra Gentiles*, trans. Charles J. O'Neil (Notre Dame: University of Notre Dame Press, 1975), 4:212–14. See also Calvin, *Institutes*, 1: book 2, chapter 1, section V.

11. Schultz, *Milton and Forbidden Knowledge*, 3, and Theodore Spencer, *Shakespeare and the Nature of Man* (Cambridge: Cambridge University Press, 1943), 1–2, 23–24, discuss these theological commonplaces for the period before 1660.

12. Glanvill, *Scepsis Scientifica* (London: E. Cotes, 1665), 5. Cf. Wilkins, *Sermons Preach'd Upon Several Occasions*, 111.

13. Saint Augustine, *City of God*, 2: book 2, chapter 4. Aquinas, *Summa Theologica*, trans. Dominican Fathers (London: Eyre and Spottiswood, 1963–76), Ia2ae, quest. 77, art. 4, identified pride with the basis of all sin. Pascal's *Pensees* stands as the most cogent seventeenth-century exposition of this outlook.

14. Saint Paul twice connects sin with Adam's fall (Rom. 5.12–15; 1 Cor. 15.22), but no formal attempt was made to give a specific account of original sin until the time of Augustine. A clear example is contained in Patrick, *A Commentary Upon the First Book of Moses* (London: Richard Chiswell, 1695), 50, 58. See also Tillotson, "The Love of God to Men in the Incarnation of Christ," *Works*, 4:553.

15. Saint Augustine, *City of God*, 2: book 14, chapter 11.

16. Edward Reynolds, *Works*, (London: B. Holdsworth, 1826), 1:3, 60.

17. Tillotson, "The Wisdom of Being Religious," in *Works*, 1:332; Thomas Gouge, *The Principles of the Christian Religion*, in *Works* (London: Thomas Braddyll, 1706), 463, 373.

18. Gilbert Burnet, *An Exposition of the Thirty-Nine Articles*, 129–30. See also Edward Fowler's preface to John Worthington's *Great Duty of Self-Resignation to the Divine Will* (London: Walter Kettilby, 1689).

19. Patrick, *The Devout Christian*, in *Works* 2:304, 305.

20. *The Confessions of Saint Augustine*, ed. E. B. Pusey (London: J. M. Dent, 1913), book 2, IV–VI.

21. Robert Sanderson, *Thirty-Six Sermons* (London: John Hindmarsh, 1689), 405; South, *Sermons Preached Upon Several Occasions*, 1:50. Even if Scripture did not inform us of our depraved state, wrote Bishop John Cosin, "yet the universal irregularity of our whole nature . . . running counter all the time of our life to all the right rules of order and reason" would make any other conclusion untenable. Cosin, *The Works of John Cosin* (Oxford: John Henry Parker, 1843), 1:209.

22. Fowler, *The Design of Christianity* (London: Tyler and Holt, 1671), 90, 168.

23. Ibid., 128.

24. Fowler, *Sermon Preached at Bow-Church Before the Lord Mayor and Court of Aldermen* (London: Brabazon Alymer, 1690), 19. Robert Boyle made the same point in *Occasional Reflections Upon Several Subjects*, in *Works*, ed. Thomas Birch (London, 1772), 2:350.

25. Wilkins, *A Discourse Concerning the Gift of Prayer* (London, 1651), 80. In his *Of the Principles and Duties of Natural Religion* (London: A. Maxwell, 1675), 394, Wilkins declared that in mankind's "dark and degenerate state," revelation was essential to discover our duty. In a work which putatively promotes the virtues of natural religion, Wilkins insisted that "Every man at his best estate, is but a feeble infirm creature." Ibid., 191.

26. *Discourse*, 80.

27. Ibid., 77. Examples could be multiplied. Matthew Hale spoke of a corrupted and depraved nature "full of impotence, and rebellion and disorder." To his mind there was not one pure act of which man could boast, and the search for forgiveness began with the unqualified admission of our "sinful and polluted Nature, a Body of Sin and Death." Hale, "Meditations Upon the Lord's Prayer," in *The Works, Moral and Religious, of Sir Matthew Hale*, ed. T. Thirlwall (London: H. D. Symonds, 1805), 2:529, 531, 532, 544. See also "The Victory of Faith Over the World," in *Works*, 2:99, and "Of Humility," 2:167, where he writes that "pride and vain-glory is so unhappily riveted in the corrupt nature of man." In "The Folly and Mischief of Sin," *Works*, 2:349, Hale wrote that all sin is against nature "and a violation and a breach even of the law and order of nature; which is nothing else but the station, course and fame, that God, with most admirable wisdom and goodness, framed for man." John Moore observed that men generally remain proud of their weakness and vanity despite their being dead in sin, "unto every good Work reprobate, and alienated from the Life of God." John Moore, *Sermons on Several Subjects*, ed. Samuel Clarke (London: T. Pemberton, 1724), 2:35.

28. Barrow, "Of the Evil and Unreasonableness of Infidelity," in *The Theological Works of Isaac Barrow*, ed. Alexander Napier (Cambridge: Cambridge University Press, 1839), 5:19. Barrow, like More and Cudworth, remained at Cambridge after 1660. As master of Trinity from 1672 until his death in 1677, he remained friends with Tillotson, Patrick, and Wilkins.

29. Barrow, *Works*, 5:66. Simon Patrick informed his Covent Garden congregation that before we find acceptance with God, our souls "must lie as low before him as our bodies; and we must sorrowfully acknowledge that we do deserve to be utterly abandoned by him." Patrick, "A Sermon Preached at St. Paul's, Covent Garden, 13 Nov. 1678" in *Works*, 8:18–19.

30. Irene Simon, "Tillotson's Barrow," *English Studies* 45 (1964): 288, concludes that Tillotson did not substantially alter Barrow's manuscripts for publication as some scholars have assumed.

31. Quoting R. Buick Knox, "Bishops in the Pulpit in the Seventeenth Century: Continuity and Change," in Knox, ed., *Reformation, Conformity and Dissent*, 101. Cf. W. M. Spellman, "Archbishop John Tillotson and the Meaning of Moralism," *Anglican and Episcopal History* 56, no. 4 (1987): 404–22.

32. Anthony Collins, *A Discourse of Freethinking* (London, 1713), 171.

33. Tillotson's influence and popularity are acknowledged by Burnet, *History*, 1:335; John Locke, "Some Directions Concerning Reading and Study for a Gentleman," in James Axtell, ed., *The Educational Writings of John Locke* (Cambridge: Cambridge University Press, 1968), 399; Evelyn, *Diary*, 4:84, 107, 240, 244, 371, 373, 435, 505, 628; N.C., *A Modest and True Account of the Chief Points in Controversy, Between the Roman Catholicks and Protestants* (Antwerp, 1705), 2 [Attributed to Cornelius Nary and also to Nicholas Colvin. The imprint is false; possibly printed in London]; Lewis Atterbury, *A Vindication of Archbishop Tillotson's Sermons* (London: Thomas Baker, 1709), 4, 12; Bevill Higgins, *Historical and Critical Remarks on Burnet's History of His Own Time* (London: P. Meighan, 1725), 182; C. F. Secretan, *Memoirs of the Life and Times of the Pious Robert Nelson* (London: John Murry, 1860), 199–200.

34. Tillotson, "Objections Against the True Religion Answered" in *Works*, 2:477; "The Necessity of Supernatural Grace," 8:492.

35. Id., "Objections Raised Against the True Religion Answered," 2:477, 481. See also "The Goodness of God," 7:31.

36. Tillotson, "The Reasonableness of Fearing God More than Men," 10:82; "The Excellency and Universality of the Christian Religion," 8:575; "Of the Ordinary Influence of the Holy Ghost," 8:444.

37. Tillotson, "Of the Education of Children," *Works*, 3:232. Cf. Herbert Croft, *The Naked Truth*, 5.

38. On the *philosophes* and education, see Peter Gay, *The Enlightenment* (New York: Norton, 1969), 2:497–516.

39. Glanvill, *The Way to Happiness* (London: James Collins, 1670), 10, 11, 14.

40. Glanvill, *Moral Evidence of a Life to Come* (1676) in Horneck, ed., 273; *Lux Orientalis* (London: Samuel Lowndes, 1682; first published 1662), 33. Glanvill's belief in the preexistence of souls, where a primeval apostasy of souls coeval with the disobedience of the angels constituted the first taint which Adam subsequently aggravated, had frustrating implications for any scheme of education as a social palliative. Glanvill, *Lux Orientalis*, preface (unpaginated). Glanvill's work borrowed extensively from Henry More's *Immortality of the Soul*. See Jackson Cope, *Joseph Glanvill: Anglican Apologist*, 88. More agreed with Glanvill's view that the differences in the degree of human depravity observable in the world were due originally to the magnitude of one's sin in a preexistent state.

41. Barrow, "Of Industry in General" in *Works*, 3:361, 364. Cf. "The Danger and Mischief of Delaying Repentance," 3:311. Stillingfleet, "Sermon Preached Before the King" (24 February 1675), in *Works*, 1:217, 220; "Sermon Preached Before the King" (15 February 1684), in *Works*, 1:343. By 1689 Stillingfleet's view had become more pessimistic, as he complained that those who magnified man's free will viewed their subjects "not as they are, but as they ought to have been" and insisted that our natural propensity to evil has left us in a state where "there is scarce such a thing as Freedom of Will left, especially to matters of salvation." Stillingfleet, "Sermon Preached Before the Queen at White-hall" (22 February 1689), in *Works*, 1:414, 415. Compare Latitudinarian views with those of High Churchmen like Robert South, who also believed that in education, particularly the task of inculcating principles of virtue, "it were to be wished . . . that the constitution of man's nature were such, that this might be done only by the mild addresses of reason and the gentle arts of persuasion." Unfortunately, "unless youth were all made up of goodness and ingenuity, this is a felicity not to be hoped for." South, "The Virtuous Education of Youth," in *Sermons*, 3:397.

42. Locke, *Some Thoughts Concerning Education*, in James Axtell, ed., *The Educational Writings of John Locke*, 134, 325. For a discussion of Locke's views, see W. M. Spellman, *John Locke and the Problem of Depravity* (Oxford: Clarendon Press, 1988).

43. *Some Thoughts*, 166.

44. Burnet, *Thoughts on Education* (1668), ed. John Clarke (Aberdeen, Scotland: University of Aberdeen Press, 1914), 9. Simon Patrick warned that as the understandings of children are weak, "so their passions are strong, and their desires violent." Patrick, "A Sermon Preached on St. Mark's Day," in *Works*, 8:183.

45. Tillotson, "Of the Education of Children," in *Works*, 3:483.
46. Richard Schlatter, *The Social Ideas of Religious Leaders, 1660–1688* (London: Oxford University Press, 1940), 31–59, discusses the importance of education for Restoration divines.
47. Tillotson, "Of the Education of Children," in *Works*, 3:474, 481, 541 (The three sermons carried the same title).
48. Id., "Of the Nature of Regeneration," in *Works*, 5:407. Cf. "The Nature of Benefit and Consideration," 2:96–97; "Of the Advantages of an Early Piety," 3:556.
49. Tillotson, "The Deceitfulness and Danger of Sin," in *Works*, 2:21. He makes a similar point in "The Education of Children," 3:521, and "The Difficulty of Reforming Vicious Habits," 2:502; "Of the Advantage of an Early Piety," 3:565.
50. Tillotson, "Of the Education of Children," in *Works*, 3:495; "The Difficulty of Reforming Vicious Habits," 2:512.
51. Rom. 3.23; Gen. 1.26; Barclay, *Mind of St. Paul*, 187.
52. Aquinas, *Summa Theologica*, Ia2ae, quest. 4, art. 8; Hooker, *Laws*, 1, 5, 2; Herschel Baker, *The Image of Man: A Study of the Idea of Human Dignity in Classical Antiquity, the Middle Ages, and the Renaissance* (New York: Harper Torchbooks, 1961), 195; Kenneth Scott Latourette, *A History of Christianity* (New York: Harper and Row, 1975), 1:511.
53. Etienne Gilson, *The Spirit of Medieval Philosophy*, trans. A. H. C. Downes (New York: Charles Scribner's Sons, 1940), 117–19; Ernst Benz, "The Concept of Man in Christian Thought," in *The Concept of Man: A Study in Comparative Philosophy*, ed. S. Radhakrishnan and P. T. Raju (Lincoln, Nebr.: Johnsen Publishing Co., 1966), 404; Robinson, *The Christian Doctrine of Man*, 207–8.
54. Hooker, *Laws*, 1, 8, 2. See also Norman Powell Williams, *The Ideas of the Fall and Original Sin* (London: Longmans, 1929), 418. Reform was impossible without preventing grace.
55. Gilson, *Spirit of Medieval Philosophy*, 168–72; Gilson, *History of Christian Philosophy in the Middle Ages* (New York: Random House, 1955), 376; Armand A. Maurer, *Medieval Philosophy* (New York: Random House, 1964), 179–81.
56. Tillotson, "The Goodness of God," in *Works*, 7:9. The words of Genesis 1.27, "So God created man in his own image, in the image of God created he him," provided a powerful reminder of the special status of mankind. Cf. Victor Harris, *All Coherence Gone* (New York: Frank Cass, 1966), 1, 5; Somerville, *Popular Religion*, 89–90.
57. Hickes, "The Natural Excellence and Dignity of Man," in *A Collection of Sermons* (London: John Churchill, 1713), 2:323, 325, 340.
58. Ibid., 2:341.
59. Tillotson, "Objections Against the True Religion Answered," in *Works*, 2:478, 481.
60. Baxter, *Treatise of Self-Denial*, in *The Practical Works* (London: James Duncan, 1830), 11:115, 116.
61. Burnet, *Exposition of the Thirty-Nine Articles*, 41. Clarendon believed that if men did not take such great pains to corrupt their own nature, "our nature would never corrupt us." *Essays Moral and Entertaining, on the Various Faculties and Passions of the Human Mind* (London: Longman, Hurst, Rees, 1815), 1:1–2.
62. Cosin, *Works*, 1:212. See also John Moore, *Sermons*, 1:30–31, who argues that God's

commandments are all accommodated to our capabilities and take into account our infirmities.

63. Edward Hyde, *A Collection of Several Tracts of the Right Honourable Edward, Earl of Clarendon* (London: T. Woodward, 1727), 500. Glanvill repeats these sentiments when he says that without being liable to sin, "many choice vertues, excellent branches of the divine Life had never been exercised, or indeed have ever been at all." *Lux Orientalis*, 68. Arthur Lovejoy, "Milton and the Paradox of the Fortunate Fall," in *Essays in the History of Ideas* (New York: G. P. Putnam's Sons, 1960), 277–95. Lovejoy discusses the background to Milton's use of the idea. The "paradox" was embraced by Augustine, Ambrose, Leo the Great, Gregory the Great, and Francis de Sales.

64. Quoting Gilson, *Spirit of Medieval Philosophy*, 118.

65. *Summa Theologica*, Ia2ae, quest. 82, art. 3.

66. Whichcote, *Moral and Religious Aphorisms*, #42.

67. Ibid., #228.

68. Stillingfleet, *Irenicum*, in *Works*, 2:172; "Sermon Preached before the King, 24 February 1675" in *Works*, 1:217, 220.

69. Burton, "A Discourse of Repentance," in *Several Discourses* (London, 1684–85), 1:228, 241; "A Discourse of Purity and Charity," 1:15; "Of Understanding the Will of God," 2:164. See also "Of the Fruits of Repentance," 1:328.

70. Tillotson, "Concerning the Incarnation of Christ," *Works*, 3:381.

71. Id., "The Nature and Influence of the Promises of the Gospel," *Works*, 4:208.

72. Id., "The Wisdom of Religion," in *Works*, 5:175. See also "Religion, Our First and Great Concernment," 5:149.

73. Burnet, *Subjection for Conscience Sake* (London: R. Royston, 1675), links social stability to the power of religion to engage men in an obedience to law. Cf. Herbert Croft, *The Legacy of the Right Reverend Herbert Lord Bishop of Hereford* (London: Charles Harper, 1679), 7, who opined that "Vertuous persons never resist authority." Hill, "The Necessity of Religion," in *Essays*, 2:11–18, discusses this point.

74. Baker, *Wars of Truth*, 66–67, 78.

75. Jacob Viner, *The Role of Providence in the Social Order* (Philadelphia: American Philosophical Society, 1970), 88; Angus McInnes, "The People and the Revolution," in Geoffrey Holmes, ed., *Britain after the Glorious Revolution* (London: Macmillan, 1969), 88–89; Roy Porter, *English Society in the Eighteenth Century* (Harmondsworth, England: Penguin, 1982), 67.

76. Christopher Hill, *World Turned Upside Down*, 130–36; id., "Sin and Society," in *Essays*, 2:119–20, 126, 127, 129; Ernst Troeltsch, *The Social Teaching of the Christian Churches*, trans. Olive Wyon, (London: George Allen and Unwin, 1931), 2:711–12.

77. Hooker, *Laws*, and Pym, "Speech at the Trial of Strafford," quoted in Hill, "Sin and Society," 2:125, 126.

78. Tillotson, "The Duty and Reason of Praying for Governers," *Works*, 4:535. Like Hobbes, Tillotson's state of nature was "a state of perpetual feud and war with all mankind." Ibid., 537.

79. Tillotson, "The Wisdom of Being Religious," *Works*, 1:321. Elsewhere he apologized for having to speak "of such dreadful and tragical things" as the eternal torments of body and soul awaiting the unrepentant sinner and found it espe-

cially disturbing that even such "harsh and unwelcome words" did but little "to awaken the greatest part of mankind to a due consideration of their ways." "The Reasonableness of Fearing God More than Men," in *Works*, 10:98. See also "The Distinguishing Character of a Good and a Bad Man," 2:143.

80. South, *Sermons on Several Occasions*, quoted in Hill, "Necessity of Religion," in *Essays*, 2:16.

81. I have borrowed these terms from John Passmore, *The Perfectibility of Man* (London: Gerald Duckworth and Co., 1970), 19.

82. Even obedientiary perfection, were that possible after man's initial declension, would, as Simon Patrick put it, be without merit, since full obedience is merely what we owe God in the first place.

4 : Revelation and the Remains of Reason

1. John Standish, *A Sermon Preached Before the King at Whitehall* (London: Henry Brome, 1676), 24–25.

2. As a busy London curate, Patrick seemed particularly resentful of Standish's comfortable circumstances at Peterhouse, Cambridge, and his insensitivity toward the task of those who labored in the city. Patrick, *An Earnest Request to Mr. John Standish*, in *Works*, 6:433, 439. See also Patrick's response to Arthur Annersley's defense of Standish, published as *Falsehood Unmasked*, in *Works*, 6:460. In the same year as Standish's attack, another fellow of Peterhouse and a royal chaplain, Miles Barnes, delivered a sermon in which he associated Latitudinarianism with libertinism. *The Authority of Church Guides Asserted*, quoted in Gasciogne, *Cambridge in the Age of Enlightenment*, 45.

3. Patrick, *An Earnest Request*, 439.

4. Reedy, *Bible and Reason*, 17. Fideism was not a Catholic monopoly, for Protestant sectaries disparaged the use of reason in religion as well.

5. Standish, *Sermon Preached before the King*, 25.

6. Collins, *A Discourse of Freethinking*, 171.

7. Harth, *Contexts of Dryden's Thought*, 99.

8. Early seventeenth-century Puritans limited reason's purview to civil and human affairs. See Morgan, *Godly Learning*, 48, and Perry Miller, *The New England Mind* (Boston: Beacon Press, 1965), 181–206. See also Allen, *Doubt's Boundless Sea*, 114, and Cragg, *Freedom and Authority*, 145.

9. Spurr, "Rational Religion in Restoration England," *Journal of the History of Ideas* 49, no. 4 (1988): 270–71; Christopher Hill, "Reason and Reasonableness in Seventeenth-Century England," *British Journal of Sociology* 20, no. 3 (1969): 235–52.

10. Reynolds, *Works*, 3:410. Cf. Tillotson, "Institutional Religion Not Intended to Undermine Natural," in *Works*, 5:298, 312–13; George Rust, *A Discourse of the Use of Reason in Matters of Religion*, trans. Henry Hallywell (London: Henry Hills, 1683), 24.

11. Baker, *Wars of Truth*, 4–6. Jerald C. Brauer, "Types of Puritan Piety," *Church History* 56, no. 1 (1987): 50, indicates that according to the rationalist strain within Puritanism, God had built rationality into the core of the cosmos.

12. See, for example, Baxter, "Knowledge and Love Compared," in *Works*, 15:46, 186.

"All knowledge that kindleth not the love of God in us," he maintained, "is so narrow and small that it deserveth not indeed the name of knowledge." Ibid., 199. See also Etienne Gilson, *Reason and Revelation in the Middle Ages* (New York: Charles Scribner's Sons, 1938), 81–85.

13. On Augustine's outlook, see John Mahoney, *The Making of Moral Theology: A Study of the Roman Catholic Tradition* (Oxford: Clarendon Press, 1991), 103. The discussion of Hooker is based on Phillip Harth's study *Swift and Anglican Rationalism* (Chicago: University of Chicago Press, 1961), 21–51, and John New, *Anglican and Puritan: The Basis of Their Opposition*, 20–26.

14. Hooker, *Laws*, 3.8.4.

15. Ibid.

16. For Aquinas's relation to classical thought here, see Vernon J. Bourke, *St. Thomas and the Greek Moralists* (Milwaukee, Wis.: Marquette University Press, 1947), 22–29; Werner Jaeger, *Humanism and Theology* (Milwaukee, Wis.: Marquette University Press, 1943), 17–19; Etienne Gilson, *The Philosophy of St. Thomas Aquinas*, trans. Edward Bullough (New York: Dorset Press, n.d.), 9–23.

17. Quoting Harth, *Swift and Anglican Rationalism*, 27; id., *Contexts of Dryden's Thought*, 106–7.

18. Hooker, *Laws*, 3.8.10.

19. Ibid., preface, 3.2.

20. Quoting Lake, *Anglican and Puritan?*, 149.

21. Sanderson, *Thirty-Six Sermons*, 484. See also Tenison, *A Discourse Concerning a Guide in Matters of Faith* (London: Benjamin Tooke, 1683), 26; and Tillotson's sermon preached at Whitehall on 4 April 1679 in *Works*, 1:257, where he declares that "Whatever doctrines God reveals to man are proportioned to their understandings, and by this faculty we are to examine all doctrines which pretend to be from God, and upon examination to judge whether there be reason to receive them as Divine, or to reject them as impostures."

22. Cosin, *Works*, 1:311. Cf. John Pearson, *An Exposition of the Creed* (London: Roger Daniel, 1659), 21.

23. Sprat, *Sermons Preached on Several Occasions*, 2, 28, 194. G. Reedy, *Bible and Reason*, 12.

24. Ronald Knox, *Enthusiasm: A Chapter in the History of Religion* (Oxford: Clarendon Press, 1950), 2–3.

25. Michael Hyde, "The Reaction to Enthusiasm in the Seventeenth Century: Towards an Integrative Approach," *Journal of Modern History* 53, no. 2 (1981): 258–80, provides a good overview of the recent literature on the subject.

26. Edward Fowler, *The Principles and Practices of Certain Moderate Divines of the Church of England* (London: L. Lloyd, 1670), 45.

27. See South, "Of the Nature and Measures of Conscience," in *Sermons*, 2:179; "The Christian Pentecost," in *Sermons*, 2:545, 546.

28. South, "Of the Nature and Measures of Conscience," in *Sermons*, 2:179, 180. South thought that Christianity "may be justly called the last and most correct edition of the law of nature." *Sermons*, 7:1.

29. Glanvill, *The Agreement of Reason and Religion*, in *Essays* (London: John Baker, 1676), 26. Cope says that all the Latitudinarians feared "the uncontrolled, mel-

ancholic prompting of the dissenter's inner light—it was this which they represented to their time as the dangerous voice of anti-reason." See Cope, "The Cupri-Cosmits," 272.

30. For the literary reaction, see George Williamson, "The Restoration Revolt Against Enthusiasm," in id., *Seventeenth-Century Contexts* (Chicago: University of Chicago Press, 1969), 202–39; R. F. Jones, "Science and English Prose Style in the Third Quarter of the Seventeenth Century," in Jones, ed., *The Seventeenth Century: Studies in the History of English Thought and Literature from Bacon to Pope* (Stanford, Calif.: Stanford University Press, 1951), 75–100.

31. Ellen More, "Congregationalism and the Social Order: John Goodwin's Gathered Church, 1640–1660," *Journal of Ecclesiastical History* 38, no. 2 (1987): 210.

32. Glanvill, *The Agreement of Reason and Religion* in *Essays*, 1–2, 6, 8, 11.

33. On Dryden's fideism, see Harth, *Contexts of Dryden's Thought*.

34. The book was reissued eight times by 1709. Popkin, "Philosophy of Bishop Stillingfleet," 305, and Carroll, *Common Sense Philosophy*, 43. Pepys, *Diary*, 6:296–97, gave the book a mixed review.

35. *Origines Sacrae*, in *Works*, 2:69. Stillingfleet's argument was later directed against Deists and atheists. See *A Rational Account of the Protestant Religion* (1668), where the Catholic menace is considered more directly. Later, in his 1688 *Discourse on the Nature and Grounds of the Certainty of Faith*, he expanded the areas where certain knowledge was impossible to include natural philosophy. Other examples of the argument for moral certainty include Tillotson's *Rule of Faith*; "The Christian Life, A Life of Faith," in *Works*, 4:188; Wilkins, *Principles and Duties of Natural Religion*, 22–30; Fowler, *Principles and Practices*, 61–62; Patrick, "An Answer to a Book Spread Abroad by the Romish Priests," in *Works*, 7:187; Moore, *Works*, 2:42.

36. Pearson, *Exposition of the Creed*, 21. Tillotson thought that there was nothing more reasonable than to believe "whatever we are sufficiently assured is revealed to us by God, who can neither be deceived himself, nor deceive us." Tillotson, "Of Self-Denial and Suffering for Christ's Sake," in *Works*, 4:227. Cf. William Sherlock, "The Reasonableness of Faith," in *Sermons Preached Upon Several Occasions* (London: R. Wrae, 1755), 1:383–84; Burnet, *Exposition of the Thirty-Nine Articles*, 37; George Rust, *Discourse of the Use of Reason*, 26.

37. Baxter, *Christian Directory*, in *Works*, 2:13. See also Patrick, *An Earnest Request to Mr. John Standish*, in *Works*, 6:439.

38. Baxter, *The Judgement of Non-conformists, of the Interest of Reason in Matters of Religion* (London, 1676), 9.

39. Ibid., 12. Dissenters were compelled to counter charges of "enthusiasm" made against them by Sheldon's chaplain Parker in the 1670s. See Ashcraft, *Revolutionary Politics*, 54.

40. Baxter, *Treatise of Self-Denial*, in *Works*, 11:321. No matter how weak the light of reason in man since the Fall, said William Sherlock, it still has the power to direct us to a safer guide, "For Reason itself teaches us to believe God, who cannot deceive us, and can itself judge of the external and visible Marks of a Revelation; that is, can judge when God speaks." Sherlock, "The Danger of Confounding the Distinctions of Good and Evil," in *Sermons*, 1:423–24.

41. South, *Sermons*, 5:74. See also Stillingfleet, "The Mysteries of the Christian Faith Asserted and Vindicated" in *Works*, 3:348, and William Sancroft, *Occasional Ser-*

mons, (London: Thomas Bassett, 1694), 75, who stated that "For though God's Judgments may be secret, yet they cannot be unjust: Like the great Deep indeed, an Abyss unfathomable, But though we have no Plumb-line of Reason, that can reach it, our Faith assures us, there's Justice at the Bottom."

42. Cosin, *Works*, 1:310. Boyle made the same point in *A Discourse of Things Above Reason*. See Richard Westfall, *Science and Religion in Seventeenth-Century England* (Ann Arbor: University of Michigan Press, 1973), 169.

43. Baxter illustrated the socially dangerous implications of Biblicism when he observed that "All Protestants disclaim that inhumane, atheistical assertion, that in Religion, Inferiors must believe all that their Superiors assert, and do all that they shall command . . . without using their own Reason to discern judicio privato whether it be agreeable, or contrary to the Laws of God." Baxter, *Judgement of Non-conformists*, 18. The pamphlet was endorsed by Bates, Manton, and other Dissenters.

44. I owe this observation to John Spurr's article "Rational Religion," 569. See also H. D. McDonald, *Ideas of Revelation: An Historical Study* (London: Macmillan, 1959), 35–36.

45. John W. Yolton, *John Locke and the Way of Ideas* (Oxford: Clarendon Press, 1956), 29. As Yolton points out, the principles that were normally listed as innate were those which buttressed the existing values of the society. Ibid., 29, 39.

46. John Wilkins, *Principles and Duties of Natural Religion*, iv–v (preface is unpaginated). See also Tillotson, *Works*, 1:349; 2:257–58, 478; 5:281–82. Cf. Burnet, *Thirty-Nine Articles*, 120.

47. Hale, *The Primitive Origination of Mankind* (London: William Gobbid, 1677), 2.

48. Ibid., 352.

49. Barrow, *Works*, 1:271. Compare "The Duty of Thanksgiving," where he says that God has impressed on our minds "perspicacious characters of his own divine essence," 1:362. See also Tillotson, *Works*, 1:349.

50. William Sancroft, *Occasional Sermons*, 65. See also Cosin, *Works*, 1:214.

51. Baxter, *The Reason of the Christian Religion*, in *Works*, 21:6–7.

52. Tillotson, "Of the Difficulty of Reforming Vicious Habits," in *Works*, 1:509. Pearson, *Exposition of the Creed*, 52, seems to have been alone in doubting the innate idea of a deity.

53. Moore, *Sermons*, 1:28, 29, 156, 416. Stillingfleet believed that the soul of man would "degenerate from itself" if not constantly improved (*Origines Sacrae*, in *Works*, 2:4), while Barrow insisted that only religion provided us with clear notions of our nature, our origins, the way to happiness, and our final end, "points about which otherwise by no reason, no history, no experience we could be well resolved or satisfied." In fact, "mere ratiocination" about such matters "doth ever grope in the dark, doth rove after shadows of truth." Barrow, "Of the Excellency of the Christian Religion," in *Works*, 5:462–63; id., "Virtue and the Reasonableness of Faith," 5:43.

54. Such had been the view of the early Latin Fathers toward the Greeks. See Allen, *Doubt's Boundless Sea*, 112.

55. Moore, *Sermons*, 1:399, 401. See also id., "The Excellency of the Christian Religion," 2:306.

56. Tillotson's preface to Wilkins's *Principles and Duties of Natural Religion*, vi–vii. Tillot-

son thought that man must take "due care to inform his conscience aright," a position which belied the idea that conscience was a fully operative moral guide. Tillotson, "A Conscience Void of Offence," in *Works*, 3:152. Stillingfleet wrote that the world was lost in disputes over such questions as the nature, condition, and immortality of the soul before the promulgation of divine Revelation. *Origines Sacrae*, in *Works*, 2:380.

57. Tenison, *Sermon Preached at the Anniversary Meeting of the Clergymens' Sons* (London: Richard Chiswell, 1691), 7.

58. Sanderson, *Thirty-Six Sermons*, 554.

59. William Sancroft, *Occasional Sermons*, 67.

60. For the details of this exchange, see Yolton, *Way of Ideas*, 48–64.

61. Bredvold, *Intellectual Milieu of John Dryden*, 22; Morgan, *Godly Learning*, 51.

62. Irene Simon, *"Pride of Reason" in the Restoration and Earlier Eighteenth Century* (Brussels: Marcel Didier, 1960), discusses the literary aspects of this continuing distrust of reason.

63. Hooker, *Laws*, 1, 12, 1. Aquinas, *Summa Theologica*, 1a2ae, quest. 109, art. 2, had not hesitated to acknowledge that "for the knowledge of any truth, man needs divine assistance so that his intellect may be moved by God to actualize itself." See also Etienne Gilson, *The Philosophy of St. Thomas Aquinas*, 357.

64. Even Locke conceded that reason, while "speaking ever so clearly to the wise and virtuous, had never authority enough to prevail on the multitude. . . ." *The Reasonableness of Christianity* in *Works*, 10 vols. (London: Thomas Tegg, 1823), 7:135.

65. Taylor, *Ductor Dubitantium*, in *Works*, ed. Reginald Heber (London: Ogle, Duncan and Co., 1822), 12: book 2, chapter 1, rule 2. See also Allen, *Doubt's Boundless Sea*, 122.

66. Sherlock, "The Purification of Our Lives by God's Word," in *Sermons*, 2:87, 89.

67. Tillotson, "Christ the Author, and Obedience the Condition of Salvation," in *Works*, 6:96. See also "The Advantages of Religion to Society," 1:420, and Barrow, "Of the Excellency of the Christian Religion," in *Works*, 2:222; id., "The Forgiveness of Sins," 2:512; id., "Virtue and the Reasonableness of Faith," 5:43.

68. Sanderson, *Thirty-Six Sermons*, 657.

69. Hoopes, *Right Reason*, 121.

70. "Royal Society, Boyle Papers," quoted in Richard Westfall, *Science and Religion in Seventeenth-Century England*, 168.

71. Locke, *Reasonableness of Christianity*, in *Works*, 7:139.

72. Cosin, *Works*, 1:286. Cf. Fowler, *Principles and Practices*, 69. Cf. Locke, *Reasonableness of Christianity*, 7:139.

73. Patrick, "A Sermon Preached on St. Mark's Day" (1686), in *Works*, 8:186.

74. Robert Hoopes, *Right Reason*, 56.

75. Fowler, *Design of Christianity*, 274.

76. Glanvill, *Agreement of Reason and Religion*, 21; Hoopes, *Right Reason*, 85. In a now much-disparaged book, Carl Becker pointed to the "faith" in human reason of the eighteenth-century philosophes, arguing that their claims regarding the uniformity of reason and the laws of nature had little empirical evidence to support them. *The Heavenly City of the Eighteenth-Century Philosophers* (New Haven: Yale University Press, 1930).

77. Tillotson, "The Necessity of Supernatural Grace," *Works*, 8:489.

78. South, "False Foundations Removed, and True Ones Laid," in *Sermons*, 2:327. See also Baxter, *Christian Directory*, in *Works*, 2:24, where he writes that God's grace cures men of the folly of sin "and make us reasonable again."

5 : The Succor of Grace

1. John Wilkins, *Sermons Preach'd Upon Several Occasions*, 309–10.
2. Wilkins, *A Discourse Concerning the Gift of Prayer* (London, 1653; first published in 1651), 96, 107, 109.
3. Barbara Shapiro, *Probability and Certainty*, 88, has written that "as a group, the rationalists rarely discussed Christ. Their emphasis was on God, God the Creator, not the God who in his mercy gave His Son to man." Allison, *Rise of Moralism*, and Alister E. McGrath, *Iustitia Dei: A History of the Christian Doctrine of Grace* (Cambridge: Cambridge University Press, 1987), 2:105–10, argue that the late Caroline divines associated justification with inherent righteousness.
4. Willey, *Christianity Past and Present* (Cambridge: Cambridge University Press, 1952), 19, 29, 37.
5. Barclay, *Mind of St. Paul*, 183–93; Baker, *Dignity of Man*, 130; N. P. Williams, *The Grace of God* (London: Longmans, 1930), 10–14.
6. Rom. 3.10.
7. For Paul, "law" meant legalism, or the view of salvation as something to be earned. The apostle's own instantaneous conversion strongly suggested that one could not prepare for grace. See Williams, *Grace of God*, 12; Cave, *Christian Estimate of Man*, 36.
8. James A. Carpenter, *Nature and Grace: Toward an Integral Perspective* (New York: Crossroad Publishers, 1988), 1–17; Norman Pettit, *The Heart Prepared* (New Haven: Yale University Press, 1966), 22–23; Hastings Rashdall, *The Idea of Atonement in Christian Theology* (London: Macmillan, 1920), 330–50.
9. Saint Augustine, *On Grace and Free Will*, in *The Basic Writings of St. Augustine*, ed. Whitney J. Oates (New York: Random House, 1948), 1:555.
10. Quoted in Roger Haight, *The Experience and Language of Grace* (New York: Paulist Press, 1979), 36. See also Williams, *Grace of God*, 21–23; Eugene A. TeSelle, "The Problem of Nature and Grace," *Journal of Religion* 45, no. 2 (1965): 238–49.
11. Quoting McGrath, *Iustitia Dei*, 1:27.
12. P. Gregory Stevens, *The Life of Grace* (Englewood Cliffs, N.J.: Prentice Hall, 1963), 44–45; Haight, *Experience and Language of Grace*, 32, says that on the issue of grace, Augustine's thoughts "were written into the doctrine of Western Christianity."
13. John 15.5. Canon 5 of the Council of Orange stated that "if anyone denies that even the beginnings of faith and the disposition to believe . . . is bestowed by the gift of grace . . . and asserts that the beginning of faith is in us by nature, he proves himself an adversary of apostolic doctrine." Quoted in Williams, *Grace of God*, 56.
14. *Summa Theologica*, Ia2ae, quest. 109, art. 1, 2.
15. Ibid., Ia2ae, quest. 109, art. 6.
16. Ibid., Ia2ae, quest. 109, art. 8. Haight, *Experience and Language of Grace*, 67; Williams, *Grace of God*, 69.
17. *Summa Theologica*, Ia2ae, quest. 109, art. 9.
18. Calvin, *Institutes*, 2, 3, 5.

19. Edmund Morgan, *Visible Saints: The History of a Puritan Idea* (New York: New York University Press, 1963), 67.

20. The New Testament variously describes Christ's work as one of salvation (Luke 2.11), deliverance or rescue (Gal. 1.4), redemption (Rom. 3.24), reconciliation (2 Cor. 5.18), and rebirth (John 10.10). See Linwood Urban, *A Short History of Christian Thought* (New York: Oxford University Press, 1986), 101.

21. Miller, *The New England Mind: The Seventeenth Century* (Boston: Beacon Press, 1964), 253, 260, 285.

22. Laud, *Works* (Oxford; J. H. Parker, 1847–60), 2:280.

23. Thomas Wood, *English Casuistical Divinity During the Seventeenth Century* (London: Society for Promoting Christian Knowledge, 1952), vii.

24. Arminius quoted in Kendall, *Calvin and English Calvinism*, 143.

25. Stevens, *Life of Grace*, 54–56; McGrath, *Iustitia Dei*, 2:2; Cassirer, *Philosophy of Enlightenment*, 140.

26. Zwingli quoted in Pettit, *Heart Prepared*, 2. Cf. Calvin, *Institutes*, 2: book 3, chapter 15, sections i, ii.

27. Wallace, *Puritans and Predestination*, 3–28. Nicholas Tyack, *Anti-Calvinists*, 1–9.

28. Articles X, XIII, printed in John H. Leith, ed., *Creeds of the Churches* (Atlanta: John Knox Press, 1977), 270.

29. H. Outrem Evennett, *The Spirit of the Counter-Reformation* (Cambridge: Cambridge University Press, 1968), 33–34; Herbert Jedin, *A History of the Council of Trent*, trans. Ernst Graff (Edinburgh: Thomas Nelson, 1961), 2:307–09.

30. Saint Augustine, "On the Spirit and the Letter," in Oates, ed., *Basic Writings*, 1:463–64.

31. Ibid., 57, 61. Wallace, *Puritans and Predestination*, viii; TeSelle, "Problem of Nature and Grace," 245.

32. *Summa Theologica*, Ia2ae, quest. 112, art. 2; Otto W. Heick, *A History of Christian Thought*, (Philadelphia: Fortress Press, 1965), 1:289; Pettit, 24–26.

33. *Treatise on Grace*, quest. 109, art. 6. quoted in R. Niebuhr, *Nature and Destiny of Man* (London: Nisbet and Co., 1945), 2:122.

34. Acts 20.21.

35. Norman Pettit, *The Heart Prepared*, 1–18; Wallace, *Puritans and Predestination*, 72–73, 75–76; Charles and Catherine George, *The Protestant Mind of the English Reformation*, 46–48.

36. Joseph Hall, *Works* (London, 1863), 9:493–94, quoted in Pettit, *Heart Prepared*, 126.

37. See above the view of Aquinas and Wilkins's statement regarding restraining grace.

38. Leith, ed., *Creeds of the Churches*, 271.

39. Cudworth, "Sermon Preached Before the Honorable House of Commons," 31 March 1647, in *Works*, 4:300. Cf. Whichcote, "The Arguments by Which a Man Should be Persuaded to Reconcile Unto God," in *Works*, 2:356.

40. For a discussion of Anglican thought on grace during the Cromwellian period, see Wallace, *Puritans and Predestination* 120–30.

41. Hammond, *A Pacifick Discourse of God's Grace and Decrees* (London, 1660), quoted in Wallace, 125.

42. Robert Sanderson, *Thirty-Six Sermons*, 49. Cf. Cudworth, "Sermon Before Commons," in *Works*, 4:371–73.

43. Reynolds, *Works*, 2:27.

44. South, "The Doctrine of Merit Stated, and the Impossibility of Men's Meriting of God," in *Sermons*, 2:232.

45. H. John McLachlan, *Socinianism in Seventeenth-Century England* (Oxford: Oxford University Press, 1951), 11–12, 15, 54–102. Tillotson deeply lamented the fact that all men who inquired into the rational grounds of the faith were quickly branded Socinians. "The Efficacy, Usefulness, and Reasonableness of Divine Faith," in *Works*, 9:271. Socinianism (from Fausto Paolo Sozzini, 1539–1604) was an extension of the doctrine of Arius (ca. 250–ca. 336) who held that Christ was divine but not co-equal with the Father. Socinians held that Christ is not divine and that his role was one of moral exemplar.

46. Burton, "Of the Fruits of Repentance," in *Works*, 1:328, 332. Cf. Rust, *Discourse of the Use of Reason*, 33. Burnet, *Thirty-Nine Articles*, 118–19, insists that we need both preventing grace and assisting grace. See also id., *A Discourse Wherein is Held Forth the Opposition of the Doctrine, Worship and Practice of the Roman Church, to the Nature, Designs, and Characters of the Christian Faith* (London: J. Watts, 1688), 7, 26.

47. Tillotson, "Of the Ordinary Influence of the Holy Ghost, on the Minds of Christians," in *Works*, 8:444–45. Compare "The Necessity of Supernatural Grace," 8:489, where he says that "this supernatural grace of Christ is that alone which can enable us to perform what he require of us." See also id., "The Possibility and Necessity of Gospel Obedience," 6:130.

48. Fowler, *Principles and Practices of Certain Moderate Divines*, 227.

49. Fowler, *The Design of Christianity* (London: E. Tyler, 1671), 129; id., *Principles and Practices*, 240. Stillingfleet preached that "meer Repentance can never make any satisfaction to God for the Breech of his Laws." "Sermon Preached before the King and Queen at White-Hall" (25 December 1693), in *Works*, 1:503. See also Moore, *Sermons on Several Occasions*, 1:33, 158; Burnet, *Thirty-Nine Articles*, 129–30.

50. Patrick, *The Devout Christian*, in *Works*, 2:195, 196, 204, 208, 212, 305. See also *A Friendly Debate*, in *Works*, 5:274.

51. Patrick, *Sermon Preached at St. Paul's, Covent Garden*, in *Works*, 8:19.

52. Hale, "Meditations Upon the Lord's Prayer," in *Works*, 2:569. Cf. the letter Hale wrote to his grandson while the latter was recovering from smallpox, admonishing him to acknowledge the goodness of God since "your deliverance was not the purchase of your own power, nor of your own desert, it was an act of the free and undeserved goodness of God." Hale, *Works*, 1:234.

53. Thomas Ken, "God's Attributes and Perfections," in *Works* (London: John Wyat, 1721), 2:28. Even the Platonist Whichcote believed that God must enable men to reform through the gift of grace. See "The Conversion of a Sinner," in *Works*, 4:209, 263.

54. 1 Cor. 4.7.

55. Moore, *Sermons*, 2:342.

56. Etymologically, "antinomianism" means antagonism or opposition to the law. The European antinomians were followers of Johannes Agricola (b. 1494), a disciple and later opponent of Luther. See Pettit, *Heart Prepared*, 140.

57. Quoting Haight, *Experience and Language of Grace*, 11.

58. McLachlan, *Socinianism in England*, 14–15.

59. See, for example, Henry More, *An Explication of the Grand Mystery of Godliness*, in

Works (London: Joseph Downing, 1708), 91; Whichcote, "The Nature of Salvation by Christ," in *Works*, 2:87, 99, 105–6; id., "The Mediation of Christ," 2:304–5; Chillingworth, *Works*, 3:30.

60. Augustine, quoted in Placher, *History of Christian Thought*, 70–71.

61. For a discussion, see Urban, *A Short History of Christian Thought*, 106–8, 117–19.

62. Tillotson, "Concerning the Divinity of Our Blessed Saviour," in *Works*, 3:301.

63. Id., "Concerning the Incarnation of Christ," in *Works*, 3:379–80 (preached at Saint Lawrence Jewry 28 December 1680). See also "The Uncertainty of the Day of Judgement," 8:116; "Christ the Author, and Obedience the Condition of Salvation," 6:103; "The Wisdom of God in the Redemption of Mankind," 6:468. See also the views of Tillotson's Nonconformist friend Thomas Gouge, *The Principles of the Christian Religion*, in *Works*, 475.

64. Burnet, *Thirty-Nine Articles*, 55. Cf. Richard Kidder, *Twelve Sermons* (London: B. Aylmer, 1697), 26.

65. Patrick, *The Work of the Ministry Represented to the Clergy of the Diocese of Ely*, in *Works*, 8:571–73. In sermons such as "One Mediator" and "One Sacrifice," Patrick reiterated the argument that Christ's sacrifice alone has placed us within the purview of eternal salvation, not for the merit of anything we can do. Patrick, *Works*, 8:212, 213, 216, 234, 244.

66. Patrick, *Mensa Mystica, or A Discourse Concerning the Sacrament of the Lord's Supper*, in *Works*, 1:101. For a discussion of Patrick's teaching on the eucharist, see C. W. Dugmore, *Eucharistic Doctrine in England from Hooker to Waterland* (London: Society for Promoting Christian Knowledge, 1942), 111–16.

67. Patrick, *A Book for Beginners*, in *Works*, 1:594. Compare the account in *Mensa Mystica* in *Works*, 1:99–100. Christ's propitiatory sacrifice is also discussed in *Advice to a Friend*, 4:434. John Worthington had encouraged Patrick to complete this particular work.

68. *Book for Beginners*, in *Works*, 1:598. Patrick suggests special prayers to be repeated before and after communion, all of which reiterate the special nature of Christ's work and man's utter inability to merit salvation.

69. Barrow, "A Sermon upon the Passion of Our Blessed Saviour," in *Works*, 1:135. See also "Of the Virtue and Reasonableness of Faith," 5:58.

70. Barrow, in *Works*, 1:135. See also *An Exposition of the Creed*, 7:152, 156, 168, 201, 223.

71. See, for example, John Moore, *Works*, 1:26, 207, 259, 410–11, 422; 2:23, 30, 33, 77, 239, 272–73, 293; Hezekiah Burton, *Several Discourses*, 1:59, 334, 407; Tillotson, "Concerning the Sacrifice and Satisfaction of Christ," in *Works*, 3:406; Fowler, *Design of Christianity*, 83; Patrick, *An Answer to a Book*, in *Works*, 7:255; Glanvill, *Anti-Fanatical Religion*, 22–23.

72. Urban, *Short History of Christian Thought*, 121–22.

73. Abelard, "Exposition of the Epistle to the Romans," in Placher, 145.

74. Baxter, *A Treatise of Conversion*, in *Practical Works*, 7:24, 25. The very work of man's conversion "is so much carried on by God's exciting of our reason." Baxter, "A Sermon on Repentance," 17:131.

75. Tillotson, "The Care of Our Souls, the One Thing Needful," in *Works*, 3:65. Compare "The Precepts of Christianity Not Grievous," 1:474; "Of the Nature of Regeneration," 5:382.

76. Id., "Of the Nature of Regeneration," in *Works*, 5:381.

77. 1 Cor. 15.10; Tillotson, "Of the Nature of Regeneration," in *Works*, 5:397. Cf. John Moore, *Works*, 1:33.

78. *Christian Directory*, 2:103. Cf. Fowler, *Principles and Practices*, 56–57, 60, 65.

79. Patrick, *Parable* in *Works*, 4:381. See also Matthew Hale, *A Brief Abstract of the Christian Religion*, in *Works*, 1:248–59.

80. Gilson, *Spirit of Medieval Philosophy*, 148–49.

81. Baker, *Wars of Truth*, 13.

82. Calvin, *Institutes*, 1: book I, chapter 16, section iv.

83. Willey, *Eighteenth-Century Background*, 3–4. Paul Johnson, *A History of Christianity* (Harmondsworth, England: Penguin, 1978), 334, repeats the common assumption that the Latitudinarians rejected the idea of an active providence.

84. Stillingfleet, "Sermon Preached on the Fast Day at St. Margaret's, Westminster 13 Nov 1678," in *Works*, 1:252.

85. Id., "Sermon Preached at the Assizes of Worcester" (21 September 1690), in *Works*, 1:451.

86. Westfall, *Science and Religion*, 87. Cf. Barrow, "The Being of God Proved From Supernatural Effects," in *Works*, 5:266–67, where Barrow sought to prove the being of God from the evidence of particular providence where the course of nature was occasionally overturned.

87. Viner, *The Role of Providence in the Social Order*, 19. See also Dudley W. R. Bahlman, *The Moral Revolution of 1688* (New Haven: Yale University Press, 1957), 10–13; Gerald M. Straka, *Anglican Reaction to the Revolution of 1688* (Madison: State Historical Society of Wisconsin, 1962), 65–79; J. C. D. Clark, *English Society, 1688–1830* (Cambridge: Cambridge University Press, 1986), 124, who writes that providence remained the leading explanation for natural and historical causation into the eighteenth century.

88. Taylor, *The Rules and Exercises of Holy Dying*, in *Works*, 4:I, ii.

89. Clark, *English Society*, 124; J. Sears McGee, *The Godly Man in Stuart England* (New Haven: Yale University Press, 1976), 32–36.

90. For a discussion, see Baker, *Wars of Truth*, 18–19.

91. Wilkins, *Principles and Duties*, 86.

92. Wilkins, *Discourse Concerning Gift of Prayer*, 147. Wilkins's popular *Discourse Concerning the Beauty of Providence* (London, 1649) was designed to comfort those troubled by the violent course of events during the Civil War and advocated a Stoic response. See Shapiro, *John Wilkins*, 69–70. Richard Westfall, *Science and Religion*, 79, shows how Wilkins attempted the impossible task of defending both particular providence and the rule of necessary laws.

93. Barrow, "The Unsearchableness of God's Judgments," in *Works*, 3:473, 477, 481.

94. Moore, *Works*, 1:121, 142.

95. Tillotson, "The End of Judgments, and the Reason of Their Continuance," in *Works*, 2:2–3. Cf. Burnet, *Some Sermons Preach'd on Several Occasions* (London: John Churchill, 1713), 34.

96. Patrick, *Autobiography*, 418; Patrick to Elizabeth Gauden, 9 November 1665, 14 December 1665, in *Works*, 9:597. See also *Advice to a Friend*, 4:493, where Patrick exhorts his readers "to exercise a great faith in God's good providence, which rules in all affairs." See also 4:496, where he says "it is most for our ease to recommend

all we have and do to God's good providence, and resolutely to rest satisfied in what he determines."

97. See, for example, "An Exhortation to the Clergy of the Diocese of Ely," in *Works*, 8:633; "Sermon before the King and Queen at Whitehall," 16 April 1690, 8:437; "Sermon Preached on the Fast-Day 11 April 1679," 8:80; *Angliae Speculum: A Glass that Flatters Not*, 7:629, 631.

98. Patrick, "Thanksgiving Sermon for the Deliverance of this Kingdom," 31 January 1689, in *Works*, 8:348, 358; "Sermon Before the Lord's Spiritual and Temporal," 16 April 1691, in *Works*, 8:449.

99. Baxter, *Reliquia*, Part II, 387.

6 : Practical Theology and the Meaning of Moralism

1. Quoted in S. C. Carpenter, *Eighteenth-Century Church and People* (London: John Murray, 1959), 127–28. Tenison had replaced Thomas Barlow after the latter's death in 1691 and immediately took up the task of inquiring into local conditions.

2. Barrow, "The Pleasantness of Religion," in *Works*, 1:169. Burnet attributed the decay in piety in his own day to the general reaction to mid-century religious enthusiasm. See *Some Sermons Preach'd on Several Occasions*, 12.

3. Fowler, *Design of Christianity*, 130.

4. Bicknell, *Thirty-Nine Articles*, 264, 267.

5. H. R. McAdoo, *The Structure of Caroline Moral Theology* (London: Longmans, Green and Co., 1949), 10.

6. Morgan, *Godly Learning*, 23–40. See, for example, Tillotson's tutor, the dissenter John Clarkson, "Of Repentance," in *Sermons and Discourses*, 13, who stated that "So proud is corrupt nature, as it is loath to deny its own, to depend on another's satisfaction."

7. Tillotson, "Excellency of the Christian Religion," in *Works*, 1:455. See also Fowler, *Principles and Practices*, 234–46; George Rust, *The Remains of that Reverend and Learned Prelate, Dr. George Rust*, ed. Henry Hallywell (London: M. Flesher, 1686), 21.

8. Patrick, *Parable*, in *Works*, 4:11–14.

9. Hale, *A Discourse of Religion*, in *Works*, 1:294.

10. *Reliquiae*, Part II, 139. Cf. Clarkson, "Of Repentance," in *Sermons and Discourses*, 41.

11. Moore, *Sermons*, 1:7, 16, 19, 22. The fullest exposition of this thesis by Moore is contained in his sermon titled "Of Faith and Works," in 2:129–52. According to Barrow, Saint Peter "exhorts us to use diligence to make our calling and election sure, but he doth not bid us know it to be sure." Barrow, "Of Justifying Faith," in *Works*, 5:140.

12. Moore, *Sermons*, 1:23; Reedy, *Bible and Reason*, 13.

13. Chillingworth, *Works*, 3:28.

14. Baker, *Image of Man*, 293; Hiram Haydn, *The Counter Renaissance* (New York: Grove Press, 1960), 37–38, 51–52.

15. Cosin, *Works*, 1:319–320. Cf. Pearson, *Exposition of the Creed*, 53–54; Sancroft, *Occasional Sermons*, 97, 106, 107.

16. Sanderson, *Sermons*, 376, 485; John Pearson, *An Exposition of the Creed*, 53–54; Rey-

nolds, *Works*, 5:iv–v, 65, 66; Baxter, *Christian Directory*, 2:322, 323; id., *The Life of Faith*, 12:355.

17. Duppa, *Holy Rules and Helps to Devotion* (London: W. Hensman, 1683), 63.

18. Sancroft, *Sermons*, 106, 107, 149.

19. Wilkins, *Sermons Preach'd on Several Occasions*, 73.

20. Burton, "Of Doing Good and Evil," in *Discourses*, 2:490; Kidder, *A Discourse Concerning the Grounds of Christian Fortitude* (London: W. Kettilby, 1680), 9; Barrow, "Of the Virtue and Reasonableness of Faith," in *Works*, 5:68; id., *The Young Man's Duty* (London, 1671), 4.

21. Glanvill, *The Unreasonable Contempt* (London, 1676), 98. See also Glanvill, *Way of Happiness*, 12–16, 17, and Barrow, "Provide Things Honest in the Sight of God," in *Works*, 3:227–28.

22. Glanvill, *Way of Happiness*, 167.

23. Patrick, *Jewish Hypocrisy*, in *Works*, 5:46. Cf. Richard Kidder, *The Christian Sufferer Supported* (London: Walter Kettilby, 1680), 9.

24. Burton, "A Discourse of Repentance," in *Discourses*, 1:178, 180; id., "Of the Fruits of Repentance," 1:331.

25. Evelyn, *Diary*, 4:240. Tillotson, "Of the Difficulty of Reforming Vicious Habits," in *Works*, 2:502.

26. Tillotson, "The Precepts of Christianity Not Grievous," in *Works*, 1:483.

27. Tillotson, "The Wisdom of Being Religious," in *Works*, 1:388. We should value nothing here below, was Tillotson's message at the funeral of his friend Thomas Gouge, "For what is there in this world, this waste and howling wilderness, this rude and barbarous country which we are put to pass through, which should detain our affections here, and take off our thoughts from our everlasting habitation." See "Sermon Preached at the Funeral of Thomas Gouge," in *Works*, 2:331. Elsewhere he indicated that God had made the world troublesome and uneasy to men in order to convince them of its vanity. *Works*, 1:524.

28. Sanderson, *Sermons*, 542–43; Hales, "The Profit of Godliness," in *Works*, 3:34–35.

29. Hickes, "Two Sermons Explaining the Doctrine of Justification," in *A Collection of Sermons*, 2:283.

30. More, *A Collection of Aphorisms* (London: J. Downing, 1704), 5; id., *An Explication of the Grand Mystery of Godliness*, in *Theological Works*, 37. Cf. Hales, "Profit of Godliness," in *Works*, 3:36.

31. Fowler, *A Sermon Preached to the Societies for the Reformation of Manners* (26 June 1699) (London: B. Aylmer, 1699), 5, 6, 7, 9, 12, 20. See also Burnet, *Some Sermons Preach'd on Several Occasions*, 19–20, 215, 223. In an essay written for the direction of a young clergyman, Glanvill told him that "The end of preaching must be acknowldg'd to be the instruction of the hearers in Faith and Good Life, in order to the Glory of God, and their present, and future happiness." The order in which he placed the goals was no coincidence. Glanvill, *An Essay Concerning Preaching* (London: H. Brome, 1678), 10.

32. Christopher Hill has identified this principle as central to the Protestant view of works. See "Protestantism and the Rise of Capitalism," in *Change and Continuity in Seventeenth-Century England* (Cambridge: Harvard University Press, 1975), 84.

33. Stillingfleet, "Sermon Preached before the Queen" (13 March 1692), in *Works*,

1:485, 491. The dissenter Thomas Gouge, whose Welsh Bible scheme Stillingfleet supported in 1674, insisted that we should not perform works of charity out of hope for reward, "but rather for conscience sake, in obedience to the Command of God . . . and in testimony of our Thankfulness unto him, for what he hath graciously bestowed on us." Gouge, *The Surest and Safest Way of Thriving*, in *Works*, 125–26.

34. See, for example, Richard Kidder, *A Discourse Concerning Sins of Infirmity and Wilful Sins* (London: Joseph Downing, 1704), 6.

35. For a discussion, see Thomas Wood, *English Casuistical Divinity During the Seventeenth Century*, 116–39; H. R. McAdoo, *The Structure of Caroline Moral Theology* (London: Longmans, Green and Co., 1949), 99–120. K. E. Kirk, *The Vision of God: The Christian Doctrine of the Summum Bonum* (London: Longman, 1931), 292–98, discusses the medieval position.

36. Jacob, *Newtonians and the English Revolution*, chapter 1.

37. Croft, *The Legacy of the Right Reverend Herbert Lord Bishop of Hereford* (London: Charles Harper, 1679), 7, 12–13; Burnet, *Subjection for Conscience-Sake* (London: R. Royston, 1675), 17; Barrow, "The Father Almighty," in *Works*, 5:349–50; "Of the Virtue and Reasonableness of Faith," 5:97; "Of Quietness, and Doing Our Own Business," 2:212; "Of Industry in Our General Calling, As Christians," 2:415; "Of Contentment," 3:37–38; John Moore, "Of Patience and Submission to Authority," in *Sermons*, 1:70–106.

38. Burton, "A Discourse of Purity and Charity," in *Discourses*, 1:14, 15.

39. Ibid., 26, 41.

40. Patrick, "A Sermon Preached on St. Mark's Day" (1686) in *Works*, 8:183, 193–94. John Moore took it to be a general observation that "much Prosperity corrupts men's Morals, and tempts them to rely upon their own Powers," thereby becoming indifferent to the constant assistance of God in the successful prosecution of all their endeavors. *Sermons on Several Subjects*, 2:142. See also Barrow's Spittal Sermon for 1671 in *Works*, 1:33.

41. See Patrick's letters to Elizabeth Gauden in *Autobiography*. Tennison was another who refused to leave his parishioners in Cambridge during the plague. Stillingfleet apparently left London.

42. Barrow, *Works*, 1:33.

43. Barrow, *Works*, 1:31–32. See also Thomas Gouge, *Christian Directions Shewing How to Walk with God All the Day-Long*, in *Works*, 237.

44. Barrow, *Works*, 1:41. Barrow had little sympathy for the man whose whole happiness was tied up "in bags and barns," the drive for money and lands (Barrow, *Works*, 1:42), and he referred to the grasping and indolent gentleman as "the most inconsiderate, the most despicable, the most pitiful and wretched creature in the world." Barrow, "Of Industry in Our Particular Calling," *Works*, 3:419. In "Of Self-Confidence, Self-Complacence, Self-Will, and Self-Interest," Barrow described excessive self-interest as "the great root of all the disorders and mischiefs in the world." *Works*, 4:123.

45. Barrow, *Works*, 1:63. Barrow reserved special criticism for those whose wealth was built on the backs of the laboring poor. Although he taught respect for the existing social order, he challenged the complacency of the ruling classes by preaching that

"It is an insufferable pride for any man to pretend or conceit himself to differ so much from his brethren, that he may be allowed to live in ease and sloth, while the rest of mankind are subject to continual toil and trouble." Barrow, "Of Industry in Our Particular Calling, as Gentlemen and Scholars," in *Works*, 3:427.

46. Barrow, "The Profitableness of Godliness," in *Works*, 1:207.

47. Barrow, "Of the Truth and Divinity of the Christian Religion," in *Works*, 5:477.

48. Barrow, "Against Foolish Talking and Jesting," in *Works*, 2:13.

49. W. Fraser Mitchell, *English Pulpit Oratory from Andrewes to Tillotson* (London: Society for Promoting Christian Knowledge, 1932); Charles Smyth, *The Art of Preaching* (London: Society for Promoting Christian Knowledge, 1940); C. F. Richardson, *English Preachers and Preaching, 1640–1670* (London: Society for Promoting Christian Knowledge, 1928); F. P. Wilson, *Seventeenth-Century Prose* (Cambridge: Cambridge University Press, 1960); R. F. Jones, "The Attack on Pulpit Eloquence in the Restoration," in Jones, ed., *The Seventeenth Century* (Stanford: Stanford University Press, 1950), 111–42; Arthur Pollard, *English Sermons* (London: Longmans, 1963).

50. John Wilkins's book on the gift of preaching has long been known as an important landmark in the adoption of the plain style. Supporting the idea that matters necessary to salvation are manifest in Scripture, he advised that the clergy "Beware of that vain affectation of finding something new and strange in every text, though never so plain." Those who attempted such in the pulpit were guilty of the sin of pride, said Wilkins. Wilkins, *Ecclesiastes, or, A Discourse Concerning the Gift of Preaching* (London: Samuel Gellibrand, 1651; first published in 1646), 12. See also Glanvill, *A Seasonable Defence of Preaching: and the Plain Way of It* (London: M. Clark, 1678), and Sprat, *Sermons Preached on Several Occasions*, 2, 28, 194.

51. Tillotson, "The Necessity of Repentance and Faith," in *Works*, 7:254. See also, "The General and Effectual Publication of the Gospel by the Apostles," 4:363. See also Sprat, *Sermons Preached on Several Occasions*, 2–6.

52. Barrow, *An Exposition on the Creed*, in *Works*, 7:20, 94.

53. Stillingfleet, "Bishop of Worcester's Charge to the Clergy of His Diocese," in *Works*, 3:627. Pepys, *Diary*, 6:87, applauded Stillingfleet's "most unconcerned and easy yet substantial manner" in the pulpit. Cf. *Diary*, 6:80; 9:548.

54. Cope, *Glanvill*, 41. The strictures of John Eachard, *The Grounds and Occasions of the Contempt of the Clergy and Religion* (London, 1670), later repeated by Macaulay in the nineteenth century, were not accepted by the Latitude-men as valid explanations.

55. Glanvill, *Anti-Fanatical Religion, and Free Philosophy* in *Essays*, 14, 18–19. Burnet, *Discourse of Pastoral Care*, vi, indicates that "the Bulk of Mankind is so made, that there is no working on them, but by moving their Affections, and commanding their Esteem," while Wilkins, *Ecclesiastes*, 26, said that the motives to religion "must properly and powerfully work upon the affections."

56. Glanvill, *The Zealous and Impartial Protestant* (London: Henry Brome, 1681), 54; id., *The Unreasonable Contempt*, 106, 108.

57. Patrick, *The Work of the Ministry Represented to the Clergy of the Diocese of Ely* (1697), in *Works*, 8:563. See also *An Exhortation Sent to the Clergy of the Diocese of Ely* in *Works*, 8:633. Burnet, "Sermon Preached at Hampden Court, June 1689," in *Some Sermons Preached on Several Occasions*, 12, connected the decline in private prayer

with the church's reaction against the enthusiasm of the Commonwealth period.

58. Stillingfleet, "Of the Particular Duties of the Parochial Clergy" (1696), in *Works*, 3:667, 668; "Of the Nature of the Trust Committed to the Parochial Clergy" (1696), in *Works*, 3:644, 657.

59. Stillingfleet, "Sermon Preached at Whitehall, 27 March 1672," in *Works*, 1:148, 150. Latitudinarian descriptions of the judgment and of Hell belie aspects of D. P. Walker's thesis, *The Decline of Hell: Seventeenth-Century Discussions of Eternal Torment* (Chicago: University of Chicago Press, 1965). See, for example, Barrow, "No Respect of Persons With God," in *Works*, 4:256; Patrick, *Aqua Genitalis: A Discourse Concerning Baptism* (1659), in *Works*, 1:45; Tillotson, "The Reasonableness of Fearing God More than Men," in *Works*, 10:84–86; Burnet, *Thirty-Nine Articles*, 67.

60. Stillingfleet, "Particular Duties," in *Works*, 3:670–73; "A Discourse Concerning the Bonds of Resignation to Benefices, in Point of Law and Conscience," in *Works*, 3:716–40.

61. Id., "The Bishop of Worcester's Charge to the Clergy of His Diocese, 1690," in *Works*, 3:631.

62. Ibid., 627, 632–35. Stillingfleet warned his clergy that their parishioners "do not pretend to fineness of thoughts, and subtlety of reasoning, but they are shrewd Judges whether Men mean what they say, or not." "Of the Obligations to Observe the Ecclesiastical Canons and Constitutions," in *Works*, 3:712–13. See also "An Ordination Sermon Preached at St. Peter's, Cornhill" (15 March 1685), in *Works*, 1:375.

63. See chapter 3.

64. See Burton, "Of Education," in *Discourses*, 2:431–32; Barrow, "The Danger and Mischief of Delaying Repentance," in *Works*, 3:332. Compare the view of High Churchmen like Sprat, who wrote that the minds of children "are generally clear spotless, white untainted, unprejudiced," while acknowledging that due to original sin "a pure, simple, undefil'd disposition of mind, by nature we cannot pretend to." *Sermons Preached on Several Occasions* (London: Charles Brome, 1697), 10.

65. Burton, "Of Education," in *Discourses*, 2:459; Glanvill, *Lux Orientalis*, 9. The dissenter Thomas Gouge wrote that "the Curse of God hangs over those Families in which Religious Duties are altogether neglected." *The Christian Householder*, in *Works*, 325, 328.

66. "Bishop of Worcester's Charge to the Clergy of His Diocese," in *Works*, 3:627, 628; "Sermon Preached before the Queen at Whitehall" (22 February 1689) in *Works*, 1:414. Stillingfleet told his clergy that "He that would reform the World to purpose, must begin with the Youth, and train them up betimes in the Ways of Religion and Vertue." Stillingfleet, "Bishop of Worcester's Charge," 3:627. See also Moore, *Works*, 2:171.

67. Fowler, *A Discourse of Offenses* (London: Brabazon Aylmer, 1683), 29. See Barrow, "Of Walking As Christ Did" in *Works*, 2:531.

68. Moore, *Sermons*, 2:168.

69. Fowler's concern led him to publish Worthington's little *Scripture Catechism* which, according to Fowler, contained "the main body of simple, pure Christianity, without the adulterations and spurious notions of man-made divinity." John Worthington, *A Scripture Catechism Shewing What a Christian is to Believe and Practice in Order*

to Salvation (Glasgow: R. Foulis, 1747), preface, iii.

70. Patrick, *The Devout Christian*, in *Works*, 2:212–98 provides a good sampling.

71. Id., *The Work of the Ministry Represented to the Clergy of the Diocese of Ely* (1697), in *Works*, 8:576–77.

72. Quoted in Edward Carpenter, *Thomas Tenison: Archbishop of Canterbury* (London: Society for Promoting Christian Knowledge, 1948), 27.

73. Tenison, *A Sermon Concerning Holy Resolution* (London: Richard Chiswell, 1694), 23.

74. Fowler, *A Sermon Preached at Bow-Church Before the Lord Mayor and Court of Alderman* (London: Brabazon Alymer, 1690), 28, 29.

75. Barrow, "Of Contentment," in *Works*, 3:54; "Provide Things Honest in the Sight of God," 3:227–28.

7 : *Revolution and the Measure of Influence*

1. F. G. James, "The Bishops in Politics, 1688–1714" in *Conflict in Stuart England: Essays in Honor of Wallace Notestein*, ed. W. A. Aiken and B. D. Henning (London: Jonathan Cape, 1960), 232, 233. Jonathan I. Israel, "William III and Toleration," in Ole Peter Grell, Jonathan I. Israel, and Nicholas Tyacke, ed., *From Persecution to Toleration* (Oxford: Clarendon Press, 1991), 163–64; Coward, *The Stuart Age*, 422, John Kenyon, *Stuart England* (Harmondsworth, England: Penguin, 1978), 294; Straka, *Anglican Reaction to the Revolution of 1688*, 18; Rupp, *Religion in England*, 55; Cragg, *Church in the Age of Reason*, 61, Every, *High Church Party*, 67, and a contemporary, Burnet, *History*, 4:136–37, agree with this assessment.

2. All of the preferments, save Burnet's and Patrick's, were granted in April and May 1691. Robert Grove was selected for Chichester after Patrick's translation to Ely.

3. Quoting John S. Morrill in Kenneth O. Morgan, ed., *The Oxford History of Britain* (Oxford: Oxford University Press, 1988), 390. On the condition and morale of the clergy after 1689, see Geoffrey Holmes, *The Trial of Dr. Saceverell* (London: Eyre Methuen, 1973), 27–28.

4. Burnet, *History*, 1:342; Patrick, *Brief Account*, 11–12.

5. G. V. Bennett, "King William III and the Episcopate," in Bennett and J. D. Walsh, eds., *Essays in Modern Church History* (New York: Oxford University Press, 1966), 111; Thomas, "The Seven Bishops and Their Petition," 56–70; Every, *The High Church Party*, 20–25.

6. Quoted in Sykes, *Church and State*, 30. Cf. S. C. Carpenter, *Eighteenth Century Church and People*, 17–18.

7. G. V. Bennett, "Conflict in the Church" in Geoffrey Holmes, ed., *Britain after the Glorious Revolution, 1689–1714* (London: Macmillan, 1969), 156; id., "King William and the Episcopate," 106–8. R. A. Beddard, "The Commission for Ecclesiastical Appointments, 1681–84: an Instrument of Tory Reaction," *Historical Journal* 110 (1967): 17, 39, writes that the commission emerged as the "clerical counterpart of the *quo warranto* campaign" while its members "represented the avant-garde of the Tory Reaction."

8. Patrick, *Autobiography* (Oxford: J. H. Parker, 1839), 141; Sykes, *From Sheldon to Secker*, 85–86. According to Burnet, *Supplement to Burnet's History*, 317, Sancroft had given his leave for the group to draw up a bill.

9. Bennett, "William III," 115; Israel, "William III and Toleration," 151–52; H. Horwitz, *Revolution Politicks: The Career of Daniel Finch, Second Earl of Nottingham, 1647–1730* (1968); Burnet, *History*, 4:20.

10. Speck, *Reluctant Revolutionaries*, 186; Henry Horwitz, *Parliament, Policy, and Politics* (Manchester: University of Manchester Press, 1977), 22; id., *Revolution Politicks*, 88. William was a Calvinist who had a history of appointing advisors based on talent rather than religious conviction. But he showed much indiscretion after his arrival in England in his open sympathy for the plight of Dissenters. His recognition of a Presbyterian church-order in Scotland, for example, infuriated M.P.s who suspected the king's Calvinism. See Burnet, *History*, 4:50; Bennett, "Conflict in the Church," 160.

11. Bennett, "William III," 116; Horwitz, *Revolution Politicks*, 90–93; Carpenter, *Eighteenth Century Church and People*, 20–21.

12. Birch, *Life of Tillotson*, 2d ed. (London, 1753), 165–66.

13. Burnet, *History*, 4:55–58; George Every, *The High Church Party*, chapter 2; Sykes, *Sheldon to Secker*, 87–89.

14. Holmes, *Politics, Religion and Society in England*, 191; Bennett, *Tory Crisis in Church and State*, 47; Sykes, *Sheldon to Secker*, 45. Jane was Dean of Gloucester at the time. The vote for Jane was fifty-five to twenty-eight.

15. Hill, *The Century of Revolution, 1603–1714* (New York: Norton, 1961), 291; Burnet, *History*, 4:16–17.

16. Geoffrey Holmes, *Politics, Religion and Society*, 192; Hugh Trevor-Roper, "Toleration and Religion after 1688," in *Persecution to Toleration*, 391; B. R. White, "The Twilight of Puritanism in the Years Before and After 1688," in ibid., 314–15.

17. John Kenyon, *Revolution Principles: The Politics of Party, 1689–1720* (Cambridge: Cambridge University Press, 1977), 84. For a longer perspective on seventeenth-century occasional conformity, see Christopher Hill, "Occasional Conformity and the Grindalian Tradition," in *Essays*, 2:301–20.

18. Sacheverell, *The Political Union: A Discourse Showing the Dependence of Government on Religion*, quoted in Kenyon, *Revolution Principles*, 93; Bennett, "Conflict," 168. The Whig-controlled Upper House, with the use of wrecking amendments, killed three Occasional Conformity Bills in 1703 and 1704. On Burnet's defense, see *History and Proceedings of the House of Lords* (London: Ebenezer Timberland, 1742), 2:56–64.

19. Leonard J. Trinterud, "A.D. 1689: The End of the Clerical World," in *Theology in Sixteenth and Seventeenth-Century England* (Los Angeles: William Andrews Clark Memorial Library, 1971), 31.

20. Israel, "William III and Toleration," 161.

21. Locke's *Letter on Toleration* (1689) argued that the responsibility of the state is not to see to the salvation of men but rather to maintain public order in this life.

22. On efforts in the 1690s see H. Horwitz, "Comprehension in the Later Seventeenth Century: A Postscript," *Church History* 34, no. 3 (1965): 342–48.

23. Clark, *English Society*, 277.

24. Israel, "William III and Toleration," 164; Holmes, *Saceverell*, 30–31.

25. Roland Stromberg, *Religious Liberalism in Eighteenth-Century England*, 5; Cragg, *Puritanism in the Age of Great Persecution*, 251; R. A. Beddard, "Vincent Alsop and

the Emancipation of Restoration Dissent," *Journal of Ecclesiastical History* 24, no. 2 (1973); 166; Stoughton, *Religion in England*, 5:90; Moore, *Works*, 1:183.

26. Hill, *Century of Revolution*, 293–94; Coward, *Stuart England*, 426; Geoffrey Holmes, "Post-Revolution Britain and the Historian," in Holmes, ed., *Britain After the Glorious Revolution*, 25; E. D. Bebb, *Nonconformity and Social and Economic Life, 1660–1800* (London, 1935), 46–50. On the dissenting academies see J. W. Ashley Smith, *The Birth of Modern Education: the Contribution of the Dissenting Academies, 1660–1800* (London, 1954); Irene Parker, *Dissenting Academies in England* (Cambridge: Cambridge University Press, 1913); H. McLachlan, *English Education Under the Test Acts* (Manchester: University of Manchester Press, 1931).

27. Holmes, *Politics, Religion and Society*, 193. Rupp, in *Religion in England*, 55, says the number is 2,356 places of worship licensed. The 940 dissenting congregations of 1690 grew modestly to around 1,200 by 1716, but most Tories thought the growth much greater. They also exaggerated the number of dissenting academies, which actually only grew from around ten in 1689 to thirty in 1714. Tories rightly saw these as training grounds for the next generation of Dissenters.

28. Holmes, *Politics, Religion and Society*, 189.

29. G. N. Clark, *The Later Stuarts*, 23.

30. F. C. Mather, "Worship 1714–1830," *Journal of Ecclesiastical History* 36, no. 2 (1985): 255–83; and Davies, *Worship and Theology, 1690–1850*, 19–37, discuss the differences between church and dissent after 1688.

31. Birch, *Life of Tillotson*, 103; Bennett, *Tory Crisis in Church and State*, 5. Anonymous broadside titled *A Dialogue between the Lord R's Ghost, and the D. of C.* castigates Tillotson for his hypocrisy. The text is printed in Louis Locke, *Tillotson*, 169–72. Cf. Hutton, *English Church*, 236.

32. The habit of deference to authority, connected to patriarchal principle, was still the norm in the late seventeenth century. See Gorden Schochet, *Patriarchalism in Political Thought* (Oxford: Oxford University Press, 1975).

33. Kenyon, *Revolution Principles*, 24–26; Straka, *Anglican Reaction to the Revolution of 1688*, 66. Clark, *English Society*, 121–40, discusses some of the uses of divine right theory after 1688. Most of those who accepted the change in monarchy attributed it to particular providence, but Tenison admitted in private that "there had been irregularities in our settlement; that it was wished things had been otherwise, but we were now to make the best of it, and to join in the support of this government, as it was, for fear of worse." Clarendon, *Diary*, quoted in Jacob, *Newtonians*, 92–93. William Sherlock's acceptance of the new king after the Battle of the Boyne is the most interesting example of providential factors. See C. F. Mullett, "A Case of Allegiance: William Sherlock and the Revolution of 1688," *Huntingdon Library Quarterly* 10 (1947–48): 83–103.

34. Horwitz, *Parliament, Policy and Politics*, 26; Every, *High Church Party*, 36; Burnet, *History*, 4:14–16; Stoughton, *Religion in England*, 77–78.

35. Charles Leslie, *The Case of the Regale and of the Pontificate Stated in a Conference Concerning the Independency of the Church*, quoted in Rupp, *Religion in England*, 8. On the non-jurors see John Findon, "The Nonjurors and the Church of England" (D. Phil. diss., Oxford University, 1979); L. M. Hawkins, *Allegiance in Church and State: The Problem of the Nonjurors in the English Revolution* (London: Routledge and

Sons, 1928), and Carpenter, *Eighteenth Century Church and People*, 56–70.

36. Within the ranks of the non-jurors there was a great deal of disagreement over the status of the church under Tillotson. Some, like George Hickes, refused to take communion or attend public prayers with his conforming brethren, while more moderate men such as Thomas Ken and Robert Frampton were willing to keep communion with the church that had disowned them while avoiding controversy whenever possible. See Rupp, *Religion in England*, 5–28; Kenyon, *Revolution Principles*, 21.

37. Burnet, *Supplement*, 358. Tillotson's letters to Lady Russell, printed in Locke, *Tillotson*, 43, 49, 50, reveal the depth of his opposition to the honor being bestowed on him. According to Every, *High Church Party*, 66, there is evidence to suggest that William threatened to leave the non-juror bishops in their sees until their deaths unless Tillotson accepted the appointment.

38. Burnet, *History*, 1:343. He continued to hold both positions until assuming his archiepiscopal functions.

39. Birch, *Life of Tillotson*, 246; E. F. Carpenter, *The Protestant Bishop: Henry Compton*, 162–63. Stephen Baxter, *William III and the Defense of European Liberty, 1650–1702* (New York: Harcourt, Brace and World, 1966), 275, indicates that William disliked the High-Church bishop of London.

40. Pruett, *Parish Clergy Under Later Stuarts*, 175–78, corrects the misperceptions of contemporaries like Eachard regarding clerical poverty and ignorance. Tillotson had praised the Socinians for their fair way of disputing religious questions. See Reedy, *Bible and Reason*, 127.

41. Hutton, *Church in England*, 251; Burnet, *Supplement*, 506. Attacks on Tillotson included Charles Leslie's *The Charge of Socinianism Against Dr. Tillotson Considered* (London, 1695). In 1693 Tillotson published *Four Sermons Concerning the Incarnation of Our Blessed Saviour* in order to counter charges of Socinianism.

42. Sykes, *Church and State in the Eighteenth Century*, 93.

43. Burnet, *Supplement*, 505–6.

44. Pruett, *Parish Clergy*, 179–80, on influence of local clergymen.

45. Bennett, *Tory Crisis in Church and State*, 47.

46. Michael Hunter, *Science and Society in Restoration England* (Cambridge: Cambridge University Press, 1981), 162.

47. Burnet, *History*, 4:387; Prideaux quoted in Every, *High Church Party*, 67. Cf. Bahlman, *The Moral Revolution of 1688*, 1–9.

48. Firmin supported the work of Stephen Nye, Anglican rector of Hertfordshire and author of a number of Socinian tracts published between 1691 and 1695. See Reedy, *Bible and Reason*, 120–21.

49. Warburton quoted in Davies, *Worship and Theology in England*, 73. See Sykes, *Church and State in England in the Eighteenth Century*, 260; Smyth, *The Art of Preaching*, chapter 4.

50. On the popularity of Tillotson's sermons in the eighteenth century, see L. P. Curtis, *Anglican Moods of the Eighteenth Century* (Hamden, Conn.: Archon Books, 1966), 42; James Downey, *The Eighteenth-Century Pulpit* (Oxford: Clarendon Press, 1969), 15–16; Richardson, *English Preachers and Preaching, 1640–1670*, 73; F. P. Wilson, *Seventeenth Century Prose*, 110; Arthur Pollard, *English Sermons*, 19–21; W. G. Humphrey, "Tillotson: The Practical Preacher," in J. E. Kempe, ed., *The Classic Preachers*

of the English Church (New York: E. P. Dutton, 1877), 2:135–44; Norman Sykes, "The Sermons of Archbishop Tillotson," *Theology* 58 (1978): 297–302.

51. Evelyn, *Diary*, 4:308, wrote of "the insuperable paines he takes & care of his Parish" while Tenison was at Saint Martin-in-the-Fields.

52. Carpenter, *Thomas Tenison: Archbishop of Canterbury* (London: Society for Promoting Christian Knowledge, 1948), 115–16, 127, 132. See also Carpenter, *Cantour: The Archbishops in Their Office* (Oxford: Mawbray, 1988), 229–40. The High Church hope that the old alliance between church and state might be restored through decisive parliamentary action appeared naive to Tenison.

53. Holmes, *Saceverell*, 34, argues that the voluntary idea was a distinctly Low Church program.

54. Rupp, *Religion in England*, 290–93; D. Owen, *English Philanthropy, 1660–1964* (Cambridge, Mass.: Belknap Press, 1964), 18–19.

55. Thirty-two parishes in London/Westminster participated in the scheme, and in twelve of these there were two or more schools, making a total of fifty-four. The total annual subscription for these schools was £2164. See M. G. Jones, *The Charity School Movement: A Study of Eighteenth-Century Puritanism in Action* (Hamden, Conn.: Archon Books, 1964), 57. For details on the London poor, see S. M. MacFarlane, "Studies in Poverty and Poor Relief in London at the End of the Seventeenth Century" (D. Phil. diss., Oxford University, 1982).

56. Tenison, *A Sermon Concerning the Folly of Atheism* (1691), quoted in Hunter, *Science and Society*, 164.

57. Gregory King, *Natural and Political Observations and Conclusions upon the State and Condition of England* (1696), quoted in Angus McInnes, "The People and the Revolution," in Holmes, ed., *Britain After the Glorious Revolution*, 86.

58. Owen, *English Philanthropy*, 63–64. Simon Patrick had opened a school for the poor at Saint James, Westminster, in April 1688.

59. Ibid., 28–29.

60. Tina Isaacs, "The Anglican Hierarchy and the Reformation of Manners, 1688–1738" *Journal of Ecclesiastical History* 33, no. 3 (1982): 393; Robert Harvey, "The Problem of Social-Political Obligation for the Church of England in the Seventeenth Century" *Church History* 40 (1971): 156–69.

61. *His Majesty's Letter to the Bishop of London*, quoted in Isaacs, 392–93. See also Bahlman, *Moral Revolution*, 16–18.

62. Owen, *English Philanthropy*, 38.

63. Ibid., 8.

64. W. A. Speck, "The Societies for the Reformation of Manners: A Case Study in the Theory and Practice of Moral Reform," *Literature and History* 3 (1976): 45–64; Rupp, *Religion in England*, 298; Owen, *English Philanthropy*, 21. One overzealous Middlesex justice, Ralph Hartley, issued warrants wholesale and secured convictions on the flimsiest of evidence. See Bahlman, *Moral Revolution*, 20–21.

65. Fredrick Seaton Seibert, *Freedom of the Press in England, 1476–1776* (Urbana: University of Illinois Press, 1965), 237–63, discusses government control of the press during the Restoration. For background on English Deism, see Richard Popkin, "The Deist Challenge," in *From Persecution to Toleration*, 195–210. Charles Blount, *Oracles of Reason* (1693), is generally credited with inaugurating the Deist controversy of the 1690s. See Harth, *Contexts of Dryden's Thought*, 62.

206 : Notes to Pages 146–151

66. The association continues today. See, for example, Jeffrey Burton Russell, *Mephistopheles: The Devil in the Modern World* (Ithaca: Cornell University Press, 1986), 130, where Deism is described as "the logical extension of Latitudinarianism." Cf. Holmes, *Sacheverell*, 25.

67. Stephen, *History of English Thought*, 1:68–69. The point is made anew by Rupp, *Religion in England*, 258. See also David A. Pailin, *Attitudes to Other Religions: Comparative Religion in Seventeenth and Eighteenth-Century Britain* (Manchester: University of Manchester Press, 1984); Hazard, *European Mind*, chapter 1.

68. Peter Byrne, *Natural Religion and the Religion of Nature* (London: Routledge, 1989), 23.

69. Rupp, *Religion in England*, 260, observes that the Deists contributed to the classical revival of the period. Cf. Peter Gay, *The Enlightenment*, vol. 1 (New York: Norton, 1969).

70. The book was published anonymously, but its author was soon well known. On Toland's life and thought, see Stephen H. Daniel, *John Toland: His Methods, Manners, and Mind* (Montreal: McGill-Queen's University Press, 1984), chapter 1; Sullivan, *Toland and the Deist Controversy*.

71. Toland, *Christianity Not Mysterious: or, A Treatise Shewing, that there is Nothing in the Gospel Contrary to Reason, Nor Above It* (London: Sam. Buckley, 1696), preface, vii–viii.

72. Ibid., 1.

73. Toland quoted Tillotson ("Nor need we to desire a better Evidence that any Man is in the wrong, than to hear him declare against Reason, and thereby to acknowledge that Reason is against him.") on the title page of *Christianity Not Mysterious*. As Gerard Reedy has shown, *Bible and Reason*, 164, n. 4, Tillotson goes on to claim that Christianity is reasonable because God has revealed it, a method of proof that Toland rejects. Anthony Collins called Tillotson "the most pious and rational of all priests," while Tindale referred to him as "the incomparable Archbishop Tillotson." Collins, *Discourse of Freethinking*, 69, and Tindale, *Christianity as Old as Creation*, 199, quoted in Cragg, *Reason and Authority*, 64.

74. Aquinas, *Summa Contra Gentiles*, 1: 3.

75. Peter Gay, ed., *Deism: An Anthology* (Princeton: D. Van Nostrand Company, 1968), 12.

76. Dryden, *Religio Laici*, in *The Poems of John Dryden*, ed., James Kinsley (Oxford: Clarendon Press, 1958), 2:62–64.

77. Paul Hazard, *The European Mind*, 253.

78. Stillingfleet, *A Letter to a Deist*, in *Works*, 2:118, 119.

79. Locke repeatedly dissociated himself from Toland. See E. S. DeBeer, ed., *The Correspondence of John Locke* (Oxford: Clarendon Press, 1973–89), 6:#2254, 2277.

80. Toland, *Christianity Not Mysterious*, 56–57.

81. Ibid., 57, 58.

82. Locke, *First Vindication of the Reasonableness of Christianity*, in *Works*, 7:165.

83. For a discussion of these connections, see Spellman, *John Locke and the Problem of Depravity*, 87.

84. Locke to Richard King (25 August 1703), in *Works*, 10:306.

85. Tillotson, "On the Education of Children," in *Works*, 3:526, 538; Locke, "Paci-

fick Christians" (Bodleian Library MSS, Locke c. 27, fol. 80), quoted in *Locke and Depravity*, 95.

86. Locke to Philip Limborch (11 December 1694), in *Correspondence of John Locke*, 5:#1856.

87. *An Essay Concerning Human Understanding*, ed. Peter Nidditch (Oxford: Clarendon Press, 1975), Book 4, chapter 18, section 2.

88. Locke, *Essay*, 4.19.3.

89. Locke, *Essay*, 4.19.4. Cf. Reedy, *Bible and Reason*, 136.

90. Anthony Collins, *A Discourse of Free Thinking* (London, 1713). As an old man Locke praised Collins and was perhaps taken in by the younger man's admiration for him.

91. Locke, *Reasonableness*, in *Works*, 7:26.

92. See John C. Biddle, "Locke's Critique of Innate Ideas and Toland's Deism," *Journal of the History of Ideas* 37 (1976): 418–20; Jacob, *Newtonians*, 214; Daniel, *John Toland*, 43.

93. Locke, *Reasonableness*, in *Works*, 7:5.

94. Ibid., 10, 11, 14. See Locke's rebuttal to John Edwards's claim that the author ignored Christ's satisfaction in *A Vindication of the Reasonableness of Christianity*, in *Works*, 163.

95. Locke, *Vindication*, in *Works*, 7:172.

96. Locke, *Reasonableness*, in *Works*, 7:135.

97. Ibid., 140.

98. Ibid., 146. Toland had asked, in his usual optimistic style, "For why may not the vulgar be judges of the true sense of things?" *Christianity Not Mysterious*, preface.

99. *Reasonableness*, in *Works*, 7:140.

100. Ibid., 83, 84, 93.

101. Ibid., 84.

102. Ibid., 93.

103. For Butler, the Deists' characteristic appeal to nature was based on the mistaken assumption that nature was an open book whose aims and purposes were clear to all. They would deny the mysteries of Christianity and yet blithely accept our still-considerable ignorance of the workings of nature. See Cragg, *Reason and Authority*, 93–124; Willey, *Eighteenth-Century Background*, 27–34.

Conclusion

1. More and Cross, ed., *Anglicanism*, xx.

2. Article VI.

3. Johnson, *History of Christianity*, 332.

4. Henry Sacheverell, *The True Character of a Low Churchman* (London, 1701), 3.

5. Patrick, *Brief Account*, 11, 12, 24.

6. Cassirer, *Philosophy of the Enlightenment*, 13.

7. C. S. Lewis, *The Problem of Pain* (London: Centenary Press, 1940), 68. See also Emil Brunner, *Man in Revolt* (London: Lutterworth Press, 1939), 129–33.

8. See John Hick, *Evil and the Love of God* (New York: Harper and Row, 1966), 49–52.

9. Ronald H. Nash, *Faith and Reason: Searching for a Rational Faith* (Grand Rapids, Mich.: Academie Books, 1988), 44.

10. Matt. 5.12; 6.1, 4, 6, 18; 10.41; 16.27; 18.23–24; 25.31–46; Luke 6.35.
11. Rudolf Schnackenburg, *The Moral Teaching of the New Testament* (New York: Herder and Herder, 1966), 25; Bicknell, *Theological Introduction to the Thirty-Nine Articles*, 113.
12. Bicknell, 114.

BIBLIOGRAPHY

Primary Sources

Atterbury, Lewis. *A Vindication of Archbishop Tillotson's Sermons.* London: Thomas Baker, 1709.

Aquinas, St. Thomas. *Summa Contra Gentiles.* 4 vols. Translated by Charles J. O'Neil. Notre Dame, Ind.: University of Notre Dame Press, 1975.

————. *Summa Theologica.* 61 vols. Translated by the Fathers of the English Dominican Province. London: Eyre and Spottiswood, 1963–76.

Aubrey, John. *Brief Lives.* Edited by Oliver L. Dick. Ann Arbor: University of Michigan Press, 1957.

Augustine. *The Basic Writings of St. Augustine.* 2 vols. Edited by Whitney J. Oates. New York: Random House, 1948.

————. *The City of God.* 2 vols. Translated by John Healey. London: J. M. Dent, 1945.

————. *Confessions of St. Augustine.* Edited by E. B. Pusey. London: J. M. Dent, 1913.

Barrow, Isaac. *The Theological Works of Isaac Barrow.* 9 vols. Edited by Alexander Napier. Cambridge: Cambridge University Press, 1839.

————. *The Young Man's Duty.* London, 1671.

Baxter, Richard. *Reliquiae Baxterianae.* Edited by Matthew Sylvester. London: T. Parkhurst, 1697.

————. *The Judgement of Non-conformists, of the Interest of Reason in Matters of Religion.* London, 1676.

————. *The Practical Works.* 23 vols. London: James Duncan, 1830.

Boyle, Robert. *Works.* 6 vols. Edited by Thomas Birch. London, 1772.

Bunyan, John. *A Defence of the Doctrine of Justification, By Faith in Jesus Christ.* London: Francis Smith, 1672.

Burnet, Gilbert. *A Discourse Wherein is Held Forth the Opposition of the Doctrine, Worship and Practice of the Roman Church, to the Nature, Designs, and Characters of the Christian Faith.* London: J. Watts, 1688.

————. *A Discourse of Pastoral Care.* London: Richard Chiswell, 1692.

————. *An Exposition of the Thirty-Nine Articles of the Church of England.* London: R. Roberts, 1699.

————. *A History of My Own Time*. 6 vols. Oxford: Oxford University Press, 1833.

————. *A Modest Survey of the Most Considerable Things in a Discourse Lately Published, Entitled Naked Truth*. London: Moses Pitt, 1676.

————. *Some Sermons Preach'd on Several Occasions*. London: John Churchill, 1713.

————. *Subjection for Conscience-Sake*. London: R. Royston, 1675.

————. *Supplement to Burnet's History*. Edited by H. C. Foxcroft. Oxford: Clarendon Press, 1902.

————. *Thoughts on Education*. Edited by John Clarke. Aberdeen, Scotland: Aberdeen University Press, 1914.

Burton, Hezekiah. *Several Discourses*. 2 vols. London, 1684–85.

Calvin, John. *Institutes of the Christian Religion*. 2 vols. Translated by John Allen. Philadelphia: Westminster Press, 1936.

Cary, Lucius. *Discourse of the Infallibility of the Church of Rome*. London: R. Royston, 1651.

Chillingworth, William. *Works*. 3 vols. Oxford: Oxford University Press, 1838.

Clarkson, David. *Sermons and Discourses on Several Divine Subjects*. London: Thomas Parkhurst, 1696.

Collins, Anthony. *A Discourse of Freethinking*. London, 1713.

Cosin, John. *The Works of John Cosin*. 5 vols. Oxford: John Henry Parker, 1843.

Croft, Herbert. *The Legacy of the Right Reverend Herbert Lord Bishop of Hereford*. London: Charles Harper, 1679.

————. *The Naked Truth or the True State of the Primitive Church*, 1675.

Cudworth, Ralph. *The Works of Ralph Cudworth*. 4 vols. Oxford: D. A. Talboys, 1829.

Dryden, John. *The Poems of John Dryden*. 4 vols. Edited by James Kinsley. Oxford: Clarendon Press, 1958.

Duppa, Brian. *Holy Rules and Helps to Devotion*. London: W. Hensman, 1683.

Eachard, John. *The Grounds and Occasions of the Contempt of the Clergy and Religion*. London, 1670.

Erasmus-Luther. *Discourse on Free Will*. Translated and edited by Ernst F. Winter. New York: Frederick Ungar Publishing, 1961.

Evelyn, John. *The Diary of John Evelyn*. 7 vols. Edited by E. S. de Beer. Oxford: Clarendon Press, 1955.

Fowler, Edward. *The Design of Christianity*. London: Tyler and Holt, 1671.

————. *A Discourse of Offenses*. London: Brabazon Alymer, 1683.

————. *The Principles and Practices of Certain Moderate Divines of the Church of England*. London: L. Lloyd, 1670.

————. *Sermon Preached at Bow-Church Before the Lord Mayor and Court of Aldermen*. London: Brabazon Alymer, 1690.

————. *A Sermon Preached to the Societies for the Reformation of Manners*. London: B. Aylmer, 1699.

Glanvill, Joseph. *An Essay Concerning Preaching*. London: H. Brome, 1678.

————. *Essays on Several Important Subjects in Philosophy and Religion*. London: John Baker, 1676.

————. *Lux Orientalis*. London: Samuel Lowndes, 1682.

————. *Scepsis Scientifica: or Confest Ignorane, the Way to Science*. London: E. Cotes, 1665.

————. *A Seasonable Defence of Preaching: and the Plain Way of It*. London: M. Clark, 1678.

————. *Some Discourses, Sermons and Remains of the Reverend Mr. Joseph Glanvill.* London: Henry Mortlock, 1681.

————. *The Unreasonable Contempt, Which the Church, and Its Ministers Suffer, from Prophane and Fanatick Enemies.* London, 1676.

————. *The Vanity of Dogmatising.* Edited by Stephen Medcalf. Hove, England: Harvester Press, 1970.

————. *The Way to Happiness.* London: James Collins, 1670.

————. *The Zealous and Impartial Protestant.* London: Henry Brome, 1681.

Grotius, Hugo. *The Truth of the Christian Religion.* London: Richard Royston, 1680.

Grove, Robert. *A Vindication of the Conforming Clergy.* London: Walter Kettilby, 1676.

Hale, Matthew. *The Primitive Origination of Mankind.* London: William Gobbid, 1677.

————. *The Works, Moral and Religious.* 2 vols. Edited by T. Thirlwall. London: H. D. Symonds, 1805.

Hales, John. *The Works of the Ever Memorable Mr. John Hales of Eton.* 3 vols. Glasgow: Robert and Andrew Foulis, 1765.

Hammond, Henry. *A Practical Catechism.* London: M. Flesher, 1684.

————. *Of the Reasonableness of the Christian Religion.* London: M. Flesher, 1684.

Herbert of Cherbury. *De Religione Laici.* Translated and edited by Harold R. Hutcheson. New Haven: Yale University Press, 1944.

Hickes, George. *A Collection of Sermons.* 2 vols. London: John Churchill, 1713.

Higgins, Bevill. *Historical and Critical Remarks on Burnet's History of His Own Time.* London: P. Meighan, 1725.

Hooker, Richard. *Laws of Ecclesiastical Polity.* 2 vols. Oxford: Oxford University Press, 1875.

Hyde, Edward. *A Collection of Several Tracts of the Right Honourable Edward, Earl of Clarendon.* London: T. Woodward, 1727.

————. *Essays Moral and Entertaining, on the Various Faculties and Passions of the Human Mind.* 2 vols. London: Longman, Hurst, Rees, 1815.

————. *History of the Rebellion and Civil Wars in England.* 6 vols. Edited by W. D. MacRay. Oxford: Clarendon Press, 1888.

Ken, Thomas. *Works.* 4 vols. London: John Wyat, 1721.

Kidder, Richard. *The Christian Sufferer Supported.* London: Walter Kettilby, 1680.

————. *A Discourse Concerning the Grounds of Christian Fortitude.* London: W. Kettilby, 1680.

————. *A Discourse Concerning Sins of Infirmity and Wilful Sins.* London: Joseph Downing, 1704.

————. *Twelve Sermons.* London: B. Aylmer, 1697.

Leslie, Charles. *The Charge of Socinianism Against Dr. Tillotson Considered.* London, 1695.

Locke, John. *The Correspondence of John Locke.* 8 vols. Edited by E. S. de Beer. Oxford: Clarendon Press, 1973–89.

————. *The Educational Writings of John Locke.* Edited by James Axtell. Cambridge: Cambridge University Press, 1968.

————. *An Essay Concerning Human Understanding.* Edited by Peter Nidditch. Oxford: Clarendon Press, 1975.

————. *Works.* 10 vols. London: Thomas Tegg, 1823.

Montaigne, Michel. *Essays.* Edited by Percival Chubb and translated by John Florio.

London: Walter Scott, n.d.

Moore, John. *Sermons on Several Subjects.* 2 vols. Edited by Samuel Clarke. London: T. Pemberton, 1724.

More, Henry. *An Account of Virtue.* London: Benjamin Tooke, 1704.

———. *A Collection of Aphorisms.* London: J. Downing, 1704.

———. *The Theological Works of Henry More.* London: Joseph Downing, 1708.

Patrick, Simon. *Autobiography.* Oxford: J. H. Parker, 1839.

———. *A Brief Account of the New Sect of Latitude-Men* (1662). Edited by T. A. Birrell. Los Angeles: University of California Press, 1963.

———. *A Commentary Upon the First Book of Moses.* London: Richard Chiswell, 1695.

———. *Works.* 9 vols. Edited by Alexander Napier. Oxford: Oxford University Press, 1858.

Pearson, John. *An Exposition of the Creed.* London: Roger Daniel, 1659.

Pepys, Samuel. *Diary.* 11 vols. Edited by Robert Latham and William Matthews. Berkeley: University of California Press, 1970–83.

Reynolds, Edward. *The Whole Works.* 6 vols. London: B. Holdsworth, 1826.

Rust, George. *A Discourse of the Use of Reason in Matters of Religion.* Translated by Henry Hallywell. London: Henry Hills, 1683.

———. *The Remains of that Reverend and Learned Prelate, Dr. George Rust.* Edited by Henry Hallywell. London: M. Flesher, 1686.

Sacheverell, Henry. *The True Character of a Low Churchman.* London, 1701.

Sancroft, William. *Occasional Sermons.* London: Thomas Bassett, 1694.

Sanderson, Robert. *Thirty-Six Sermons.* London: John Hindmarsh, 1689.

Sherlock, William. *Sermons Preached Upon Several Occasions.* 2 vols. London: R. Wrae, 1755.

South, Robert. *Sermons Preached upon Several Occasions.* 7 vols. Oxford: Clarendon Press, 1823.

Sprat, Thomas. *Sermons Preached on Several Occasions.* London: Charles Brome, 1697.

Standish, John. *A Sermon Preached Before the King at Whitehall.* London: Henry Brome, 1676.

Stillingfleet, Edward. *Works.* 6 vols. London, 1707–10.

Taylor, Jeremy. *The Whole Works of the Right Reverend Jeremy Taylor.* 15 vols. Edited by Reginald Heber. London: Ogle, Duncan, and Co., 1822.

Tenison, Thomas. *A Discourse Concerning a Guide in Matters of Faith.* London: Benjamin Tooke, 1683.

———. *A Sermon Concerning Holy Resolution.* London: Richard Chiswell, 1694.

———. *Sermon Preached at the Anniversary Meeting of the Clergymens' Sons.* London: Richard Chiswell, 1691.

Tillotson, John. *Works.* 10 vols. Edited by Thomas Birch. London: J. F. Dove, 1820.

Toland, John. *Christianity Not Mysterious: or, A Treatise Shewing, that there is Nothing in the Gospel Contrary to Reason, Nor Above It.* London: Sam. Buckley, 1696.

Whichcote, Benjamin. *Eight Letters of Dr. Anthony Tuckney, and Dr. Benjamin Whichcote.* Edited by Samuel Salter. London: J. Payne, 1753.

———. *Moral and Religious Aphorisms.* Edited by Samuel Salter. London: J. Payne, 1753.

———. *Works.* 4 vols. Aberdeen, Scotland: J. Chalmers, 1751.

Wilkins, John. *A Discourse Concerning the Gift of Prayer.* London, 1651.

———. *Ecclesiastes, or, A Discourse Concerning the Gift of Preaching*. London: Samuel Gellibrand, 1651.

———. *Principles and Duties of Natural Religion*. London: A. Maxwell, 1675.

———. *Sermons Preach'd Upon Several Occasions*. London: Richard Chiswell, 1701.

Wood, Anthony. *Athenae Oxoniensis*. 5 vols. Edited by P. Bliss. Oxford, 1813–20.

Worthington, John. *The Great Duty of Self-Resignation to the Divine Will*. London: Walter Kettilby, 1689.

———. *A Scripture Catechism Shewing What a Christian is to Believe and Practice in Order to Salvation*. Glasgow: R. Foulis, 1747.

Secondary Sources

Abbot, W. C. "English Conspiracy and Dissent, 1660–1674." *American Historical Review* 14 (1908–9).

Abernathy, George R. *The English Presbyterians and the Stuart Restoration*. Philadelphia: Transactions of the American Philosophical Society, 1965.

Aiken, W. A., and Henning, B. D., eds. *Conflict in Stuart England: Essays in Honor of Wallace Notestein*. London: Jonathan Cape, 1960.

Allen, Don Cameron. *Doubt's Boundless Sea: Scepticism and Faith in the Renaissance*. Baltimore: Johns Hopkins University Press, 1964.

Allison, C. F. *The Rise of Moralism: The Proclamation of the Gospel from Hooker to Baxter*. New York: Seabury Press, 1966.

Ashcraft, Richard. *Revolutionary Politics and Locke's Two Treatises of Government*. Princeton: Princeton University Press, 1986.

Avis, Paul. *Anglicanism and the Christian Church*. Edinburgh: T. & T. Clark, 1989.

Aylmer, G. E. *Rebellion or Revolution?: England 1640–1660*. Oxford: Oxford University Press, 1986.

Bahlman, Dudley W. R. *The Moral Revolution of 1688*. New Haven: Yale University Press, 1957.

Baker, Hershal. *The Image of Man: A Study of the Idea of Human Dignity in Classical Antiquity, the Middle Ages, and the Renaissance*. New York: Harper Torchbooks, 1961.

———. *The Wars of Truth: Studies in the Decay of Christian Humanism in the Earlier Seventeenth Century*. Gloucester, Mass.: Peter Smith, 1969.

Bangs, Carl. *Arminius: A Study in the Dutch Reformation*. Nashville: University of Tennessee Press, 1971.

———. "Arminius and the Reformation." *Church History* 30 (June 1961).

Barclay, William. *The Mind of St. Paul*. New York: Harper and Row, 1958.

Baxter, Stephen, ed. *England's Rise to Greatness*. Berkeley: University of California Press, 1983.

———. *William III and the Defense of European Liberty, 1650–1707*. New York: Harcourt, Brace and World, 1966.

Bebb, E. D. *Nonconformity and Social and Economic Life, 1660–1800*. London: Epworth, 1935.

Becker, Carl. *The Heavenly City of the Eighteenth-Century Philosophers*. New Haven: Yale University Press, 1930.

Beddard, R. A. "The Commission for Ecclesiastical Appointments, 1681–4." *Historical Journal* 10 (1967).

————. "Sheldon and Anglican Recovery." *Historical Journal* 19 (1976).

————. "Vincent Alsop and the Emancipation of Restoration Dissent." *Journal of Ecclesiastical History* 24 (1973).

Bedford, R. D. *The Defence of Truth: Herbert of Cherbury and the Seventeenth Century.* Manchester: University of Manchester Press, 1979.

Bennett, G. V. *The Tory Crisis in Church and State: The Career of Francis Atterbury.* Oxford: Clarendon Press, 1975.

Bennett, G. V., and Walsh, J. D., eds. *Essays in Modern Church History.* New York: Oxford University Press, 1966.

Best, G. F. A. *Temporal Pillars: Queen Anne's Bounty, the Ecclesiastical Commissioners, and the Church of England.* Cambridge: Cambridge University Press, 1964.

Biddle, John C. "Locke's Critique of Innate Ideas and Toland's Deism." *Journal of the History of Ideas* 37 (1976).

Blethen, H. Tyler. "Episcopacy and Stability in Restoration England." *Historical Magazine of the Protestant Episcopal Church* 46 (1977).

Bosher, Robert S. *The Making of the Restoration Settlement.* London: Dacre Press, 1957.

Boton, F. R. *The Caroline Tradition in the Church of Ireland.* London: Society for Promoting Christian Knowledge, 1958.

Bourke, Vernon J. *St. Thomas and the Greek Moralists.* Milwaukee, Wis.: Marquette University Press, 1947.

Brauer, Jerald C. "Types of Puritan Piety." *Church History* 56 (1987).

Bredvold, Louis. *The Intellectual Milieu of John Dryden.* Ann Arbor: University of Michigan Press, 1934.

Browning, A., ed. *English Historical Documents, 1660–1714.* Oxford: Oxford University Press, 1953.

Brunner, Emil. *Man in Revolt.* London: Lutterworth Press, 1939.

Burnyeat, Myles, ed. *The Sceptical Tradition.* Berkeley: University of California Press, 1983.

Byrne, Peter. *Natural Religion and the Religion of Nature.* London: Routledge and Kegan Paul, 1989.

Carlton, Charles. *Archbishop William Laud.* New York: Routledge and Kegan Paul, 1987.

Carpenter, Edward. *Cantour: The Archbishops in Their Office.* Oxford: Mawbray, 1988.

————. *Thomas Tenison: Archbishop of Canterbury.* London: Society for Promoting Christian Knowledge, 1948.

Carpenter, James A. *Nature and Grace: Toward an Integral Perspective.* New York: Crossroad Publishers, 1988.

Carpenter, S. C. *Eighteenth Century Church and People.* London: John Murray, 1959.

Carroll, Robert Todd. *The Common Sense Philosophy of Religion of Bishop Edward Stillingfleet.* The Hague: Martinus Nijhoff, 1975.

Carswell, John. *The Descent on England.* New York: John Day, 1969.

Carter, C. Sydney. *The English Church and the Reformation.* London: Longmans, 1915.

Caspari, Fritz. *Humanism and the Social Order in Tudor England.* Chicago: University of Chicago Press, 1954.

Cassirer, Ernst. *The Philosophy of the Enlightenment.* Princeton: Princeton University Press, 1979.

Cave, Sydney. *The Christian Estimate of Man.* London: Duckworth, 1944.

Clark, Sir George. *The Later Stuarts, 1660–1714*, 2d ed. Oxford: Clarendon Press, 1961.

Clark, J. C. D. *English Society, 1688–1830*. Cambridge: Cambridge University Press, 1986.

Clifford, Alan C. *Atonement and Justification: English Evangelical Theology, 1640–1790*. Oxford: Clarendon Press, 1990.

Collinson, Patrick. *The Elizabethan Puritan Movement*. London: Jonathan Cape, 1967.

———. *The Religion of Protestants*. Oxford: Clarendon Press, 1982.

Coolidge, John. *The Pauline Renaissance in England*. Oxford: Clarendon Press, 1970.

Cope, Jackson. "The Cupri-Cosmits: Glanvill on Latitudinarian Anti-Enthusiasm." *Huntington Library Quarterly* 17 (1954).

———. *Joseph Glanvill: Anglican Apologist*. St. Louis: Washington University Press, 1956.

Coward, Barry. *The Stuart Age*. London: Longman, 1980.

Cragg, Gerald R. *The Church in the Age of Reason*. London: Pelican, 1980.

———. *Freedom and Authority: A Study of English Thought in the Early Seventeenth Century*. Philadelphia: Westminster Press, 1975.

———. *From Puritanism to the Age of Reason*. Cambridge: Cambridge University Press, 1950.

———. *Puritanism in the Period of the Great Persecution*. New York: Russell and Russell, 1971.

———. *Reason and Authority in the Eighteenth Century*. Cambridge: Cambridge University Press, 1970.

——— ed. *The Cambridge Platonists*. New York: Oxford University Press, 1968.

Cross, Claire. *English Church and People, 1450–1660*. Atlantic Highlands, N.J.: Humanities Press, 1976.

Cruickshanks, Eveline, ed. *By Force or By Default? The Revolution of 1688*. Edinburgh: John Donald, 1989.

Curtis, L. P. *Anglican Moods of the Eighteenth Century*. Hamden, Conn.: Archon Books, 1966.

Daniel, Stephen H. *John Toland: His Methods, Manners, and Mind*. Montreal: McGill-Queens University Press, 1984.

Davies, Horton. *The English Free Churches*. London: Oxford University Press, 1963.

———. *Worship and Theology in England from Andrewes to Baxter and Foxe, 1603–1690*. Princeton: Princeton University Press, 1975.

———. *Worship and Theology in England from Watts and Wesley to Maurice, 1690–1850*. Princeton: Princeton University Press, 1961.

Downey, James. *The Eighteenth-Century Pulpit*. Oxford: Clarendon Press, 1969.

Dugmore, C. W. *Eucharistic Doctrine in England from Hooker to Waterland*. London: Society for Promoting Christian Knowledge, 1942.

Dugmore, C. W., and Duggan, Charles, ed. *Studies in Church History*. Vol. 1. London: Thomas Nelson, 1964.

Earle, Peter. *The Making of the English Middle Class*. Berkeley: University of California Press, 1989.

Edwards, David L. *Christian England: From the Reformation to the Eighteenth Century*. Grand Rapids, Mich.: William B. Eerdmans, 1983.

Eire, Carlos M. W. *War Against the Idols: The Reformation of Worship from Erasmus to Calvin*. Cambridge: Cambridge University Press, 1986.

Elson, James H. *John Hales of Eton*. Morningside Heights, N.Y.: King's Crown Press, 1948.

Evennett, H. Outrem. *The Spirit of the Counter-Reformation*. Cambridge: Cambridge University Press, 1968.

Every, George. *The High Church Party, 1688–1718*. London: Society for Promoting Christian Knowledge, 1956.

Faulkner, Robert K. *Richard Hooker and the Politics of a Christian England*. Berkeley: University of California Press, 1981.

Fawcett, Thomas J. *The Liturgy of Comprehension, 1689*. Southend-on-Sea, England: Alcuin Club, 1973.

Feiling, Keith. *A History of the Tory Party*. Oxford: Clarendon Press, 1924.

Ferreira, Jamie. *Scepticism and Reasonable Doubt*. Oxford: Clarendon Press, 1986.

Findon, John. "The Nonjurors and the Church of England." D. Phil. diss., Oxford University, 1979.

Gascoigne, John. *Cambridge in the Age of Enlightenment*. Cambridge: Cambridge University Press, 1989.

———. "Politics, Patronage and Newtonianism: The Cambridge Example." *The Historical Journal* 27 (1984).

Gay, Peter. *The Enlightenment*. 2 vols. New York: Norton, 1969.

———, ed. *Deism: An Anthology*. Princeton: D. Van Nostrand Company, 1968.

George, Charles and Catherine. *The Protestant Mind of the English Reformation*. Princeton: Princeton University Press, 1961.

George, Edward A. *Seventeenth-Century Men of Latitude*. New York: Charles Scribner's Sons, 1908.

Gilmore, Myron P. *The World of Humanism*. New York: Harper Torchbooks, 1962.

Gilson, Etienne. *History of Christian Philosophy in the Middle Ages*. New York: Random House, 1955.

———. *The Philosophy of St. Thomas Aquinas*. Translated by Edward Bullough. New York: Dorset Press, n.d.

———. *Reason and Revelation in the Middle Ages*. New York: Charles Scribner's Sons, 1938.

———. *The Spirit of Medieval Philosophy*. Translated by A. H. C. Downes. New York: Charles Scribner's Sons, 1940.

Green, I. M. *The Re-establishment of the Church of England, 1660–1663*. Oxford: Oxford University Press, 1978.

Grell, Ole Peter; Israel, Jonathan I.; and Tyacke, Nicholas, eds. *From Persecution to Toleration*. Oxford: Clarendon Press, 1991.

Haight, Roger. *The Experience and Language of Grace*. New York: Paulist Press, 1979.

Haller, William. *The Rise of Puritanism*. New York: Columbia University Press, 1938.

Hardacre, Paul H. "The Genesis of the Declaration of Breda, 1657–1660." *Journal of Church and State* 15 (1973).

Harris, Tim. *London Crowds in the Reign of Charles II*. Cambridge: Cambridge University Press, 1987.

Harris, Victor. *All Coherence Gone*. New York: Frank Cass, 1966.

Harrison, A. W. *Arminianism*. London, 1937.

Harth, Phillip. *Contexts of Dryden's Thought*. Chicago: University of Chicago Press, 1968.

———. *Swift and Anglican Rationalism*. Chicago: University of Chicago Press, 1961.

Harvey, Robert. "The Problem of Social-Political Obligation for the Church of England in the Seventeenth Century." *Church History* 40 (1971).

Hawkins, L. M. *Allegiance in Church and State: The Problem of the Nonjurors in the English Revolution*. London: Routledge and Sons, 1928.

Haydn, Hiram. *The Counter-Renaissance*. New York: Grove Press, 1960.

Hazard, Paul. *The European Mind, 1680–1715*. Translated by J. Lewis May. New York: Meridian, 1963.

Heick, Otto W. *A History of Christian Thought*. 2 vols. Philadelphia: Fortress Press, 1965.

Heward, Edmond. *Matthew Hale*. London: Robert Hale, 1972.

Hick, John. *Evil and the Love of God*. New York: Harper and Row, 1966.

Hill, Christopher. *The Century of Revolution*. New York: Norton, 1961.

———. *Change and Continuity in Seventeenth-Century England*. Cambridge: Harvard University Press, 1975.

———. *The Collected Essays of Christopher Hill*. 3 vols. Amherst: University of Massachusetts Press, 1985–86.

———. "Reason and Reasonableness in Seventeenth-Century England." *British Journal of Sociology* 20 (1969).

———. *Some Intellectual Consequences of the English Revolution*. Madison: University of Wisconsin Press, 1980.

———. *The World Turned Upside Down*. New York: Viking, 1972.

Holmes, Geoffrey. *Politics, Religion and Society in England, 1679–1742*. London: Hambledon Press, 1986.

———. *The Trial of Dr. Saceverell*. London: Eyre Methuen, 1973.

———, ed. *Britain After the Glorious Revolution, 1689–1714*. London: Macmillan, 1969.

Hoopes, Robert. *Right Reason in the English Renaissance*. Cambridge: Harvard University Press, 1962.

Horwitz, Henry. "Comprehension in the Later Seventeenth Century: A Postscript." *Church History* 34 (1965).

———. *Parliament, Policy, and Politics*. Manchester: University of Manchester Press, 1977.

———. "Protestant Reconciliation in the Exclusion Crisis." *Journal of Ecclesiastical History* 15 (1964).

———. *Revolution Politicks: The Career of Daniel Finch, Second Earl of Nottingham, 1647–1730*. London: Cambridge University Press, 1968.

Hughes, Trevor. *The Piety of Jeremy Taylor*. London: Macmillan, 1960.

Hunt, John. *Religious Thought in England*. 3 vols. London: Strahen and Co., 1871.

Hunter, Michael. *Science and Society in Restoration England*. Cambridge: Cambridge University Press, 1981.

Huntley, Frank Livingston. *Jeremy Taylor and the Great Rebellion*. Ann Arbor: University of Michigan, 1970.

Hutton, J. H. *The English Church: From the Accession of Charles I to the Death of Anne*. London: Macmillan, 1913.

Hutton, Ronald. *Charles the Second*. Oxford: Clarendon Press, 1989.

———. *The Restoration: A Political and Religious History of England and Wales, 1658–1667*. Oxford: Oxford University Press, 1987.

Hyde, Michael. "The Reaction to Enthusiasm in the Seventeenth Century: Towards an Integrative Approach." *Journal of Modern History* 53 (1981).

Isaacs, Tina. "The Anglican Hierarchy and the Reformation of Manners, 1688–1738." *Journal of Ecclesiastical History* 33 (1982).

Jacob, Margaret. *The Newtonians and the English Revolution.* Ithaca: Cornell University Press, 1976.

Jaeger, Werner. *Humanism and Theology.* Milwaukee: Marquette University Press, 1943.

Jedin, Herbert. *A History of the Council of Trent.* 2 vols. Translated by Ernst Graff. Edinburgh: Thomas Nelson, 1961.

Johnson, Paul. *A History of Christianity.* Harmondsworth, England: Penguin, 1978.

Jones, F. R. *The Seventeenth Century: Studies in the History of English Thought and Literature from Bacon to Pope.* Stanford: Stanford University Press, 1950.

Jones, J. R. *Country and Court: England, 1658–1714.* Cambridge: Harvard University Press, 1979.

———. *The Revolution of 1688 in England.* New York: Norton, 1972.

———, ed. *The Restored Monarchy, 1660–1688.* Totawa, N.J.: Rowman and Littlefield, 1979.

Jones, M. G. *The Charity School Movement: A Study of Eighteenth-Century Puritanism in Action.* Hamden, Conn.: Archon Books, 1964.

Jordon, Winthrop K. *The Development of Religious Toleration in England.* 4 vols. Gloucester, Mass.: Peter Smith, 1965.

Kempe, J. E., ed. *The Classic Preachers of the English Church.* 2 vols. New York: E. P. Dutton, 1877.

Kendall, R. T. *Calvin and English Calvinism.* Oxford: Oxford University Press, 1979.

Kenyon, J. P. *The Popish Plot.* London: Heinemann, 1972.

———. *Revolution Principles: The Politics of Party, 1689–1720.* Cambridge: Cambridge University Press, 1977.

———. *Stuart England.* Harmondsworth, England: Penguin, 1978.

———, ed. *The Stuart Constitution.* Cambridge: Cambridge University Press, 1966.

Kirk, Kenneth E. *The Vision of God: The Christian Doctrine of the Summum Bonum.* London: Longmans, 1931.

Knox, R. Buick, ed. *Reformation, Conformity and Dissent: Essays in Honor of Geoffrey Nuttall.* London: Epworth Press, 1977.

Knox, Ronald. *Enthusiasm: A Chapter in the History of Religion.* Oxford: Clarendon Press, 1950.

Lacey, Douglas R. *Dissent and Parliamentary Politics in England.* New Brunswick: Rutgers University Press, 1969.

Lake, Peter. *Anglicans and Puritans?: Presbyterian and English Conformist Thought from Whitgift to Hooker.* London: Unwin Hyman, 1988.

———. "Calvinism and the English Church." *Past and Present* 114 (1987).

Latourette, Kenneth Scott. *A History of Christianity.* 2 vols. New York: Harper and Row, 1975.

Lecky, William E. H. *A History of England in the Eighteenth Century.* 6 vols. London: Longmans, Green, and Co., 1888.

Lee, Maurice, Jr. *The Cabal.* Urbana: University of Illinois Press, 1965.

Leith, John H., ed. *Creeds of the Churches.* Atlanta: John Knox Press, 1977.

Lewis, C. S. *The Problem of Pain.* London: Centenary Press, 1940.

Locke, Louis. *Tillotson: A Study in Seventeenth-Century Literature.* Copenhagen: Rosen-kilde and Bagger, 1954.

Lovejoy, Arthur. *Essays in the History of Ideas.* New York: G. P. Putnam's Sons, 1960.

McAdoo, H. R. *The Spirit of Anglicanism: A Survey of Anglican Theological Method in the Seventeenth Century.* London: Adam and Charles Black, 1965.

————. *The Structure of Caroline Moral Theology.* London: Longmans, Green and Co., 1949.

Macaulay, Thomas B. *History of England from the Accession of James II.* 2 vols. London: Longmans, Green, Reader, & Dyer, 1876.

McConica, James K. *English Humanists and Reformation Politics.* Oxford: Clarendon Press, 1965.

McDonald, H. D. *Ideas of Revelation: An Historical Study.* London: Macmillan, 1959.

MacFarlane, S. M. "Studies in Poverty and Poor Relief in London at the End of the Seventeenth Century." D. Phil. diss., Oxford University, 1982.

McGee, J. Sears. *The Godly Man in Stuart England.* New Haven: Yale University Press, 1976.

McGiffert, Arthur C. *Protestant Thought Before Kant.* London: Duckworth, 1911.

McGrath, Alister. *The Intellectual Origins of the European Reformation.* Oxford: Basil Blackwell, 1987.

————. *Iustitia Dei: A History of the Christian Doctrine of Grace.* 2 vols. Cambridge: Cambridge University Press, 1987.

McLachlan, H. *English Education Under the Test Acts.* Manchester: University of Manchester Press, 1931.

McLachlan, H. John. *Socinianism in Seventeenth-Century England.* Oxford: Oxford University Press, 1951.

Mahoney, John. *The Making of Moral Theology: A Study of the Roman Catholic Tradition.* Oxford: Clarendon Press, 1991.

Manuel, Frank. *The Religion of Isaac Newton.* Oxford: Oxford University Press, 1974.

Marshall, John S. *Hooker and the Anglican Tradition.* London: Adam and Charles Black, 1963.

Mather, F. C. "Worship 1714–1830." *Journal of Ecclesiastical History* 36 (1985).

Matthews, A. G. *Calamy Revised.* Oxford: Clarendon Press, 1934.

Maurer, Armand A. *Medieval Philosophy.* New York: Random House, 1964.

Miller, John. "The Crown and the Borough Charters in the Reign of Charles II." *English Historical Review* 100 (1985).

————. *James II: A Study in Kingship.* Hove, England: Wayland Publishers, 1977.

————. *Popery and Politics in England.* Cambridge: Cambridge University Press, 1973.

Mitchell, W. Fraser. *English Pulpit Oratory from Andrewes to Tillotson.* London: Society for Promoting Christian Knowledge, 1932.

More, Ellen. "Congregationalism and the Social Order: John Goodwin's Gathered Church, 1640–1660." *Journal of Ecclesiastical History* 38 (1987).

More, Paul Elmer, and Cross, Frank Leslie, ed. *Anglicanism: The Thought and Practice of the Church of England: Illustrated from the Religious Literature of the Seventeenth Century.* London: Society for Promoting Christian Knowledge, 1935.

Morgan, Edmund. *Visible Saints: The History of a Puritan Idea.* New York: New York University Press, 1963.

Morgan, John. *Godly Learning: Puritan Attitudes Towards Reason, Learning and Education,*

1560–1640. Cambridge: Cambridge University Press, 1986.

Morgan, Kenneth O., ed. *The Oxford History of Britain*. Oxford: Oxford University Press, 1988.

Morrill, John, ed. *Reactions to the English Civil War, 1642–1649*. New York: St. Martin's Press, 1982.

Mullett, C. F. "A Case of Allegiance: William Sherlock and the Revolution of 1688." *Huntingdon Library Quarterly* 10 (1947–48).

Munz, Peter. *The Place of Hooker in the History of Thought*. London: Routledge and Kegan Paul, 1952.

Nankivell, James. *Edward Stillingfleet, Bishop of Worcester, 1689–1699*. Worcester, England: Ebenezer Baylis, 1946.

Nash, Ronald H. *Faith and Reason: Searching for a Rational Faith*. Grand Rapids, Mich.: Academie Books, 1988.

New, J. F. H. *Anglican and Puritan: The Basis of Their Opposition, 1558–1640*. Stanford, Calif.: Stanford University Press, 1964.

Nicholson, Marjorie. "Christ's College and the Latitude Men." *Modern Philology* 27 (1929).

————., ed. *The Conway Letters*. New Haven: Yale University Press, 1930.

Niebuhr, R. *The Nature and Destiny of Man*. 2 vols. London: Nisbet and Co., 1945.

Nuttall, Geoffrey F., and Chadwick, Owen, eds. *From Uniformity to Unity, 1662–1962*. London: Society for Promoting Christian Knowledge, 1962.

Olin, John C., ed. *Luther, Erasmus and the Reformation*. New York: Fordham University Press, 1969.

Orr, Robert R. *Reason and Authority: The Thought of William Chillingworth*. Oxford: Clarendon Press, 1967.

Osmond, P. H. *Isaac Barrow: His Life and Time*. London: Society for Promoting Christian Knowledge, 1944.

Overton, J. H. *Life in the English Church, 1660–1714*. London: Longmans, 1885.

Owen, D. *English Philanthropy, 1660–1964*. Cambridge, Mass.: Belknap Press, 1964.

Packer, John W. *The Transformation of Anglicanism, 1643–1660*. Manchester: University of Manchester Press, 1969.

Pailin, David A. *Attitudes to Other Religions: Comparative Religion in Seventeenth and Eighteenth-Century Britain*. Manchester: University of Manchester Press, 1984.

Parker, Irene. *Dissenting Academies in England*. Cambridge: Cambridge University Press, 1913.

Passmore, John. *The Perfectibility of Man*. London: Gerald Duckworth and Co., 1970.

Patterson, M. W. *A History of the Church of England*. London: Longmans, Green and Co., 1933.

Pattison, Mark. *Essays*. 2 vols. Edited by Henry Nettleship. Oxford: Clarendon Press, 1889.

Patrides, C. A., ed. *The Cambridge Platonists*. Cambridge: Cambridge University Press, 1971.

Penelhum, Terence. *God and Scepticism: A Study in Scepticism and Fideism*. Dordrecht, Holland: D. Reidel Co., 1983.

Pettit, Norman. *The Heart Prepared: Grace and Conversion in Puritan Spiritual Life*. New Haven: Yale University Press, 1966.

Peyton, S. A. "The Religious Census of 1676." *English Historical Review* 48 (1933).

Pinkham, Lucille. *William III and the Respectable Revolution*. Hamden, Conn.: Archon Books, 1969.

Placher, W. C. *A History of Christian Theology*. Philadelphia: Westminster Press, 1983.

Pollard, Arthur. *English Sermons*. London: Longmans, 1963.

Popkin, Richard. *The History of Scepticism from Erasmus to Spinoza*. London: University of California Press, 1979.

———. "The Philosophy of Bishop Stillingfleet." *Journal of the History of Philosophy* 9 (1971).

Porter, Roy. *English Society in the Eighteenth Century*. Harmondsworth, England: Penguin, 1982.

Powicke, Frederick J. *The Cambridge Platonists*. London: J. M. Dent, 1924.

Pruett, John H. *The Parish Clergy Under the Later Stuarts: The Leicestershire Experience*. Urbana: University of Illinois Press, 1978.

Radhakrishnan, S., and Raju, P. T. *The Concept of Man: A Study in Comparative Philosophy*. Lincoln, Nebr.: Johnsen Publishing Co., 1966.

Rashdall, Hastings. *The Idea of Atonement in Christian Theology*. London: Macmillan, 1920.

Reardon, Bernard M. G. *Religious Thought in the Reformation*. New York: Longmans, 1981.

Redwood, John. *Reason, Ridicule and Religion: The Age of Enlightenment in England, 1660–1750*. London: Thames and Hudson, 1976.

Reedy, Gerard, S. J. *The Bible and Reason: Anglicans and Scripture in Late Seventeenth-Century England*. Philadelphia: University of Pennsylvania Press, 1985.

Reeve, L. J. *Charles I and the Road to Personal Rule*. Cambridge: Cambridge University Press, 1989.

Richardson, C. F. *English Preachers and Preaching, 1640–1670*. London: Society for Promoting Christian Knowledge, 1928.

Roberts, J. D. *From Puritanism to Platonism in Seventeenth-Century England*. The Hague: Martinus Nijhoff, 1968.

Robertson, John M. *A Short History of Freethought*. 2 vols. London: Watts and Co., 1915.

Robinson, H. Wheeler. *The Christian Doctrine of Man*. Edinburgh: T. & T. Clark, 1947.

Robinson, M. W. *A History of the Church of England*. 2d ed. London: Longmans, Green and Co., 1933.

Rupp, Gordon. *Religion in England, 1688–1791*. Oxford: Oxford University Press, 1986.

Russell, Conrad. *Origins of the English Civil War*. Oxford: Clarendon Press, 1990.

Russell, Jeffrey Burton. *Mephistopheles: The Devil in the Modern World*. Ithaca: Cornell University Press, 1986.

Schlatter, Richard. *The Social Ideas of Religious Leaders, 1660–1688*. London: Oxford University Press, 1940.

Schnackenburg, Rudolf. *The Moral Teaching of the New Testament*. New York: Herder and Herder, 1966.

Schochet, Gorden. *Patriarchalism in Political Thought*. Oxford: Oxford University Press, 1975.

Schultz, Howard. *Milton and Forbidden Knowledge*. New York: Modern Language Association, 1955.

Seaward, Paul. *The Cavalier Parliament and the Reconstruction of the Old Regime, 1661–*

1667. Cambridge: Cambridge University Press, 1989.

Secretan, C. F. *Memoirs of the Life and Times of the Pious Robert Nelson*. London: John Murry, 1860.

Seibert, Fredrick Seaton. *Freedom of the Press in England, 1476–1776*. Urbana: University of Illinois Press, 1965.

Shapiro, Barbara. *John Wilkins: An Intellectual Biography*. Los Angeles: University of California Press, 1969.

——— . *Probability and Certainty in Seventeenth-Century England*. Princeton: Princeton University Press, 1983.

Simon, Irene. *"Pride of Reason" in the Restoration and Earlier Eighteenth Century*. Brussels: Marcel Didier, 1960.

——— . "Tillotson's Barrow." *English Studies* 45 (1964).

——— , ed. *Three Restoration Divines: Barrow, South, Tillotson*. Paris, 1967.

Simon, William. "Comprehension in the Age of Charles II." *Church History* 31 (1962).

——— . *The Restoration Episcopate*. New York: Bookman Associates, 1965.

Smith, J. W. Ashley. *The Birth of Modern Education: The Contribution of the Dissenting Academies, 1660–1800*. London, 1954.

Smith, Perseved. *The Social Background of the Reformation*. New York: Collier Books, 1967.

Smyth, Charles. *The Art of Preaching*. London: Society for Promoting Christian Knowledge, 1940.

Snell, Alan P. F. *The Great Debate: Calvinism, Arminianism and Salvation*. Worthing, England: H. E. Walter, 1982.

Somerville, John. "The Anti-Puritan Work Ethic." *Journal of British Studies* 20 (1981).

——— . *Popular Religion in Restoration England*. Gainesville: University of Florida Press, 1976.

Speck, W. A. *Reluctant Revolutionaries*. Oxford: Oxford University Press, 1988.

——— . "The Societies for the Reformation of Manners: A Case Study in the Theory and Practice of Moral Reform." *Literature and History* 3 (1976).

Spellman, W. M. "Archbishop John Tillotson and the Meaning of Moralism." *Anglican and Episcopal History* 56 (1987).

——— . *John Locke and the Problem of Depravity*. Oxford: Clarendon Press, 1988.

Spencer, Theodore. *Shakespeare and the Nature of Man*. Cambridge: Cambridge University Press, 1943.

Spurr, John. "The Church of England, Comprehension, and the Toleration Act of 1689." *English Historical Review* 104 (1989).

——— . "Latitudinarianism and the Restoration Church." *The Historical Journal* 31 (1988).

——— . "Rational Religion in Restoration England." *Journal of the History of Ideas* 49 (1988).

Stevens, P. Gregory. *The Life of Grace*. Englewood Cliffs, N.J.: Prentice-Hall, 1963.

Stoughton, John. *History of Religion in England, from the Opening of the Long Parliament to the End of the Eighteenth Century*. 6 vols. London: Hodder and Stoughton, 1888.

Straka, Gerald. *Anglican Reaction to the Revolution of 1688*. Madison: State Historical Society of Wisconsin, 1962.

Stranks, C. J. *The Life and Writings of Jeremy Taylor*. London: Society for Promoting Christian Knowledge, 1952.

Stromberg, Roland. *Religious Liberalism in Eighteenth-Century England*. Oxford: Clarendon Press, 1954.

Sullivan, Richard E. *John Toland and the Deist Controversy*. Cambridge: Harvard University Press, 1982.

Sutch, Victor D. *Gilbert Sheldon, Architect of Anglican Survival*. The Hague: Martinus Nijhoff, 1973.

Sutherland, James. *English Literature of the Late Seventeenth Century*. Oxford: Oxford University Press, 1969.

Sykes, Norman. *Church and State in England in the Eighteenth Century*. New York: Octagon Books, 1975.

——— . *The Church of England and Non-Episcopal Churches in the Sixteenth and Seventeenth Centuries*. London: Society for Promoting Christian Knowledge, 1948.

——— . *From Sheldon to Secker: Aspects of English Church History, 1660–1768*. Cambridge: Cambridge University Press, 1959.

——— . "The Sermons of Archbishop Tillotson." *Theology* 58 (1978).

Symonds, Richard. *Alternative Saints: The Post-Reformation British People*. London: Macmillan, 1988.

Tavard, George. *Holy Writ or Holy Church*. New York: Harper and Brothers, 1955.

Tawney, R. H. *Religion and the Rise of Capitalism*. Gloucester, Mass.: Peter Smith, 1962.

Todd, Margo. *Christian Humanism and the Puritan Social Order*. Cambridge: Cambridge University Press, 1987.

Trevelyan, G. M. *England Under the Stuarts*. New York: G. P. Putnam's Sons, 1946.

Trevor-Roper, Hugh. *Catholics, Anglicans and Puritans: Seventeenth-Century Essays*. Chicago: University of Chicago Press, 1988.

——— . *Religion, the Reformation and Social Change*. London: Macmillan, 1972.

Trinterud, Leonard J. "A.D. 1689: The End of the Clerical World." In *Theology in Sixteenth and Seventeenth-Century England*. Los Angeles: William Andrews Clark Memorial Library, 1971.

Troeltsch, Ernst. *The Social Teaching of the Christian Churches*. Translated by Olive Wyon. 2 vols. London: George Allen and Unwin, 1931.

Tulloch, John. *Rational Theology and Christian Philosophy in the Seventeenth Century*. 2 vols. Edinburgh: Blackwood, 1872.

Tyacke, Nicholas. *Anti-Calvinists: The Rise of English Arminianism*. Oxford: Clarendon Press, 1986.

——— . "The Rise of Arminianism Reconsidered." *Past and Present* 115 (1987).

Underdown, David. *Revel, Riot, and Rebellion: Popular Politics and Culture in England, 1603–1660*. Oxford: Oxford University Press, 1988.

Urban, Linwood. *A Short History of Christian Thought*. New York: Oxford University Press, 1986.

Van Leeuwen, Henry G. *The Problem of Certainty in English Thought, 1630–1690*. The Hague: Martinus Nijhoff, 1963.

Viner, Jacob. *The Role of Providence in the Social Order*. Philadelphia: American Philosophical Society, 1970.

Von Ranke, Leopold. *A History of England, Principally in the Seventeenth Century*. 5 vols. Oxford: Clarendon Press, 1875.

Walker, D. P. *The Decline of Hell: Seventeenth-Century Discussions of Eternal Torment*. Chicago: University of Chicago Press, 1965.

Wallace, Dewey D. *Puritans and Predestination: Grace in English Protestant Theology, 1525–1695*. Chapel Hill: University of North Carolina Press, 1982.

Watts, Michael R. *The Dissenters: From the Reformation to the French Revolution*. Oxford: Clarendon Press, 1978.

Weber, K. *Lucius Cary: Viscount Falkland*. New York: Columbia University Press, 1940.

Western, J. R. *Monarchy and Revolution: The English State in the 1680s*. Totawa, N.J.: Rowman and Littlefield, 1972.

Westfall, Richard. *Science and Religion in Seventeenth-Century England*. Ann Arbor: University of Michigan Press, 1973.

Whiteman, A. O. "The Episcopate of Dr. Seth Ward, Bishop of Exeter." D. Phil thesis, Oxford University, 1951.

Whiting, C. E. *Studies in English Puritanism from the Restoration to the Revolution, 1660–1688*. London: Frank Cass and Co., 1931.

Williams, N. P. *The Grace of God*. London: Longmans, 1930.

Williams, Norman Powell. *The Ideas of the Fall and Original Sin*. London: Longmans, 1929.

Willey, Basil. *Christianity Past and Present*. Cambridge: Cambridge University Press, 1952.

——— . *The Eighteenth-Century Background*. Boston: Beacon Press, 1961.

——— . *The Seventeenth-Century Background*. London: Chatto and Windus, 1934.

Williamson, George. *Seventeenth-Century Contexts*. Chicago: University of Chicago Press, 1969.

Wilson, F. P. *Seventeenth-Century Prose*. Cambridge: Cambridge University Press, 1960.

Wood, Thomas. *English Casuistical Divinity During the Seventeenth Century*. London: Society for Promoting Christian Knowledge, 1952.

Wormald, B. M. H. *Clarendon*. Cambridge: Cambridge University Press, 1951.

Yolton, John W. *John Locke and the Way of Ideas*. Oxford: Clarendon Press, 1956.

INDEX